KUNDALIN

IN SEARCH OF THE

Volume

Bhagwan Shree Rajneesh
is now known simply
as Osho.

Osho has explained that
His name is derived
from William James' word
'oceanic' which means
dissolving into the ocean.
Oceanic describes the
experience, He says,
but what about
the experiencer? For that
we use the word 'Osho'.
Later He came to find out
that 'Osho' has also been used
historically in the Far East
meaning
"The Blessed One, on whom
the Sky Showers Flowers."

Published by
Sterling Publishers Private Limited

KUNDALINI YOGA

IN SEARCH OF THE MIRACULOUS

Volume II

OSHO

A Sterling Paperback

STERLING PAPERBACKS
An imprint of
Sterling Publishers (P) Ltd.
L-10, Green Park Extension, New Delhi-110016
Tel : 6191023, 6191784/85; Fax : 91-11-6190028
E-mail: ghai@nde.vsnl.net.in
Website : www.sterlingpublishers.com

Kundalini Yoga: In Search of the Miraculous — Volume II

ISBN 81 207 1954 9
Reprint 1998, 1999, 2000

Originally published under the title
In Search of the Miraculous Vol. II and
'JIN KHOJA TIN PAIYAN' (CH. 11 to 19) in HINDI language.

Editing by Swami Yoga Chinmaya,
Swami Krishna Prabhu
Coordination by Swami Amano Surdham

Published by Sterling Publishers Pvt. Ltd., New Delhi-110016.
Lasertypeset by Vikas Compographics, New Delhi.
Printed at Prolific Incorporated, New Delhi-110020.

CONTENTS

INTRODUCTION

"YES, NO AND WOW are the only words we really need...." This pearl was passed on to me many years ago as a friend and I were hiking awestruck through the Colorado Rockies and I have recalled it often in the last week as I struggled to write an introduction to this book.

So...WOW! Now I feel better and can manage a little story. About two years ago, I was looking up references from Osho about bodywork in the research library when my hands fell like magnets on a mysterious manuscript called "The Mystic Experience" in which Osho introduces Dynamic Meditation and discusses the movement of *kundalini* energy in the body in the precise and detailed way that a scientist might describe the movement of electrons in an atomic explosion.

I sat entranced for the rest of the day, as Osho showered insight after insight on the laws of "inner explosion." Then I ran to the people in the Publications Department, demanding why such precious material was not available in the Commune's bookstore. "There, there," said the Publications people, "the first nine chapters have already been published as *In Search Of The Miraculous: Volume One* and the rest is scheduled for publication...."

And so we arrive at the present movement, and discover Osho speaking on the most "esoteric" subjects in an utterly practical and earthly manner:

"Your *kundalini* is your sleeping energy. Its boundaries extend from the sex centre to the brain....

"What is the most interesting is the fact that between these two extremes you cannot rest anywhere, you cannot pause anywhere....

"To tarry in the middle is neither proper, nor natural, nor meaningful. It is as if a man climbs a ladder and stops halfway. To him we would say, 'Do one of the two: either go up or come down,' because the ladder is not the house, to stop in between is meaningless. There cannot be a more useless person than one who stops halfway up the ladder. Whatever he has to do he can do either at the top of the ladder or at the bottom of the ladder.

"So the spine is the ladder, so to speak. In this ladder, each vertebra is a step. The *kundalini* starts from the lowest centre and reaches to the very top. If it reaches the highest centre, explosion is inevitable. If it remains at the lowest centre it is sure to take the form of sexual discharge. The explosion is inevitable in the first case and the discharge in the second case. These two things should be understood well."

How to climb the ladder? This book is a road map, a guidebook to the science of inner alchemy.

What does it mean to receive *shaktipat* from a master? What is grace? How does the movement of *kundalini* energy differ in men and women? How does it manifest as it moves through the seven *chakras*? What does it really mean to talk of merging with the inner man, the inner women? What is the meaning of *tantra,* and how can lovers help each other move from the lowest centre to the highest?

And through it all, again and again, Osho reminds us that the search for the miraculous is an inner search, and not to become lost in the other, be it lover or master:

"Take the hint from wherever you get it: it will disappear time and again. It cannot be permanent, because it comes from another.... Therefore, take what you get silently, be grateful and move on. And if you feel that something had come but become lost again, then seek the source within from which it can never be lost. There is no way of losing then, for your own treasure is infinite. That which is bestowed by another stands the chance of becoming lost. Do not be a beggar who keeps asking from others. That which you receive from another should start you on your own search."

Yes, Osho, yes.

Ma Deva Nirvesha

1

OUTER HELP IN THE GROWTH OF KUNDALINI ENERGY

***You said at** the Nargol meditation camp that the meaning of shaktipat—transmission of the divine energy—is that the energy of the divine descends into the meditator. Later on, You said that there is a difference between shaktipat and grace. These two statements seem contradictory. Please explain.*

There is a slight difference between the two and there is a little similarity between the two also. Actually the field of each extends into the other. *Shaktipat* is the energy of the divine. In fact, there is no other energy except the energy of the divine. In *shaktipat,* however, a person functions as a medium. Although ultimately the person is also a part of the divine, in the initial stage the individual functions as a medium.

It is just like the lightning that flashes across the sky and the electric light that lights the house: they are the same but the light that burns in the house is brought about through a medium and the hand of man is clearly evident behind it.

The lightning that flashes in the rain is the same energy of the divine but it is not brought about by man. If man becomes extinct the lightning will still flash across the sky but the electric bulb will no longer work. *Shaktipat* is like the electric bulb in which man is the medium; grace is the lightning in the sky that comes without the help of a medium.

A person who has attained to this energy level, one who is in contact with the divine, can function as a medium because he is a better vehicle than you are for this happening. He is familiar with the energy and its workings. The energy can enter you more quickly through him. You are totally unacquainted, immature; this man is a well matured vehicle. If the energy enters you through him, it comes about easily as he is an efficient medium.

Secondly, that person is a narrow channel from which you will receive energy, but only according to your capacity. You can sit under the electric light in the house and read as it is a regulated light; you cannot read under the lightning in the sky because it follows no regulation.

So if suddenly by chance a person happens to be in a state in which the grace can descend on him or a sudden situation is created in which *shaktipat* happens to him without a medium, then there is every possibility of his freaking out or becoming insane. The energy that has descended on him may be too much and his capacity to hold it too little; hence, he can be completely shattered. Then unknown, unfamiliar experiences of joy become painful and unbearable.

It is as if a man used to staying in darkness for years is suddenly brought out into the daylight: the darkness will deepen all the more and he will not yet be able to see the light of the sun. His eyes were accustomed to seeing in the darkness, so they cannot stand the glare of light and will close.

So sometimes it happens that such a situation can come about within you in which the unlimited energy of grace can descend unknowingly on you; but its effect can be fatal, destructive, if you are not ready. You have been caught unawares, so the happening can turn into a disaster. Yes, grace can also become harmful and destructive.

In the case of *shaktipat* the chances of accident are very few, almost nil, because there is a person who is functioning as a medium, as a vehicle. Passing through a medium the energy becomes gentle and mild, and the medium can also regulate the intensity of the energy. He can allow only that amount of energy to flow into you which you can hold. But remember, the medium is only a vehicle and not the source of this energy.

So if a person says that he is doing *shaktipat,* that he is doing the transmission of the energy, then he is wrong. It would be just like the bulb declaring that it is the giver of light. Because the light is always emitted through the bulb, the bulb may be deluded that it is the creator of light. This is not so. It is not the primal source of light but merely a medium for its manifestation. So a person who declares that he can perform *shaktipat* is under the same illusion as the bulb.

The energy that is transmitted is always the energy of the divine. But if a person becomes a medium, then we can call it *shaktipat*. If there is no medium and this energy descends suddenly it can be harmful. But if a man has waited long enough, if a man has meditated with infinite patience, then *shaktipat* too can happen in the form of grace. Then there will be no medium, but then there will be no mishap. His infinite waiting, his boundless patience, his unwavering devotion, his everlasting resolve, develop his ability to allow the infinite. Then there will be no mishap. And the happening can take place both ways—with or without a medium. But in the absence of a medium he will not feel it as *shaktipat* but as grace from the beyond.

So there are similarities as well as differences between the two. I am in favour of grace as far as it is possible; as far as possible there should not be a medium. But in certain cases this is possible and in certain cases it is not possible. So instead of the latter category of people wandering for endless lives, some person can be made a medium to bring down the divine energy to them. Only that person can be a medium, however, who is no longer an individual ego. Then the hazard is almost nil, because such a person, while becoming the medium, does not become a guru: there is no person left to become a guru. Understand this difference well.

When a person becomes a guru he becomes a guru in reference to you; when a person becomes a medium he does so in relationship to the universal being; then he has nothing to do with you. Do you understand the difference?

Ego cannot exist in any state brought about in relationship to you. So the real guru is one who does not become a guru. The definition of a sadguru, a perfect master, is one who does not become a guru. This means that all who call themselves guru do not have the qualification to be a guru. There is no greater disqualification than a claim of guruship; that shows the presence of ego in such a person, and that is dangerous.

If a person suddenly reaches a state of void, where ego has completely disappeared, he can become a medium. Then *shaktipat* can happen near him, in his presence, and there is no possibility of danger. There is no danger to you or to the medium through which the energy is flowing.

And yet, basically, I am in favour of grace. When the ego has died and the person is no longer an individual, when these conditions are fulfilled, *shaktipat* almost becomes grace.

If the individual is not self-conscious of this state, then *shaktipat* is very near to grace. Then just being near him can bring about the happening. This person appears to you as a person but in actuality he has become one with the divine. It would be better to say that he has become the hand of the divine extended towards you. He is close to you. Now such a man is wholly instrumental. If that person speaks in the first person in such a state of consciousness we tend to misunderstand him. When such a person says 'I', he means the supreme self— but it is difficult for us to understand his language.

That is why Krishna can say to Arjuna, "Leave all else and surrender unto me." For thousands of years we will be pondering on what sort of a person this is who says, "Surrender unto me." His statement seems to confirm the presence of an ego. But this man could say it this way simply because he is no more an ego. Now his 'I' is the outstretched hand of someone, and it is that someone who is behind him saying, "Surrender unto me—the only one." These words, the only one, are priceless. Krishna says, "Surrender unto me, the only one." The 'I' is never the only one—it is many. Krishna is speaking from a place where the 'I' is the only one, and this is not the language of the ego.

But we understand only the language of the ego; therefore, we feel that Krishna has made an egoistic statement by telling Arjuna to surrender unto him. But this is a mistake. We always have two ways of looking at things: one is through our own point of view, from where we are invariably deluded; and the other is from the point of view of the divine, from where there is no question of delusion. So the happening can take place through a person like Krishna in whose person individual ego plays no part.

Both happenings, *shaktipat* and grace, are very contrary at the periphery; both are very close to one another at the centre. I am in favour of that space where it is difficult to distinguish between *shaktipat* and grace. That alone is useful; that alone is valuable.

A monk in China was observing the birthday of his guru with great celebration. People asked him whose birthday he was celebrating, as he always said that he had no guru and that there was no need for a guru. Then what was all this about? He begged them not to question him, but they kept on insisting, "Today is the day of the guru—have you a guru?"

The monk said, "Don't put me in difficulty. It is good that I keep quiet."

But the more he kept quiet, the more the people insisted, "What is the matter? What is it that you are celebrating?—because this is master's day celebration. Do you have a master?"

The monk said, "If you go on insisting, then I have to say something about it. Today I remember the man who refused to be my guru, because if he had accepted me as a disciple I would have gone astray. That day when he refused me I was very angry with him, but today I want to bow down to him in great gratitude. Had he wished he could have been my guru, because it was I who begged him to accept me, but he did not agree."

So the people asked, "Then what do you thank him for when he refused you?"

The monk said, "It is enough to say that by not becoming my guru this man did for me what no guru could do. Therefore, my obligation is doubled. If he had been my guru there would have been some give and take on both sides. I would have touched his feet, offered my veneration and respects, and the matter would have been concluded. But this man did not ask for respect and he did not become my guru. Therefore, my obligation to him is double. This has been absolutely one-sided: he gave and I could not even thank him, because he left no place even for that."

Now in such a situation as this, there will not remain any difference between *shaktipat* and grace. The more the difference the more you should keep away from it; the less the difference the better it is. Therefore, I emphasize grace. The day *shaktipat* has come very close to grace, so close that you cannot distinguish between *shaktipat* and grace, know that the right happening has taken place. When the electricity of your house becomes like the unhindered and natural lightning in the sky and becomes a part of the infinite energy, that moment you should know that if *shaktipat* happens then it is equivalent to grace. Remember what I have said.

In the Nargol meditation camp You have said that either the energy rises from within and reaches up to the divine or the energy of the divine descends and merges within. You said that the first is rising of the *kundalini* and the second is the grace of the divine. Then later on You have said that when the sleeping energy within meets the enormous energy of the infinite, an explosion takes place which is *samadhi*. Is the union of the awakened *kundalini* and grace absolutely necessary for *samadhi*? Or, is the evolution of the *kundalini* up to the *sahasrar* similar to the happening of divine grace?

Explosion never takes place with only one energy. Explosion is the union of two energies. If the explosion was possible with one energy, then it would have happened long ago.

It is as if you have a matchbox and you place a matchstick near it: they can lie like this indefinitely and no flame will result. No matter how small the distance between the two—half a centimetre or a quarter of a centimetre makes no difference—there will be no result. For that explosion the friction of the two is necessary; then only will you get fire. Fire is hidden in both of them but there is no way of producing it with only one of the two.

The explosion happens when the two energies meet. Thus, the sleeping energy within the individual must rise up to the *sahasrar* and then only is the union, the explosion, possible. No union is possible except at the point of the *sahasrar*. It is just as if your doors are closed and the sun is shining outside. The light stays outside your door. You move inside the house up to the door, but still you will not meet the light of the sun. Only when the door opens do you come in contact with the sunlight.

So the ultimate point of the *kundalini* is the *sahasrar*. That is the door where grace awaits us. The divine is always waiting at this door. It is you who are not at the door: you are away within somewhere. You have to come to the door. There the union will take place, and that union will be in the form of an explosion. It is called explosion because then you will immediately disappear; you will no longer be. The matchstick will have been burnt in the explosion though the matchbox will still be. The matchstick that is you turns into ashes and merges into the formless.

In the happening you will be no more. You will be lost; you will be broken and scattered; you will no longer be. You will not be what you were behind the closed door. All that was yours will be lost. Only the one who waits outside the door will remain, and you will become a part. This cannot happen to you alone, by yourself. For this explosion it is very necessary for you to reach up to the infinite cosmic energy. The sleeping energy within has to be awakened and made to rise upwards to the *sahasrar* where the cosmic energy forever awaits. The journey of the *kundalini* starts from your sleeping centre and ends at the place, at the boundary, where you disappear.

So there is one boundary which is of the physical, which we have taken for granted. But this is not the greater boundary. If my hand is cut off it does not make much difference to me. If my feet are cut off, the body will not suffer much, because I still remain. In other words, I still remain in spite of the changes within these limits. Even if the eyes and ears are not, I still remain. So your actual boundary is not the boundary of the body; your actual boundary is the *sahasrar* centre, after which you no longer exist. No sooner do you encroach on this boundary than you are gone; you cannot remain.

Your *kundalini* is your sleeping energy. Its boundaries extend from the sex centre to the centre at the top of the head. That is why we are continuously aware that we may be able to disidentify ourselves with the other parts of the body, but we cannot break our identity with the face, with the head. It is easy to recognise that "I may not be the hand," but to see one's face in the mirror and to conceive that "I am not this face" is very difficult. The face and the head—this is the limit. Therefore, man is ready to lose everything but not his intellect.

Socrates was once talking about contentment, saying that it is a great treasure. Someone asked him whether he would prefer to be a discontented Socrates or a contented pig. Socrates replied, "I would prefer to be a discontented Socrates than a contented pig, because the contented pig has no knowledge of his contentment. A dissatisfied Socrates will at least be conscious of his dissatisfaction." This man, Socrates, is saying that man is willing to lose all, but not his intellect—even if it is a dissatisfied intellect.

The intellect is also very near the centre of *sahasrar,* the seventh and last *chakra*. Rightly speaking, we have two boundaries. One is the sex centre; below this centre the world of nature begins. At the centre of sex there is no difference between trees, birds, animals and ourselves. This centre is the ultimate limit for them, whereas for man it is the first point, the starting line. When we are based in the sex centre we too are animals. Our other limit is the intellect. It is near our second boundary line beyond which is the divine. Beyond this point we are no longer ourselves; then we are the divine. These are our two frontier lines, and between these two our energy moves.

Now, the reservoir where all our energy lies asleep is near the sex centre. That is why ninety-nine per cent of man's thoughts, dreams and activities are spent around this reservoir. No matter how much culture may be displayed, whatever the false pretexts the society may bring out, man lives there and there alone: he lives around the sex centre. If he earns money it is for sex; if he builds a house it is for sex; if he earns prestige he does so for sex. At the root of it all we will find sex.

Those who understood talked of two goals—sex and liberation. The other two goals, wealth and religion, were only the means. Wealth is a resource of sex; therefore, the more sexual the era the more wealth-oriented it will be. The more in search of liberation an age is the more it will be thirsty for religion. Religion is just a means as wealth is a means. If you long for liberation religion becomes the means. If you wish for sexual satisfaction wealth is the means. So there are two goals and two means—because we have two frontiers.

It is interesting that between these two extremes you cannot rest anywhere, you cannot stop anywhere. Many people find themselves in great difficulty as they have no desire for liberation, and if for some reason they become antagonistic towards sex they find themselves in a terrible predicament. They start staying away from the sex centre, but they won't go anywhere near the centre for liberation. They fall into doubt and uncertainty, and that is very difficult, very painful, and really a hell. Their lives are filled with inner turmoil.

To linger in the middle is neither right nor natural nor meaningful. It is as if a man climbs a ladder and stops halfway. To him we would say, "Do one of the two: either go up or come down, because the ladder is not a house and to stop in between is meaningless." There cannot be a more useless person than one who stops halfway up the ladder. Whatever he has to do, he can do it either at the top of the ladder or at the bottom of the ladder.

So the spine is the ladder, so to speak. On this ladder each vertebra is a step. The *kundalini* starts from the lowest centre and reaches to the very top. If it reaches the highest centre explosion is inevitable. If it remains at the lowest centre it is sure to take the form of sexual discharge, ejaculation. These two things should be understood well.

If the *kundalini* is at the lowest centre a discharge of sexual energy is inevitable. If it reaches the highest centre explosion is certain. Both are explosions and both require the participation of the other. In the discharge of sex the other is necessary, even if it is an imaginary other. But all your energy does not become scattered from here, because this is only the beginning point of your being. You are much more than that, and you have progressed much from there. The animal is fully satisfied at this point and therefore does not seek liberation.

If animals could write scriptures there would be written in them only two goals worth striving for: wealth and sex. Wealth will be in forms suitable to the animal world. The animal that has more flesh, more strength, will be the richer one. He will win over the others in a competition of sex; he will gather ten females around him. And this also is a form of wealth. The extra fat within his body is his wealth.

A man too has riches which can be converted into "fat" at any time. A king can keep a thousand queens. There was a time when a man's wealth was measured by the number of wives he possessed. If a man is poor, how can he afford four wives? Today's criteria of education and bank balance are a much later development. In the olden days the number of women was the only criterion of wealth. This is why in extolling the affluence of our ancient heroes we have had to inflate the number of their women, and this was many times false.

For instance, the sixteen thousand queens of Krishna. In Krishna's time there was no other way of expressing his greatness: "If Krishna is a great man, then how many wives does he have?" So we had to conjure up the colossal figure of sixteen thousand—which was an impressive number then, though today it might not seem so due to the population explosion. In those days there were not so many people. In Africa even now there are communities that consist of only three people. So if they are told that a man has four wives it would be an impossible figure because they do not know anything beyond the figure of three.

In the realm of sex the presence of the other is required. If the other person is not present, even imagining the other produces the necessary effect. This is why it was thought that if God is present even in imagination, the explosion can take place. Therefore, the long tradition of *bhakti,* the path of devotion, developed in which imagination was used as the means for explosion. If ejaculation is possible through the imagination, why cannot the energy explosion take place in the same way at the *sahasrar*? This gave rise to the possibility of meeting God in the head through the use of imagination. But this was not really possible. Ejaculation is possible in imagination because it has actually been experienced; therefore it can be imagined. But we have had no meeting with God; therefore He cannot be imagined. We can only imagine that which has been experienced by us.

If a man has experienced a certain kind of pleasure he can always sit back, recall the experience and enjoy it again. A deaf person cannot hear in his dreams no matter how hard he tries; he cannot even imagine sound. Similarly, a blind man cannot envisage light. But if a man has lost his eyes he can always dream of light. Rather, now he can only see light in his dreams, because he no longer has eyes to see it. So we can envisage our experiences, but there is no way to imagine what has never been experienced.

Explosion is not our experience; therefore, imagination does not work here. We will actually have to go within, and then the actual happening can take place. So the *sahasrar chakra* is your ultimate boundary, where you end.

As I said before, man is a ladder. Nietzsche's words in this context are very precious. He said, "Man is a bridge between two eternities." There is one eternity—that of nature, which has no end—and there is the other, of the divine, which is also infinite, limitless. Man is a bridge swaying between these two. Therefore, man is not the resting place. One either goes forwards or backwards. There is no place to build a house on this bridge. Whoever tries to settle on it repents, because a bridge is not a place to have a house; it is only meant for crossing over from one end to the other.

In Fatehpur Sikri, Akbar tried to build a temple of all religions. He dreamed of one religion, which he named Din-i-Ilahi—the essence of all religions. So he had inscribed a sentence on the entrance door which is a saying of Jesus Christ. It reads: This world is only a resting place and not a permanent home. You may halt here for some time but you cannot stop here forever. This is only a place of rest on your journey. It is a camping ground, a traveller's bungalow where one can stay the night and resume travelling in the morning. We halt here only so that we may rest the night and start again at daybreak. There is no other purpose. We do not stop here for all time.

The human being is a ladder that has to be climbed; therefore he is always tense. It is not correct to say that a man is tense: rather, man is tension. A bridge is always tense; it is a bridge because it is tense. It is that which lies between two extremes. Man is an inevitable tension; therefore, he is never at peace, never tranquil. Only when he becomes like an animal does he experience a little peace, or else he attains perfect peace when he becomes the divine. The tension loosens when he becomes an animal; then he has climbed down the steps of the ladder to stand on the ground, the place with which he has been familiar for thousands of lives. He has relieved himself of all bother about tension. So man seeks freedom from tension in sex, or in other experiences related to sex such as alcohol, drugs, etcetera, that can take him into temporary unconsciousness. But you can be there for a short while only; even if you wish, you cannot stay in the animal state permanently. Even a man of the worst quality can stay in the animal state only for a short while.

The man who commits murder does so in the moment when he becomes an animal. Had he waited a moment longer, perhaps, he might have been unable to do it. Our becoming like animals is somewhat like a man jumping: for a moment he is in the air; then he comes back on the ground. So the worst of men is not bad forever; he cannot be. He is so only during moments; otherwise, he is normal like any other person. For one moment he derives comfort, because he falls back onto the known ground where there are no tensions. This is why we find no tensions in animals.

Look into their eyes: there is no tension. The animal never goes mad or commits suicide; he suffers no heart disease. But all this becomes possible for animals which are in the bondage of man—when they pull man's wagon or become his domestic pets. This is a different thing altogether. When man tries to pull the animal across the bridge the complications start.

Now, if a stray dog enters this room he will move about as he pleases, but if a pet dog enters he will go and sit where he is ordered. Now this pet dog has entered the world of man and left his animal world behind. He is bound to land himself in trouble. He is an animal that has been made to undergo the tensions of a human being. Thus, he is forever in distress. He eagerly awaits the order to run out of the room.

Man can fall back into the animal state only momentarily. This is why we say that all our joys are shortlived. Joy can also be eternal, but where we look for it, it is only a transitory state. We try to find happiness in the animal state, and this can be only for a very short while. We cannot remain in the animal state for long. It is difficult to go back into our previous state of existence. If you want to go back to yesterday you can close your eyes and visualise—but for how long? When you open your eyes you will find yourself where you are.

You cannot go back. You can forcibly do it for a moment or so, but then you always repent. Therefore, all momentary pleasures bring repentance in their course. You are left with a feeling that your efforts have gone in vain, but after a few days you forget again and fall again into the same mistake. Momentary joy can be attained on the animal level, but eternal joy is attained only upon merging into the divine. This journey has to be completed within your own being. You have to cross from one end of your bridge to the other; only then does the second happening take place.

Therefore, I consider sex and *samadhi* equivalent. There is a reason for this. In fact, these are the only two happenings that are equivalent. In sex we are at one end of the bridge, the lowest rung of the ladder where we are one with nature; in *samadhi* we are at the other end of the bridge, the topmost rung of the ladder where we are one with the divine. Both are unions; both are explosions in a certain way. In both cases you lose yourself in a particular sense: in sex you lose yourself for a moment, and in *samadhi,* forever. In both cases you cease to exist. The former is a very momentary explosion, and after it you recrystallise, because where you had gone was a lower state to which you cannot revert. But once you merge into the divine you cannot recrystallise.

This reversal is as impossible as the one into the animal state. It is absolutely impossible. It is just like expecting an adult man to get into his baby clothes. You have become one with the absolute, so you cannot revert back to the individual. Now the individual self has become such a narrow and insignificant place that you can no longer enter there. Now you cannot even imagine how you can be in it. The matter of the individual ends here.

For the explosion to happen both things are needed: your journey within must reach the point of the *sahasrar,* to meet with the grace there....

Why we call this centre *sahasrar* needs to be explained. These names are not coincidental, though language always develops accidentally and by constant use. We use the word door: any other name could have been easily used to denote the same thing. There are thousands of languages in the world and there must be thousands of words that mean door and are capable of conveying the same meaning. But when a thing is not accidental there occurs a similarity in all languages. So the meaning of door, or *dwar,* conveys the meaning of that through which we pass in and out. So in all languages the word used for door will convey this meaning, because this is a part of an experience and not a coincidental arrangement. The idea of the space through which entrance and exit are possible is conveyed by this word door.

Thus the word *sahasrar* has been coined as a result of experiences, and it is not accidental. No sooner do you attain the experience than you feel as if a thousand flower buds have bloomed within you all of a sudden. We say a thousand, meaning infinite, and we liken it to flowers because the experience is like a flowering. Something within that was closed like a bud has opened. The word flower is used in the context of flowering, of blossoming. And not only have one or two things blossomed—infinitely many things have blossomed.

So to call this experience "the opening of a thousand-petalled lotus" is natural. Have you seen a lotus opening in the rays of the morning sun? Watch carefully. Go near a lotus pond and observe silently as the lotus bud slowly opens its petals. Then you can visualise what the feeling would be if a thousand-petalled lotus opened in this way in the head. Then you will be able to imagine the experience somewhat.

There is another wonderful experience: that of sex. Those who go deep into the experience of sex also feel this flowering, but it is a very fleeting experience. Something within blossoms, but it closes again almost immediately.

But there is a difference between the two experiences. In the sex experience the flower is felt to be hanging downwards, whereas in *samadhi* the petals are felt to be blooming upwards. This differentiation can only be made by passing through both experiences. It is natural that the flowers that bloom downwards join you to a lower realm, while the flowers that bloom upwards join you to a higher realm. In fact, this blooming is an opening that makes you vulnerable to another realm. It is a door that opens—a door through which something enters within you for the explosion to take place.

Thus, both these things are required. You will travel up to the *sahasrar* and there someone is always awaiting you. It is not correct to say that someone will come there when you reach; that someone is already there waiting for the happening to take place in you.

Does the kundalini unfold toward the sahasrar only by shaktipat? Does the explosion take place only then?

If this is so, then does it mean that samadhi can be obtained through somebody else?

This has to be understood properly. In existence, in life, there is no happening which is so simple that you can understand it just by one aspect of it; it has to be viewed from many dimensions. Now if I strike a door with a hammer and the door opens, I can say that the door opened with the blow of my hammer. This is also correct in the sense that had I not struck the door, the door would not have opened. Now with the same hammer I strike another door, but the hammer may break and the door may not open—then.... Then one other factor comes into our knowledge: when I struck the first door and it opened, it was not entirely because of the hammer. The door was fully ready to open. It may have been old, it may have been weak, but whatsoever the case it was ready to open. So the door had as much a hand as the hammer in this happening. In one instance the hammer struck and the door opened; in another, the hammer broke and the door did not open.

So when the happening takes place in *shaktipat,* it is not entirely due to *shaktipat*. At the other end, the meditator in such a case is inwardly prepared and ready, so a slight push becomes effective. If this push had not been given by *shaktipat,* the meditator may have taken a little longer time to reach to *sahasrar*. So the *kundalini* is not reaching to the *sahasrar* only because of *shaktipat;* it is the time element that is decreased—nothing more. The meditator would have reached in any case.

Suppose I had not hammered at the door, but this door is old and about to collapse: then it could fall with a single gust of wind. And even if there is no wind, in the course of time it will collapse on its own. Then it will be difficult to explain why and how it fell, because it is preparing to fall all the time. So at the most, the difference will be of the time gap.

For example, a glimpse of the divine happened to Swami Vivekananda near Ramakrishna. If Ramakrishna alone was responsible for the happening in Vivekananda, then it could have also happened to all the others who came to him. He had hundreds of disciples. If Vivekananda alone was responsible, it could have happened to him long before. He had gone to many before he came to Ramakrishna, but the happening did not take place. So Vivekananda was ready in his own way and Ramakrishna was capable in his own way.

When this readiness and capability meet at a particular point, the time gap of the happening is reduced. It could be that if Vivekananda had not met Ramakrishna at that particular moment, the happening may have taken place one year later, two years later, or maybe in his next birth, or, perhaps, after ten more births. The time is not important. If the person is getting ready then the happening will take place sooner or later.

The time gap can be shortened. And it is important to understand that time is fictitious, dreamlike; hence it is not of much value. In fact, time is such a dreamlike phenomenon that it has not much value. You can take a short nap and hardly a minute may pass, but in that short period you might see a dream from your childhood right up to your old age, with all the events, incidents. But in the waking state it will be hard to believe that such a long dream lasted not more than a minute. Actually, the time dimension in the dream state is very different. Dream time is capable of having many, many incidents in a very short span; hence, the illusion.

Now, there are insects that are born in the morning and are dead by the evening. We say, "The poor creatures!"—but we do not know that in that span of time such an insect lives out life in its entirety, and it experiences all that we experience in seventy years. There is no difference: such an insect builds a house, finds a wife, has children, fights with others, and even reaches the state of *sannyas*—all within twelve hours. But their perception of time is different. We pity them for the short life granted to them, and they must be pitying us that we take seventy years to do all that they can do within a period of twelve hours. How dull we must be according to them!

Time is dependent on mind; it is a mental entity. The length of time fluctuates according to the states of our mind. When you are happy, time becomes short. When you are in trouble or pain, time becomes very long. When you are sitting at the deathbed of some relative, the night never seems to end; it seems as if the sun will never rise. It seems as if it is the last night of the world and it will never end, the sun will never rise.

Sorrow prolongs time. In sorrow you want time to pass quickly. The keener you expect the time to pass the slower it seems to creep, because this is a relative experience, though time is actually moving at its normal speed. When a lover awaits his beloved he feels she is taking too long to come, when actually she is walking at her normal pace. He wants her to have the speed of an airplane.

So time appears slow in sorrow. When you are happy, when you meet your friends or loved ones, you spend the night talking and at daybreak you wonder how the night passed so quickly. Perception of time is different in moments of happiness and of sorrow.

Time is dependent on mind; therefore, changes can be brought about in time by hammering the mind with an outside agent. If I hit you on your head with a stick it is natural that your head is hurt. Your body can be hit from outside, so can your mind. But you cannot be hit by some outside force because you are neither the body nor the mind. But right now you think that you are the body and the mind, so the body and the mind can be affected. And by affecting your bodymind, the time scale can be changed in different ways; centuries can be reduced to moments, and vice versa.

The moment awakening happens to you, you will be struck with wonder. It is now two thousand years since Jesus, five thousand years since Krishna, and a great deal of time has passed since Zarathushtra and Moses. But you will be surprised that the moment you awaken you will say, "My God, they too have just been awakened!" The time gap ceases completely then. Now these thousands of years become like a dream period.

So when one awakens, all awaken. There is not even the difference of a single moment. This is difficult to understand. The moment you awaken, you become the contemporary of Buddha, Christ, Mahavira and Krishna. They will be around you as if they too have just become awakened with you. There is not a moment's difference—there cannot be.

Now if we were to make a circle and draw many lines from the centre to the circumference, we would find that at the circumference the distance between any two lines will be the most. Then, as you proceed along these lines toward the centre, the distance between the two lines becomes less and less, until at the centre point there is no distance. All the lines become one at that point. So when a person reaches the centre of that profound experience, the distances that were present at the circumference—of two thousand years, five thousand years—vanish. But it is difficult for such a person to explain his experience, because his listeners are at the periphery and their language is also that of the periphery. This is why there is the possibility of deep misunderstanding.

A man came to me. He was a devotee of Jesus. He asked me, "What do you think of Jesus?"

I replied, "It is not proper to give an opinion about oneself."

He looked at me in surprise. "Perhaps you did not hear me," he said. "I asked your opinion on Jesus."

I said, "I also feel that you have not heard. I said, 'It is not proper to give an opinion of oneself.'" He looked perplexed. Then I explained to him, "You can theorise about Jesus so long as you do not know him. The moment you know, there will be no difference between you and him. How will you form an opinion?"

Once an artist came to Ramakrishna, bringing with him a picture of Ramakrishna and showing it to him. He asked Ramakrishna how he liked the picture, but he found that Ramakrishna bowed down and touched the feet of the picture with his forehead. The people present there thought there was some mistake, some confusion. Perhaps, he did not realise that it was his own picture. So the artist reminded him that it was his own picture that he was bowing to.

"I forgot about that," Ramakrishna replied. "This picture is so deep in *samadhi*—how can it be mine? In *samadhi* there is no 'I' and no 'you'. So I bowed to *samadhi*. It is good that you reminded me or people would have laughed." But people had already laughed.

The language of the circumference is different from the language of the centre. So when Krishna says, "It was I who was Rama," and when Jesus says, "I had come before and told you," and when Buddha says, "I will come again," they speak the language of the centre, and this is difficult for us to understand. Buddhists are waiting for Buddha's coming again on earth. The truth is that he has come many times. Even if he came he would not be recognised, because there is no way of coming in the same form again. That face was a dreamlike phenomenon, and it has been lost forever.

So at the centre there is no time gap. Therefore, the time implied for the happening of enlightenment can be speeded up or slowed down; it can be speeded up very much. That can be done by *shaktipat*.

And in the last part of your question you are asking about the other person involved in the happening of *samadhi*.

The other appears as the other because of your clinging hard to the boundary of your own ego. So Vivekananda will think that the happening took place because of Ramakrishna. If Ramakrishna thought that way it would be foolish. For Ramakrishna it took place in a different way. It was as if the right hand is hurt and the left hand applies the medicine. Now, the right hand might think that someone else is treating it and might offer thanks or refuse the treatment. The right hand may say, "I don't take help from the other; I am independent." But then it does not know that the same energy is working through the left hand that works through the right hand. So when a person is helped by another it is not actually another; it is your own readiness that calls out for this help from the other part of your very own self.

There is an ancient book in Egypt in which it is said, "Never go looking for the master. He will appear at your door the moment you are ready." It also says, "Even if you set out in search of him, how will you search? How will you recognise him? If you have become qualified enough to recognise the master, then nothing else is missing in you."

Therefore, it is always the master who recognises the disciple. The disciple can never recognise the master. There is no possibility, there is no way. Since you still cannot recognise your own inner being, how will you recognise the master? The day you are ready, some hand that is really your own will be present as your guide to help you. That hand is the hand of another so long as you do not know. The day you know, you will not even wait to offer thanks.

There is a certain custom in zen monasteries in Japan. When a meditator comes to the monastery to learn meditation he brings along his mat, spreads it on the ground and sits upon it. Every day he meditates on the mat and leaves it as it is. The day his meditation is complete he rolls up the mat and leaves. The master then understands that his meditation is complete.

He expects no thanks, because where is the need? And who is to thank whom? The meditator does not say a word. The master sees the meditator rolling his mat and he understands. The time has come to roll up the mat. It is good. There is no necessity to even observe the formality of thanking. Who is to be thanked? And if the meditator commits this mistake, the master might hit him with his staff ordering him to unroll the mat as meditation has not yet happened.

So the idea of the other is due to our ignorance; otherwise where is the other? It is oneself alone in myriad forms; it is only oneself on numerous journeys; it is oneself in innumerable mirrors. It is definitely oneself alone who is in the mirror, though what one sees is other than oneself.

There is a Sufi story. A dog lost his way in a palace. The walls and the ceiling of this palace were made of mirrors, so the dog was in a great difficulty. Wherever he looked there were dogs, dogs and only dogs. He became very puzzled: so many dogs all around! He was alone and yet surrounded by so many dogs. There was no way to get out, because the doors were also of mirrors so he saw dogs there too. Then he began to bark, but all the dogs in the mirrors began to bark with him. And when his bark filled the room he was sure his fears were not unfounded and that his life was in danger. He went on barking and all the dogs barked even louder. He ran here and there to fight them; the dogs in the mirror did likewise. All night he exhausted himself barking and fighting the dogs in the mirrors, although he was alone there! In the morning he was found dead inside the palace by the guards. The dog died running, barking and fighting with the reflections, although he was alone there. When he died all noise subsided; the mirrors became silent.

There are many mirrors, and when we see the other it is our own reflection in different mirrors; therefore, the other is a fallacy. The notion that we are helping others is an illusion, and the notion that we are receiving help from the other is also an illusion. Actually, the other, as such, is an illusion.

Once this is realised life becomes simple. Then neither you do something for the other, taking him as the other nor do you let the other do something for you feeling him as the other. Then it is you yourself extended on both ends. Then if you give a helping hand to someone on the road you will have helped your own self. If someone else has given you a helping hand, then he too has only helped himself. But this comes within our understanding only after the ultimate experience. Before that, the other is definitely the other.

Once You mentioned that shaktipat proved to be harmful to Vivekananda.

It was not *shaktipat* that was harmful for Vivekananda but what followed afterwards. But the idea of gain and loss also pertains to the dream state; it is not beyond dreams.

With the help of Ramakrishna, Vivekananda had a glimpse of *samadhi* which he would have had on the basis of his own strength, but much later. Now, it is like this: I struck the door with a hammer and the door fell, but I can make the door stand again by fixing the nails into it with the same hammer. The hammer that can bring down the door can fix it also—but it is the same hammer working in both the cases.

Ramakrishna had some difficulties for which he had to make use of Vivekananda. Ramakrishna was a complete rustic, unlearned, uneducated. His experience was profound but he had no means of expressing it, conveying it. It was necessary for him to use another person as a vehicle, as a medium to make his experience known to the world. If this had not been so you would never have heard of Ramakrishna. It was out of his compassion that he tried to convey to you his experiences through another person.

If I have come upon some treasure in my house and if I am lame and I climb upon the shoulders of another man to deliver the treasure to your house, I will be making use of this man's shoulders. He will be put to a little inconvenience and trouble by carrying me, but my intention was only to deliver the treasure to you. But because I am lame, and the treasure may be unclaimed for all time, I cannot even go out and give the news.

This problem was there with Ramakrishna; it was not so with Buddha. In Buddha's personality both Ramakrishna and Vivekananda were present together. Buddha could express what he knew; Ramakrishna could not express what he knew. He needed another person who could be a vehicle for his expression. So he showed Vivekananda a glimpse of the inner treasure, but immediately told him that he would keep the key with him and he would give the key back to Vivekananda only three days before his death.

Vivekananda started crying and begged Ramakrishna not to take away what he had given him. Ramakrishna told him, "You have other work to do. If you go into *samadhi* you will be lost forever and my work will suffer. It is good that you do not experience *samadhi* before my work is over, as you would be able to do that work only before attaining to *samadhi*." Ramakrishna did not know that people have worked after attaining *samadhi* also. He could not have known it, because he himself was unable to do anything after *samadhi*.

Normally, we are guided by our own experiences. After his experience of *samadhi* Ramakrishna could not do a thing. He could not speak for long—talking was very difficult for him. Even if someone said the word Rama, he would enter into a trance. Someone would come along and say in salute to him, "Jai Ramji," and he would be lost to the world. For him it was difficult to retain consciousness even at the mention of any name of God, such as Rama. It at once reminded him of the other world. Someone would say "Allah!" and he would be gone. If he saw a mosque he would be lost in *samadhi*; he could not move from there. He would hear a devotional song while walking along the road and he would collapse in a trance, then and there.

So according to his own experience he was right in thinking that the same could happen to Vivekananda. Therefore, he told Vivekananda, "You have a great task to perform, and after that you can enter into *samadhi*." Vivekananda's whole life passed without attaining *samadhi*, and this caused him great pain.

But remember, the pain belonged to the dream world. It was like a man dreaming a bad dream. Three days before his death he was given the key, but until then there was great pain. The letters he wrote until five to seven days before his death are full of pain and anguish, and the agony increased more and more with his restless longing for that of which he had had only a glimpse.

Your longing is not yet that intense because you have no idea of what it is. One moment's glimpse and the longing will begin. You can understand it this way: you are standing in the dark with pebbles in your hands, thinking they are a treasure of precious stones. You are very happy. Then a flash of lightning comes and you find out that there are mines of diamonds ahead of you while you are holding pebbles in your hand. Then the lightning is gone, but it leaves a message behind that you have to inform others who stand holding pebbles in their hands that a priceless treasure awaits them. So the lightning will not flash for you, and you have to carry out the task of telling people about the treasure lying ahead. Thus Vivekananda was made to accomplish a particular task which was complementary to Ramakrishna and a necessity for him; what was missing in Ramakrishna he had to complement through another person.

It happens like this many times. If a single person is unable to perform a particular task, three or four other people are required. Sometimes even five to ten people are required to help spread the message of a single person. So Ramakrishna did it out of compassion, but it created some difficulty for Vivekananda.

So I say avoid *shaktipat* as much as possible. As far as possible, strive for grace. Only that *shaktipat* is useful which is as good as grace, which has no strings attached, which has no conditions along with it, which is absolutely unconditional, for which nobody says, "I am keeping the key for a certain period."

Shaktipat should take place without the medium even inquiring what happened. If you want to thank him you should not even know where to find him; then it will be easy for you. But at times, when someone like Ramakrishna needs the help of another, there is no other way of obtaining it than this; otherwise, Ramakrishna's experiences would have been lost, unexpressed. He needed a medium for expressing it and Vivekananda fulfilled it.

This is why Vivekananda always said that whatever he was saying did not belong to him. When he was honoured in America he said that he was very pained because the honour belonged to one of whom they had no idea. And when someone called him a great man he said, "I do not even deserve to be in the dust at the feet of that great man who is my master." But the fact remains that had Ramakrishna gone to America he would have been locked up in a lunatic asylum; he would have been put under psychiatric treatment. Nobody would have heard him; rather, he would definitely have been pronounced mad.

We have yet not been able to differentiate between mundane madness and divine madness, so in America both these types would be put in the asylum. Ramakrishna would have been kept under treatment, whereas Vivekananda would be given all the honour—because what Vivekananda says is intelligible. He himself was not in the state of divine madness. He was simply a messenger, a postman who carried the letter of Ramakrishna and read it to the people abroad. But he could read it well.

Mulla Nasruddin was the only literate person in his village—and you can imagine how literate he would be in that case—so everyone in the village looked to him to write their letters. One man went to him to get his letter written. Nasruddin said he would not write as his foot hurt. The man said, "What has your foot got to do with writing a letter? Won't you write with your hand?"

Nasruddin said, "You don't know. When I write a letter, only then can I read it. So I have to travel to another village to read it. I will write the letter but who will read it? My foot is in deep pain. As long as I cannot walk I will not do any letter writing."

So if people like Ramakrishna write a letter, they alone can read it, because they have forgotten your language and the language they speak is meaningless to you. We would call such people mad. So such people have to look for and choose a messenger from among us who can write in our language. Such a man is no more than a postman. Therefore, beware of Vivekananda. He has no experience of his own. What he says is another's experience. He is proficient in his art, he is an expert in using words, but it is not his experience.

It is for this reason that we find an overconfidence in the talks of Vivekananda. He stresses his points more than is required, and this is to make up for the deficiency. He himself is aware of the fact that what he is saying is not out of his own experience. The wise one, however, always hesitates: he is afraid; he may not be able to put forth his experience as clearly as he feels it. He will contemplate a thousand ways in his mind before he speaks and yet he will be concerned that what he says may not be quite what he wants to express. One who does not know goes ahead and says what he has to say. He feels no hesitation, because he knows exactly all that he has to say.

But this was very difficult for an enlightened one like Buddha. He did not give answers to certain questions. He used to say, "There is difficulty in answering these questions." So people used to say, "There are better people in our village who answer all our questions. They are wiser than Buddha. We ask them whether God is, and they reply either yes or no confidently. Buddha does not answer because he does not know."

But for Buddha it was very difficult to answer yes or no, so he hesitated and said, "Ask something else, not this." It was only natural for people to say that he did not know and that he should admit his ignorance. But this also Buddha could not say, because he knew. In fact Buddha speaks a different language from us and this is what causes the difficulty.

So it has happened time and again that many people like Ramakrishna left this world without giving their message. They could not. It is a very rare combination for a person to know and be able to convey. When this rare combination takes place we call such a person a *tirthankara,* an *avatar,* a prophet, etcetera. So the number of enlightened ones is not restricted only to those who have spoken. There have been many others who could not deliver their message.

Someone asked Buddha, "You have ten thousand bhikkhus here, and for the last forty years you have been teaching the people. How many people have reached the state of consciousness you are in?"

Buddha said, "Many have reached."

The person asked, "Then why can't we recognise them as we can recognise you?"

Buddha said, "You cannot recognise them because of the difference that I can speak and they cannot. If I too keep silent, you will not know me. You recognise only words; you cannot recognise enlightenment. It is only a matter of coincidence that I know and can also speak about it."

So there was some difficulty for Vivekananda which he must rectify in his lives to come. But this difficulty was inevitable. Therefore Ramakrishna, out of sheer necessity, brought it upon him. Vivekananda felt a loss but his loss belonged to the world of dreams. But even then, why should one undergo loss even in a dreamlike realm? If we need a dream then why not have a good dream?

There is a fable of Aesop:

Once a cat was lying under a tree dreaming. A dog comes along and he too rests under the tree. The cat seems to be dreaming a lovely dream, and the dog is curious to find out what it is all about.

When she wakes, the dog asks her what she has dreamed. The cat says, "Oh, it was a lovely dream. The sky was pouring mice."

The dog looks down in disdain and says, "You fool! It never rains mice. We also dream, and we always see bones pouring down—and our scriptures also say that it always rains bones. Mice never fall like rain, you stupid cat! If you must dream, dream of bones."

For the dog, bones are meaningful. Why should he dream of mice? But for the cat, bones are useless.

So I say to you: if you have to dream, why dream a bad dream? And if you are to awaken, then make maximum use of your own ability, your own strength, your own resolve—and do not wait for the other person to help you. Help will come, but that is another matter. You should not wait for and expect help, because the more you expect the weaker will become your resolve. Stop thinking on those lines altogether. Expect no help and make a total effort, remembering that you are all alone. Help will come from many sources—but that is a different matter altogether.

Therefore, my emphasis is on your own willpower, so that no other hindrance is created for you. And when you get something from someone it should always be unasked for and unexpected by you. It should come like the wind, and then it may go away like the wind.

This is why I said that Vivekananda suffered a loss, and as long as he lived he was acutely aware of it. His listeners sat enraptured; they even got a glimpse of what he said. But Vivekananda knew for himself that it was not happening to him. It would be a terrible thing for me to bring you the news of something tasty and have no experience of its taste myself. I may have once had a taste of it, but in a dream that then broke. Imagine if afterwards I am told, "Now you will no more dream of it, but go and tell others about it." So it was with Vivekananda. He had his own hardships. But he was a strong man; he was able to bear these hardships. This is a part of compassion, but this does not mean that you too should bear such hardships.

Vivekananda had an experience of samadhi through contact with Ramakrishna. Was it an authentic experience?

It will be good to call it a preliminary experience. The question of its authenticity is not important here. It was totally a preliminary experience in which one gets only a glimpse. This glimpse cannot be very deep or spiritual. This happening takes place at the borderline where the mind ends and the soul begins. At this depth it is only a psychic experience; therefore the glimpse was lost. But in Vivekananda's case it was not helped to go too deep because Ramakrishna was afraid. He did not allow it to go too deep; otherwise this man would be of no use to him. Ramakrishna was so deeply concerned about his vision that it never occurred to him that his concept about the experience leaving a man useless for the world was not one hundred per cent correct.

Buddha spoke for forty years after his enlightenment; the situation was similar with Jesus and Mahavira. They had no difficulty. But with Ramakrishna it was different. He had this difficulty; the difficulty was always in his own mind. Therefore, he gave Vivekananda just a fleeting glimpse. It was authentic as far as it went, but it was elementary. It did not go deep enough; otherwise he would have found it difficult to come back.

Can there be a partial experience of samadhi?

Not partial but preliminary. There is a difference between the two. The experience of *samadhi* cannot be partial, but there can be a mental glimpse of *samadhi*. The experience is spiritual; the glimpse is mental. If I stand on the top of a mountain and see the sea, I will definitely see the sea but from a distance. I will not have stood at the shore; I will not have touched or tasted of its waters; I will not have dived into it or bathed in it. I have seen the sea from the top of the mountain. Would you call this experience partial?

No. And in spite of the fact that I did not touch even a drop of the ocean, you cannot call my experience unauthentic. I have seen the ocean from the top of a mountain even though I have not become one with it. In the same way, you can see the soul from the topmost peak of your body.

The body too has its peak—its peak experiences. If you have a very deep experience of the body you can get a glimpse of the soul in it. If you are perfectly healthy and experience a feeling of well-being, if the body is overflowing with good health, you can reach a height of the body from where you can have a glimpse of the soul. You will experience that you are not the body and that you are something else. You will not have known what the soul is but you will have reached the ultimate height of the body.

The mind too has its heights. For example, when you are deeply in love—not in sex, because sex is only the possibility of the body. But even in sex, if you reach the peak of sexual experience, you get a glimpse of the soul. However, it will be a faraway glimpse—a glimpse from the farthest end. But if you have a deep experience of love, if you sit next to your loved one for a moment with not a word to break the silence, with only love moving between the two of you, without any doing or desiring but only waves of love moving from one to the other, in that peak moment of love you will reach the height from where you will have a glimpse of the soul. So lovers too get a glimpse of the soul.

An artist paints a picture. He is so absorbed in making it that for a moment he becomes God, the creator, because he experiences the same state that God must have felt when he created the world. But this height is of the mind. During the moment of the glimpse this man feels like the creator. Many times such a man makes the mistake of thinking that this experience is enough. This experience can be had from music, from poetry, from natural beauty and from other such things. But all these are faraway peaks. When you are totally dissolved in *samadhi,* the realisation happens. On the outside there are many peaks from where you can have a glimpse of the soul.

So this experience of Vivekananda happened at the level of the mind, because as I have told you, the other can go into you up to the peak of the mind and can lift you up to that peak.

Look at it this way: I take a small child on my shoulders and he looks all around. Then I put him down—because my shoulders cannot be his own. His own legs are still small and it will take a long time for him to grow up to my height. But lifted upon my shoulders he has seen, and now he can go to others and say that he has seen something. People may not believe him; they may say that it is not possible at his height. But it is possible to climb on the shoulders of another and have a view. All this is the possibility of the mind; hence, it is not spiritual.

All the same, it is not unauthentic; it is elementary. The elementary experience can take place either in the body or in the mind. And it is not partial; it is complete, but it is confined to the realm of the mind. It is not of the soul, because in the experience of the soul there is no coming back. At that level no one can keep your key; no one can say that when he returns the key, then only will it happen. Nobody else has any say there. If some special task is expected to be accomplished by a medium, then he has to be stopped before the point of transcendence; otherwise difficulty will arise.

So Vivekananda's experience was an authentic experience, but its authenticity is psychic and not spiritual. This too, however, is not a small happening; it does not happen to all. It requires a very powerful and matured mind.

Could we say that Ramakrishna exploited Vivekananda?

It could be said but it should not be said, because the word conveys an idea of condemnation behind it. He did not exploit him to gain something selfish for himself; his idea was that through Vivekananda others will be benefited. He exploited him only in the sense that he made use of him. There is a great difference between exploitation and utilisation. When I am dealing with something or using something for the sake of my ego, then it becomes exploitation. But when I am doing something for the world, for the universe, for everybody, there is no question of exploitation.

Besides, where is the certainty that if Ramakrishna had not shown him the glimpse, Vivekananda would have got it in this life by himself? This point can be decided only by those who are enlightened. I feel that would have been the case, but we cannot show any proof in such matters. When Ramakrishna told Vivekananda that three days before his death he would get the key, it could only mean that according to Ramakrishna, Vivekananda would have reached *samadhi* three days before his death as a result of his own efforts. Now, as far as returning the key is concerned, Ramakrishna was already dead, but the key was returned exactly as it had been said.

This is possible because you do not know your own personality as much as the person who has gone deep within the self. From his own depths he can know your potential. He can even tell when you will reach if you can walk at your own pace.

Let us say, you have started on a journey and there is a mountain in your path. Now, I know the path and the steps of the mountain, how long it takes to cross it and what difficulties you will encounter. I see you climbing the mountain, and I can say that you will take, for example, three months to cross it. I can tell from the speed of your walking and the manner in which you are traveling that you will take that much time. If I were to pick you up on the way and give you a glimpse of the top, then leave you again where you were, promising you that within three months you will find the goal, this cannot basically be looked upon as my making use of you. Everything within is so subtle and complex that you cannot know it outwardly.

For instance, Nirmala went home yesterday and somebody told her that she would die at the age of fifty-three. Now, I have given her a guarantee that she will not die at fifty-three. It is not I who will carry out the guarantee: it will fulfil itself on its own. So now if she does not die at the age fifty-three she will attribute it to me.

Vivekananda would say that the key had been returned three days before his death—but who was there to return the key?

Could it be that Ramakrishna knew that Vivekananda had to go through a very hard time in his spiritual endeavour with failures and pains, and so, out of compassion, he gave him a glimpse to keep up his hopes?

Never think in terms of this language, that "It could be..." because this has no end and there is no meaning in it. In this way you will go on thinking irrelevantly. It is enough to think in terms of what exactly is possible and no more, because otherwise these are meaningless paths that may lead you astray. In this pattern of thinking you will be deeply harmed, as you will go on missing that which is. So always see a fact as it is, and if you want to know a thing as it is, cut out all the could-have-beens. If you do not know the exact facts, then know that you do not know, but do not try to cover your ignorance with wise assumptions of "It could be." This is how we cover up many of our shortcomings. It is better to refrain from this.

2

RIPENING OF THE MEDITATOR ON THE PATH

***In one of** Your previous discourses You said that a sudden and direct descent of grace can become a disaster sometimes. The person might be harmed or become mad or he may even die. A question naturally arises: Is grace not always beneficial? Does grace not keep its own equilibrium? The mishap can also be due to the fact that the recipient was unfit. In that case, how can grace descend on an unqualified person?*

God is not a person but an energy. This implies that energy has no considerations for individuals; whatsoever happens to each individual happens impartially.

For example, the tree on a river bank receives its nutrition from the passing current; it will bear flowers and fruits and will grow tall and strong. But the tree that falls into the same current will be carried away with the swift tide. Now the river has nothing to do with either of these trees. Neither is it interested in feeding the former nor in destroying the latter. The river just flows. The river is a flowing energy, it is not a person.

We have always made the mistake of looking upon God as a person. Therefore, all our thinking about God is as if he were a person. We say he is very kind; we say he is merciful; we say he always blesses us. These are our expectations and desires that we impose upon God. Though we can impose our expectations on a person and if they are not fulfilled we make the person responsible for it, we cannot do this to energy. So whenever we deal with energy as if it is a person, we are bound to go off track, because then we are lost in dreams. If we deal with energy the results will be entirely different.

For instance, the force of gravity: you are able to walk on the earth because of this force, but this force is not specially meant to make you walk. Don't mistakenly think that if you don't walk, the gravitation will not exist. It was there when you were not on the earth and it will be there even after you are no more. If you walk in a wrong manner you might fall and break your legs. This will also be due to gravity; but for this you will not be able to sue anyone as there is no person to blame. Gravitation is a current of energy. You have to be careful about its laws of functioning if you want to deal with it. But it does not think at all about how to deal with you.

God's energy does not work out of consideration for anyone. In fact, it is not proper to say "God's energy," rather we should say: "God is energy." God does not think about how to behave with you; it has its own eternal law and this eternal law is religion. Religion means the laws of behaviour of the energy that is God.

If you behave with discrimination, understanding and in conformity with this energy, it becomes grace for you—not on its own, but because of you. If you do the opposite, if you go against the laws of the energy, it becomes non-grace-yielding towards you. In this case God is not ungraceful; it is so because of you.

So it will be an error to look upon God as a person. God is not a person but an energy; therefore, prayer and worship hold no meaning. It is meaningless to have expectations from God. If you wish that this divine energy becomes a blessing, grace for you, then you have to do something to your own self; hence, spiritual practice has meaning, prayer does not. Meditation has meaning, worship does not. Understand the difference clearly.

In prayer you are doing something with God: you beg, you insist, you expect, you demand. In meditation you are working upon your own self. In worship you are doing something with God; in spiritual endeavour you are doing something on your self. The effort for spiritual growth means that you are transforming yourself in such a way that you are not in a discord with existence, with religion. When the river flows you are not swept away by the current. Instead, you are on the bank where the waters of the river strengthen your roots rather than washing them away. The moment we see God as energy the whole structure of religion changes.

It is for this reason I had said that if the grace descends suddenly and directly it can sometimes become a disaster.

Another thing you have asked, "Can an unfit person be the recipient of grace?"

No, grace never descends on a person unqualified for it. It always descends on a person who is prepared for it. But sometimes an unfit person suddenly develops the necessary qualifications, and he himself is unaware of this. The happening always takes place under the right conditions, just as the light is visible only to those with eyes and not to the blind. But if a blind man has been medically treated so that he can see, and he comes out of the hospital and he sees the sun directly, he will be seriously harmed. He will have to put on dark glasses for a month or two and wait.

If an unreceptive person suddenly becomes receptive, there is bound to be a mishap. The sun cannot be blamed in the case of the blind man. He has to develop the strength of his eyes to bear the sunlight or else there is a danger that he can become totally blind. The first blindness was curable, but now it will be difficult to cure his second blindness.

Understand this well: the experience comes only to those who are deserving. But sometimes there is a possibility of an undeserving person suddenly developing the necessary qualifications due to circumstances of which he himself is not aware. Then there is always a fear of disaster, because the energy descends suddenly and you are not in a condition to bear it.

For example: a man suddenly gets a large amount of money. Usually it should not be of any harm, but if it comes suddenly it may be dangerous. A sudden happiness may also create an accident, because we need a certain capacity to bear it. We become able to bear happiness if it comes upon us gradually. If bliss comes gradually only then we become prepared for it.

This preparedness, the capacity to bear, depends on so many factors. The nerves in the brain, one's physical fitness, one's mental capacity—all have their limitations, and the energy we are talking about is unlimited. It is like the ocean falling into the drop: if the drop is not prepared in some way to receive the ocean it will merely die; it will be destroyed and it will attain nothing.

To be exact, there is a double line of action necessary for spiritual growth. We have to bring ourselves to the path and become in tune with it. But before that we have to develop our ability to absorb it. These are the two tasks to be accomplished by a seeker. On one hand we have to open the door and improve our eyesight, and on the other we have to wait even after the sight is improved in order for the eyes to be able to bear the brightness of light; otherwise too much light brings an even deeper darkness. This is a one-sided transaction—the light has nothing to do with it. The responsibility is entirely ours and we cannot blame anyone for it.

The journey of man's life is spread over many lives, and he does many things in each life. Many times it happens that he dies just as he is about to be able to receive grace. With this death he loses all the memories of this life. Working upon yourself through many lives you may have reached up to ninety-nine degrees of growth; dying you will forget all your achievements—but the existential elements of your inner growth will be carried over to the next life.

There is another person sitting next to you who has accomplished only one degree of growth in his past life. He has also forgotten all about it. You both are meditating: you two belong to a totally different level of growth. Now, if one degree of growth happens the other person will reach only the second degree of growth and grace is not going to descend on him. But with plus one degree of growth you will reach the one hundred-degree point and suddenly grace will descend upon you. This will be sudden for you because you have no idea that you are at the ninety-ninth degree. And so heaven can drop into you all of a sudden and proper preparation should be made for this.

When I say mishap I am only referring to a happening for which we are not prepared. Mishap does not necessarily mean a bad or painful event; it means only the occurrence of that event for which we are not yet ready. Now, if a man wins a lottery of one million dollars it is not a bad happening. But he can die. One million dollars!—it can stop the beating of his heart. So mishap means the occurrence of an event for which we are not prepared.

The opposite may also take place. If a man is prepared for his death and it comes, it is not necessary that his death is a bad event. If a man such as Socrates is prepared to meet death and welcomes it with open arms, then for such a person death becomes *samadhi*. He accepts death with such love and joy that he will see that reality which never dies.

We approach death with so much distress that we become unconscious before death. We do not experience death consciously. This is why, even though we have died many times, we are unaware of the process of death. Once you know what death is, then the very idea that you can die will never arise. Then the event of death will take place and you will be standing aside watching it. But this must happen with full consciousness.

So death can be a good fortune for one person and grace can be a misfortune to another. Therefore the spiritual growth is twofold: we have to call, invoke, search and move, and at the same time we have to prepare ourselves for the event so that when light reaches our door we are not blinded by it. If you remember what I have told you in the beginning there won't be any difficulty. If you take God to be a person you will find yourself in great difficulty; if you take him as an energy there won't be any difficulty.

This concept of God as a person has caused a great deal of difficulty. The mind desires him to be a person so that we can transfer all responsibility onto him, and having made him responsible we start to place the burden of every small thing onto him. If a man finds a job he thanks God; if he loses his job he becomes angry with God. If a man gets a blister he suspects it to be the doing of God; if it heals he thanks God. We never consider how we are employing God; we do not even think how egocentric is this attitude in which we assume that God should worry even about our blisters.

If we lose a coin on the road and happen to find it, we say, "By God's grace I found it." We want God to keep our accounts to the last rupee. This idea satisfies our mind because then we can stand at the centre of the world. Then our dealings with God are similar to that of a servant before a master. We expect him to stand guard at our door and take care of our possessions to the last coin. The advantage of considering God as a person is that responsibility can be easily placed upon him.

But a seeker takes responsibility upon himself. In fact, to be a seeker means to hold no one but oneself responsible for everything. If there is sorrow in my life I am responsible, and if there is happiness in my life I am responsible. If I am tranquil it is I who am responsible; if I am restless it is my own making. There is no one but myself who is responsible for whatsoever state I am in. If I fall and break my leg it is my own fault and I cannot blame gravity. If this is the attitude of the mind, then you will have understood rightly. Then the meaning of a mishap will be different.

For this reason, I say that grace is beneficial and is a blessing to a person who is well prepared for it. In fact, there is a time for everything. There is a special moment for each happening, and to miss this moment is a great tragedy.

In one of Your talks You said that the effect of shaktipat diminishes gradually; thus the seeker must maintain a regular contact with the medium. Does this not mean dependency upon some person in the form of a guru?

This can become a dependency. If someone is eager to be a guru and if someone is eager to get a guru, this state of dependency can happen. So do not make the mistake of becoming a disciple or making somebody your guru. But if there is no question of a guru or a disciple, there is no fear of dependency. Then the person from whom you are taking help is simply a part of your own self that has travelled ahead on the path. Then who is the guru and who is the disciple?

I often tell the story that Buddha told of one of his previous lives. He said, "I was an ignorant person in my previous life. A wise person had attained enlightenment, so I went to see him. I bowed down to touch his feet in reverence. But no sooner had I lifted myself up than I found to my astonishment that the old man had bent to touch my feet.

"'What is this you have done!' I exclaimed. 'That I should touch your feet is right and proper, but it is not fitting that you should touch mine.'

"The old man said, 'If you touch my feet and I do not touch yours it would be a great mistake, because I am nothing but a part of you a few steps ahead of you. And when I bow at your feet I remind you that you did well to touch mine. But do not be under the misconception that you and I are two. Also, do not make the mistake of thinking that I am wise and you are ignorant. It is a matter of time. A little more time and you too will be enlightened. It is just as when my right foot comes forward, the left remains behind to follow: actually, the left foot remains behind in order that the right may go forward.'"

The relationship of guru and disciple is harmful. However, a non-related relating between a guru and the disciple is very beneficial. Non-related means there are not two; relationship is where there are two. We can understand if a disciple feels the guru to be a separate entity from him, because the disciple is ignorant. But if the guru also feels the same, that is too much. Then it means that the blind is leading the blind—and the blind man who is leading is more dangerous, because the second blind man has total trust in him.

There is no spiritual meaning to a guru-disciple relationship. Actually, all relationships are the relationships of power. They are all relations of power politics. Someone is a father, someone is a son; if this were a relationship of love it would be a different matter. Then the father would not be conscious of his being the father, nor the son of being a son. Then the son would be the preceding form of the father and the father would be the subsequent form of the son—and this is the truth of the matter.

We sow a seed and a tree grows. Then this tree gives rise to thousands of seeds. What is the relationship between these seeds and the first seed? One came first and the others followed later. It is the journey of the same seed that fell to the ground, sprouted and dissolved in the soil. The father is the first link and the son the second in the same chain. But then there is a chain, not individual persons. Then if the son touches his father's feet he is showing his respect for the previous link. He is showing his reverence for that which is going out, because without him he could not have come into the world. He has come into existence through him.

And if the father is bringing up his son, feeding him and clothing him, he is not taking pains for someone else; it is his own extension he is nurturing. If we say that the father becomes a youth once more in his son, we would not be wrong. Then the matter is not one of relationship; it is a different matter. It is love, not a relationship.

Generally we find the relationship between father and son to be a political relationship. The father is strong and the son is weak, so the father dominates the son. He tries to make him feel, "You are nothing; I am everything." But he does not realise that soon a time will come when the son will be the strong one. Then he will dominate the father in the same way.

These relationships between the master and the disciple, the wife and the husband are perversions....Otherwise, why should there be any relationship between a husband and a wife? Two people have felt oneness between them, so they are together. But no, this is not so. The husband dominates the wife in his own way; the wife dominates the husband in her own way. Both are playing their own strength as a power politics on each other.

The same is the case with the guru and the disciple. The guru oppresses the disciple, and the latter waits for him to die so that he may become the guru. If the guru would delay dying there would be plotting and scheming against him. So it is difficult to find a guru whose disciples do not rebel against him or become his enemies. The chief disciple is bound to be the enemy of the guru. So one must be careful in choosing the chief disciple. It is almost inevitable, because the pressure of power is always met with rebellion. Spirituality has nothing to do with it.

I can understand a father pressurising the son: it is a case of two ignorant people, and they could be forgiven. It is not good but it can be excused. The husband oppressing the wife and vice versa is usual—not good, but it is very common. But when the guru suppresses his disciple it becomes difficult. This area at least should be free of any claim that "I know and you do not."

What is this relationship between a guru and a disciple? One is a claimant: he says, "I know, you do not know. You are ignorant, I am wise. The ignorant must bow to the wise." But what sort of a wise man is he who says, "You must bow in reverence"? He is the most ignorant person. He knows a few inherited secrets, he has studied some scriptures and he can repeat them from his memory. There is nothing more to him than this.

Perhaps you have not heard this story:

There was a cat who became all-knowing. She became famous among cats—so much so that she came to be looked upon as a *tirthankara*. The reason for her becoming all-knowing was that she had found a way of sneaking into a library. She knew everything about this library. By everything I mean the means of entrance and exit from the library, which set of books was the most comfortable to snuggle against, which books gave warmth in the winter and which were cool in the summer, etcetera.

So the word went around among the cats that if anybody wanted any knowledge about the library, the all-knowing cat could provide the answer. Naturally, there was no doubt about such a one who knew everything about the library being omniscient. This cat even had followers. But the fact remained that she knew nothing. All she knew about books was whether she could sit behind them comfortably, which books had cloth binding, were warm, and which ones did not. More than this she did not know. She had not the least idea of what was inside the book. And how could a cat know what is inside a book?

There are such all-knowing cats among men too, who know how to shield themselves with books. You attack them and they will at once take refuge in the *Ramayana* and try to strangle you with its verses. Or, they will say, "So says the *Gita*."

Now who is to fight with the *Gita*? If I were to say, "This is what I say," you can debate with me. But if I bring the *Gita* in I am safe. I take refuge behind the *Gita*. The *Gita* gives warmth in the cold; it gives me a vocation and becomes a protective shield against enemies. It even becomes an ornament and can be played with, but a person who does this only knows as much about the *Gita* as the cat in the library; he knows no more than she does.

It may be possible that by long association the cat might come to know what is inside the books, but these knowledgeable gurus will not know at all. The more they learn the book by heart, the less need there will be for them to know. They will then be under the illusion that they know all there is to know.

Whenever a man claims the authority of knowing, know that it is only ignorance that has become outspoken, because assertion is ignorance. But when a man hesitates even to mention that he knows, then know that he has begun to receive a glimpse, a ray of wisdom. Such a man, however, would not become a guru, he would not even dream of becoming one, because with becoming a guru comes the authority of knowledge. The meaning of guru is one who knows: he is sure that he knows, and now you need not know; he can impart his knowledge to you.

So this claim and authority kill the sense of quest and inquiry in others. Authority cannot exist without suppression, because he who wields authority is always afraid of your finding out the truth. Then what would become of his power? So he will stop you from finding out. He will gather followers and disciples around him, and within the disciples also there will be a hierarchy of chief disciples and lesser disciples. This is again a political web and it has nothing to do with spirituality.

When I say that a happening like *shaktipat*—which is the descent of the energy of the divine—takes place easily in the presence of a particular person, I do not mean that you should cling and get fixed with this person; nor do I say that you should be dependent upon him or make him into a guru. I also do not say that you should stop your search. On the contrary, whenever this event takes place through a medium you will feel that if this experience through an indirect source could bring so much joy, how much more blissful it would be to experience a direct descent of the divine energy! After all, when a thing comes through someone it does lose some of its freshness; it becomes a little stale.

I go to a garden and I am filled with the fragrance of the flowers, and then you come to see me and you feel the fragrance of the flowers through me. You will find that it will also be mingled with my body odour, and it will also have become faint by then.

So when I say initially *shaktipat* is very beneficial, what I mean is that first you should get the news that there is a garden and there are flowers so that you maybe are encouraged to set out on the journey. But if you acquire a guru you will stagnate, so do not stop at a milestone. The milestones tell us much more than the ones we call gurus. They tell us exactly how many miles more are left for the destination. No guru can give such precise information. And yet we do not worship the milestones or sit near them. If we did we would prove ourselves to be less than stones, because the stone is there to indicate how much more of the journey is left. It is not there to stop you.

If a milestone could speak, it too would call out, "Where are you going? I have given you the necessary information. You have travelled ten miles and you have twenty more to go. Now you know, so you have no need to go further. Be my disciple; follow me." But the stone cannot speak, so it cannot become a guru.

Man speaks; therefore he becomes a guru. He says, "I have shown you so much; be grateful to me. You must show your gratitude, your indebtedness to me." Remember, he who demands gratitude has nothing to give you. He is merely giving you a piece of information just like a milestone. A milestone does not know anything about the journey. There is only one piece of information engraved on it which it gives to all who pass by.

Likewise, if gratitude is demanded and expected from you, beware. Do not get stuck with an individual. Move beyond individuality towards the formless, the eternal, the infinite. However, a glimpse is possible through a person who is just a vehicle, because ultimately the individual also belongs to the divine. Just as the ocean can be known through the well, so can the infinite be known through the individual. If a glimpse can happen to you, then realisation can also happen. But do not depend on anybody or be enslaved by anything.

All relationships are binding, whether they be of husband and wife, father and son, or guru and disciple. Where there is relationship, there is slavery. So the spiritual seeker has not to form relationships. If he keeps the relationship of husband and wife there is no harm; it is not a hindrance because this relationship is irrelevant. But the irony lies in the fact that he renounces and drops out of husband-wife, father-son relationships to form a new guru-disciple relationship. This is very dangerous.

The idea of a spiritual relationship has no meaning. All relationships belong to the mundane world. Relationship as such is worldly. If we say that relationship is the world, it would not be wrong. You are alone, unassociated. This is not an egotistical statement because others too are alone and unassociated. Someone is two steps ahead of you; if you have heard the footsteps, then you have already known the direction of your journey that far. There are some who are two steps behind you, there are some others traveling along with you. So an infinite number of souls are travelling on the path. In this journey we are all fellow travellers; the only difference is that somebody is a little ahead or a little behind. Take maximum advantage of those ahead of you, but do not turn it into some kind of slavery.

Keep away from dependence and relationships, and especially from "spiritual" relationships—always. Worldly relationships are not dangerous, because the world as such is a relationship. It is not a problem. Receive the message and indications wherever they are available. I do not mean that you should not be thankful for them.

This should not create any complication in your mind. What I am saying is that if gratitude is demanded it is wrong, but if you are not grateful it is equally wrong. One should thank the milestone also for giving us information, whether it hears or not.

When we say that the guru should not ask or expect gratitude, it deludes the listener and feeds his ego. He thinks, "It is absolutely correct. There is no need even to thank him!" There we make a mistake, because then we grasp the statement from the opposite extreme. I am not saying that you should not even be grateful. What I mean is that the guru should not demand gratitude. So if you are not grateful it will be equally wrong on your part. You must be grateful, but this gratitude will not bind you because that which is never asked for never binds. If I thank you without your asking it is not binding. But if you demand thanks, whether I thank you or not, it will bind you and create troubles.

Take the hint or the glimpse from wherever you get it. It will disappear again and again. It cannot be permanent because it comes from another. Only that will last which is yours.

So you will have to undergo the happening of *shaktipat* again and again. If you are afraid of losing your freedom, seek your own experience. It is of no use being afraid of bondage, because if I bind myself to you it is bondage, and if I run away from you with the fear of being bound then also I am linked with and, hence, bound to you.

So take what you get silently; be grateful and move on. And if you feel something had come but has been lost again, then seek the source within, from where it can never be lost. There is no way of losing then, because our own treasure is infinite. With that which has its source in another there is the chance that it will be lost.

Do not be a beggar who keeps asking from others. That which you receive from another should start you on your own search. And this becomes possible only when you do not get stuck at having a relationship. Receive, offer your thanks, and move on.

You said that God is an impartial and pure energy. God is not specially interested in man's life; it has no obligation towards man's life. In the Katha Upanishad there is a sutra which means, "God comes to meet him whom he likes." What are the basis and reasons for his preference?

Actually, I did not say that God is not interested in you: if He was not you would not have been. Nor did I say He was indifferent toward you: He cannot be because you are not apart from Him. You are an extension of Him. What I said was that He does not have any special interest in you. There is a difference between these statements.

The energy that is God has no special interest in you in the sense that it will not violate its laws for your sake. If you hit your head with a stone you are bound to bleed; nature will take no special interest in you—although when you hit your head and the blood starts flowing it is flowing because God is involved in the happening. When you drown in the river, then too nature is playing its part—that of drowning you. But there is no special interest in the sense that it will save you when its law was to drown you. The law is that if you fall from the roof you will have a fracture; nature has no special interest that you should not.

Those who believe God to be a person have fabricated many stories of divine favours—for instance, that Pralad was neither burnt by fire nor hurt when he was thrown down the mountain. These stories are our wishful thinking; we wish that it should be so. We wish that God should have a special interest in us, that we should be the centre of his attention.

The workings of energy are always according to the law. Man's interest can be special; man can be partial. But energy is always impartial, impartiality is its only interest; therefore it will do what is within its law and never falls out of it. There are no miracles on the part of God.

Now about the *Katha Upanishad sutra,* its meaning is very different. It says, "He meets only those of his choice, with whom he is happy and whom he likes." Naturally, you will say this means that he has a special interest in some people. This is not so. Actually, there is great difficulty in explaining such things, because when a truth is to be explained it has to be dealt with from its manifold aspects.

Those who have attained God have invariably said, "Who are we and what value do our efforts have? We are just nobodies and our worth is not even equal to a particle of dust; yet we attained him. And if we meditated a while, of what great value was that compared to this priceless treasure we attained? There is no comparison between our efforts and our gain." So those who have attained enlightenment have maintained that it was not the result of their effort. "It was his grace, it was his wish to bless us; otherwise, could we ever have found him?" they always ask.

This is the statement of an egoless person who realises the magnificence and magnitude of his attainment. However, if this becomes the way of thinking of those who have not yet attained it will be very dangerous. When this comes from those who have attained, this statement is fitting and carries a distinct mark of refinement of feeling.

Such persons maintain, "Who are we that we should have attained him? What was our strength, our ability? What was our right? What claim did we have on him? Yet because of his compassion he blessed us to meet him." For those who have attained this statement is proper. What they mean is that they do not consider their attainment to be the direct result of their effort. It is not the achievement of the ego; it is a gift, grace.

What they say is correct, but reading the *Katha Upanishad* you will be in difficulty. Reading any of the scriptures man has been in great difficulty, because scriptures are the statement of those who know and are being read by those who do not. They take it according to their understanding and say, "Okay. If God meets only him whom he wishes to meet, according to his own liking, why should we bother? Why should we do anything?" Then the declaration of the egoless person becomes a protection for our lethargy.

There is a vast difference between the two—like between the sky and the earth. The humble and egoless statements of enlightened people become a protection for our dullness and laziness. Then we say, "Well, God meets only whom He wants to meet and He does not meet those He does not want to."

There is a similar statement of Saint Augustine which runs something like this: "Those whom God wished, He made them good; those whom He wished, He made them bad." This seems a very dangerous statement. If this is so—that God makes some bad and He makes some good as it suits His fancy—then things are crazy! Then He must be an insane God!

When you read this you can give a very negative meaning to it. But what Augustine means is totally different. He tells the good man, "Do not be conceited that you are good, because those whom God wished He made good." And to the bad man he says, "Do not be distressed, do not worry. Those whom God wished He made evil."

He is pulling out the pride from the good man's ego and he is pulling out the sting of the bad man's remorse. This statement comes from one who knows. But the bad man hears it and he says, "If that is so, I have no hand in it—for those whom God wants to be evil are evil." The good man's journey also slackens; he says, "What is there to do? Those whom God chooses to make good He makes good, and those whom He chooses not to He does not." His life becomes meaningless and stagnant.

This is what the scriptures have done to the whole world. Scriptures are the words of those who are enlightened. However, those who know do not need to read scriptures, but those who do not know do read them; then the difference in understanding is poles apart. The meaning we give to their words is our own and not the actual meaning.

I have come to feel that there should be two kinds of scriptures—words of the enlightened ones should be kept separate, and there should be separate scriptures prepared specially for the unenlightened ones. The scriptures containing the words of the enlightened ones should be totally hidden from the ignorant man, because he is bound to deduce his own meanings and then everything becomes twisted and contorted. In this way all our wisdom has become contorted. Do you understand what I am saying?

You have said that shaktipat, transmission of vital energy, takes place through the medium of an egoless person and that he who says, "I can do shaktipat," is for sure a phony and shaktipat will not happen through him. But I know many such people who practise shaktipat, and the kundalini energy starts moving and growing as written in the scriptures. Are these false processes? If so, how and why?

This is also an important point to understand. In fact, there is nothing in this world which has no false counterpart to it. False coins exist in every dimension of life. And it is always the case that the counterfeit coin is brighter in appearance than the genuine one. It has to be, because it is the brightness that will make it attractive; it is useless in its reality. A true coin works even if it is not bright. A false coin makes loud claims because it has to compensate, and because of its worthlessness it is easily available.

All spiritual achievements have their false counterparts and there is no experience without a counterfeit counterpart. If there is a real *kundalini* there is a false *kundalini* too. If there are genuine *chakras,* there are false *chakras* also. If there are true methods of yoga there are false methods as well. The difference between the two is that the genuine experiences occur on the spiritual plane, whereas the false occur on the psychic, mental plane.

For example, if a person enters into deep meditation and moves closer to his being, he will begin to experience many things. He can experience such fragrances as he has never known before; he can hear music that is out of this world; he can see colours that are not seen on earth. But all these experiences can be created by hypnosis in no time and without difficulty. Colours can be produced; melodies can be produced; tastes and fragrances can be produced. And for all this there is no need to go through deep meditation and inner transformation. All you need is to become unconscious through hypnosis; then whatsoever is suggested from without can happen within. These experiences are false coins.

Whatsoever happens in meditation can happen through hypnosis also but it will not be spiritual. It is an induced state; it is like a dream. If you love a woman in your waking state you can love her in your dreams also—and the woman in the dream will be more beautiful. If the man does not wake up and keeps on dreaming he will never know whether the dream girl is real or illusory. How will he know? Only when the dream is broken will he know that it was a dream.

So there are methods by which all kinds of dreams can be created within you. A dream of *kundalini* can be created; dreams of *chakras* can be created; many experiences can be created. You will love to revel in these dreams; they are so pleasant that you would not like them to disappear. They are such dreams that it is difficult to call them dreams, because they happen while you are awake, while you are active. They are daydreams. They can be practised and you can pass all your life in them, but in the end you will find you have reached nowhere; you have been seeing a long dream. There are means and methods to create these dreams. Another person can induce them in you and you will never be able to distinguish between the false and the true, because you have no idea of the real experience.

If a man has never seen a real coin and has always dealt with false coins, how will he know that his coins are false? To know the false the genuine must be known. So only the moment the *kundalini* unfolds itself can one find how far apart the two experiences are. The real *kundalini* is a different experience altogether.

Remember, many of the *kundalini* descriptions in the scriptures are false, and there are reasons for this. Now I will tell you a secret of the scriptures. All the sages and seers who have lived on the earth have purposely left some basic errors in each scripture for the purpose of judging the progress and authenticity of the disciple. Now, for instance, I may tell you from outside this house that there are five rooms within, but I know there are six. One day you might come and say, "I have seen the house from inside and there are five rooms only as you say." Then I will know that you have seen some other place—an illusory one—and not the house I talked about.

In this way one room has always been left out; this gives the information whether you have really experienced or not, whether your experience is genuine or not. If your experiences totally correspond with the scriptures then it is a false coin, because something has been always left out in the scriptures; it is very necessary to do so.

If your experiences tally with books, know that book-knowledge is being projected. The moment your experiences come in a different manner, a manner in which they might coincide with the scriptures in some places and not in others, then know that you are on the right track—that things are happening authentically and that you are not merely projecting the descriptions you have read in the scriptures.

So when the *kundalini* awakens authentically you will know where in the scriptures things have been devised to judge the authenticity of the experiences of the meditators. But before this you cannot know it. Every scripture had to necessarily drop some information; otherwise it would be difficult to judge the authenticity of experiences.

There was a teacher of mine. He was a professor in the university. Whatever book I mentioned he would say that he had read it. One day I mentioned a fictitious book and the name of its author. I said, "Have you read the book of so-and-so? It is a wonderful book."

He said, "Yes, I have."

"Now either you produce that book or all your previous claims of having read books are nullified," I told him. "There is no such book and no such author!"

He was surprised. "What do you mean? Is there no such book?" he said.

"No!" I said. "There was no other way to judge the authenticity of your claims."

Those who know will at once find out. If your experiences are exactly as laid down in the scriptures you will be caught, because there are gaps left in the scriptures: something false has been added, something true has been left out, and all this was absolutely necessary because otherwise it would be difficult to tell what is happening to whom.

The experiences described in the scriptures can be created; everything can be created, because the capacity of the human mind is so much. And before one enters into the innermost core of the being the mind deceives one in a thousand ways. And if you too want to deceive yourself then it is very easy.

So I say the matter of descriptions in the scriptures or someone claiming to do *shaktipat* or techniques of creating false experience are not significant points. The essential core of the matter is something different. There are many other ways of finding out the authenticity of your experience.

A man drinks water in the daytime and his thirst is quenched; he drinks water in a dream but his thirst is not quenched. In the morning he finds his throat parched and his lips dry, because drinking water in a dream cannot quench the thirst. It is actual water that quenches the thirst. Whether the water was real or unreal can be found out from your thirst—whether it is quenched or not.

So those of whom you are talking, who claim to awaken people's *kundalini* or who say that at least their own *kundalini* has become awakened, are still searching. They claim they have experienced many things, and yet their search continues. They maintain they have found water, and yet they have no idea of the lake!

It was only the day before yesterday that a friend came and said that he had reached the state of thoughtlessness, and he had come to ask for a method of meditation. Now, what to say to such a person! One man says his *kundalini* has awakened but his mind is restless; another says that the *kundalini* has awakened but he is still tortured by sex! There are intermediate devices to discover the authenticity of your experience.

If the experience is real, the search ends. Then even if God comes and offers tranquillity or bliss, the person will refuse politely and ask him to keep it for himself; he no longer needs it. So to find out the authenticity of the experience look deep into the personality of the person for some other symptoms of transformation.

One man says that he goes into *samadhi,* into superconsciousness. He buries himself underground for six days and comes out alive. But if you leave money in the house this man will steal; if he finds the opportunity he will indulge in drinking alcohol. If you did not know about his claim of *samadhi* you would not find anything of value in him. There is no fragrance, no radiance, no grace in his personality; he is just an ordinary man.

No, he does not go into *samadhi:* he has learned the trick of a false *samadhi*. He has mastered the trick of staying underground for six days by *pranayam;* he has learned how to control his breath so that within the given area of his resting place he can use the minimum amount of oxygen. Thus he can stay underground for six days. He is almost in the same state as the Siberian bear that hibernates underneath the snow for six months. He is not in any kind of *samadhi*. At the end of the rainy season the frogs lie buried underground for eight months: they are not in *samadhi*. This man has learned the same, nothing more.

Now, if you bury a man underground who has attained to the authentic state of *samadhi* he is likely to die, as *samadhi* has nothing to do with being buried underground. If Mahavira or Buddha were made to lie underground in this way there is little possibility of their coming out alive. But this man will come out alive, because this achievement has nothing to do with *samadhi*. *Samadhi* is a different matter altogether. But this man will attract the masses. If Mahavira fails and this man succeeds, he will appear to be a real *tirthankara* and Mahavira will appear to be false.

So these false psychic coins have their own false claims, and methods have been evolved for making them convincing. Thus a separate world has been created around them which has nothing to do with the reality. Such persons who are involved in trading the false coins have lost the genuine path from where the real transformation comes. Staying six days or even six months beneath the ground has nothing to do with self-realisation. But what are the inner qualities of such a man? How much peace and silence does this man have within? Is he blissful within? If he loses a coin he will not sleep at night, but he can stay comfortably underground for six days.

All this has to be considered and the real meaning behind it has to be found.

So those who claim to have the capacity of doing *shaktipat* can do so, but it is not the authentic *shaktipat*. It is intrinsically a kind of hypnosis. Deep down they have somehow learned the skills of playing with the magnetic forces. It is also not sure that they know the complete science of this subject. Neither they know the science of this process nor are they aware of the falseness of their claims. They are in a big mess.

You see a street magician in India showing his tricks. He spreads a cloth and tells a boy to lie on it. He keeps a trinket on his chest. He then asks the boy what is the number of a currency note in the pocket of an observer. The boy will tell him the number. "What is the time on the watch of the person standing there?" The boy will tell the exact time. "What is the name of this man?" The boy will tell him the name. Everyone watching is convinced of the magic of the trinket.

Then he removes the trinket from the boy's chest and repeats the questions. The boy lies silent: he cannot answer. Now this magician makes a good business with the trinkets—one rupee each! You take it home: you can put it on your chest for the rest of your life but nothing is going to happen. It is not that the boy has been taught by the magician to speak when the trinket is on his chest and to be silent when it is removed, nor is there any special quality in the trinket itself. The trick is more subtle and you will be surprised to know it.

This process is called post-hypnotic suggestion. A person is made unconscious by hypnosis, and in this state of hypnotic trance he is told to have a good look at the trinket. He is also told that as soon as this trinket is placed on his chest he must become unconscious. Then, in this state of unconsciousness, he can be made to read the number of currency bills or tell the time on the watch. There is nothing phony in it. As soon as the boy is made to lie on the sheet in a hypnotic state and the trinket is placed on his chest he goes into a hypnotic trance. Now he can tell the number of the currency bill if asked by the magician. Neither the boy nor the magician knows exactly what is happening inside.

The magician has learned a trick: a man is put into a hypnotic trance and then being shown a thing he is told, "Whenever this thing is placed on you, you will immediately become unconscious, falling into hypnotic trance again." This method works perfectly—the magician knows only this much. Neither of the two knows the inner mechanism, the dynamics of the energy phenomenon. If they were to know it they would not be performing tricks by the roadside. To know the dynamics of the process is a deep subject even though it is only a psychic phenomenon. Even Freud or Jung did not know it. Even today the greatest of the psychologists of the world do not know the dynamics of body-energy in its totality. But this magician somehow has stumbled on a trick which he utilises to earn a living.

To put on an electric switch, it is not necessary for you to know what electricity is, how it is produced, or what electrical engineering is all about. You simply press a button and the electricity starts flowing. Anybody can press the button.

The street magician has learned the art of post-hypnotic suggestion and he is using it to sell his trinkets. You buy a trinket, take it home, but it will be useless for you. The trinket had worked along with a certain process of post-hypnotic suggestion. You place it on your chest and nothing happens. Then you feel that you are wrong somewhere, because you have seen the trinket working.

So many false and pseudo experiences can be created. They are false and pseudo not in the sense that they do not exist but in the sense that they are not spiritual; they are only psychic processes. Every spiritual experience has its psychic parallel. Therefore, psychic counterparts can be created by those persons who are not spiritual yet who make claims about their psychic capacity. But it is nothing compared to the authentic spiritual experience.

The authentically spiritual man does not claim anything. He does not say, "I am doing *shaktipat*; I am doing this and that. And when it happens you will become involved and attached to me." He has become a nobody, a nothingness. Just by being near him something starts happening to you. But he has absolutely no sense of doing it.

There is an ancient Roman story of a great sage. The fragrance of his being and the rays of his wisdom spread so much that they reached up to the gods in heaven. They came to him and said, "Ask a favour. We are prepared to grant you anything you wish."

The saint replied, "What was to happen has happened; there is nothing more to desire. Please do not put me into a difficulty by asking me to desire something. Do not embarrass me with your offer. It would be bad manners if I did not ask, but the fact is that there is nothing left for me to ask for. Everything has happened to me, even that which I have never thought of."

The gods were impressed even more by his words, because his fragrance became stronger with the fact that he was beyond desire. "You must ask something," the gods insisted. "We will not leave without conferring a favour upon you."

The saint was in a fix. "What shall I ask for? I cannot think of anything," he told the gods. "You give me whatever you like; I will take it."

"We will give you a power. Just your touch will bring the dead to life and the sick back to health," they told him.

"This is good, a great help," he said, "but what about me? I will be in a great trouble, because I may have an idea that I am healing the sick, that I am bringing the dead back to life. If my ego comes back from the back door, then I am finished, then I am lost in darkness. Please save me; have compassion on me; do something so that I do not know of these miracles."

So the gods agreed. They said, "Wherever your shadow falls it will bring back the dead to life."

"That is good," said the sage. "Now do me a last favour. Please grant that my neck becomes stiff so that I cannot look back to see the effect of my shadow."

The favour was granted. The sage's neck became stiff. He went about from town to town. When his shadow fell on withered flowers they began to bloom, but by then he would have gone ahead; his neck did not allow him to look back. He never came to know. When he died he asked the gods whether their gift was fruitful or not, because he never came to know about it. I feel this story to be very lovely.

When *shaktipat* happens, it happens just like this. It happens with the shadow and the neck is stiff. The medium, through whom the divine energy flows, must be a complete void or else his head may be turned. If there is even a trace of the ego there will be the urge to look back and see whether the happening has come about or not. If it has, then the feeling of "I have done it," comes in. It will be difficult to avoid this feeling.

So wherever a man becomes empty and silent, *shaktipat* happens with great ease around him, just as the sun rises and the flowers open, or as the river flows and the trees are nourished. The river never claims that it has watered so many trees and so many trees are blooming because of it. The river does not even know all this. By the time the flowers bloom, the water that nourished the trees will have reached the ocean. Where is there time for it to wait and see? There is no way of looking back. When the happening takes place amidst such conditions it has a spiritual value. But where there is the ego, the doer, when someone says that "I am the doer," then it is a psychic phenomenon and it is nothing more than hypnosis.

Is there not a possibility of hypnosis and illusion in Your new method of Dynamic Meditation? With many participants nothing is happening; are they not on the right track? There are others in whom a lot of processes are happening; are they on the right path? Could some of these be just putting on an act?

There are two or three things which have to be properly understood. Hypnosis is a science and it can be easily used for creating deceptions. However, hypnosis can also be used to help you. Science is always a two-edged sword.

Atomic energy can produce wheat in the fields; it can also wipe out the whole humanity at a stroke. Both the possibilities are there. The electric current that moves the fans in your house can also kill you, but you will not hold electricity responsible for it. If an egoist makes use of hypnosis he will do so to suppress, destroy and delude the other. But the opposite of this is also possible.

Hypnosis is a neutral energy; it is a science. It can be used to break the dreams that go on inside you, and your deep-rooted illusions can also be eradicated by it.

The method I am using is hypnosis at its initial phase, but with this is joined a fundamental element which will protect you from being hypnotised—and that is witnessing. This is the only difference between hypnosis and meditation, but this is a very great difference. When you are hypnotised you are made to become unconscious. Only then can you be worked upon. However, I say that in meditation hypnosis is useful, but only when you become the observer. Then you are awake and alert, and you know what is happening all the time. Then nothing can be done against your will; you are always present. In hypnosis the suggestions can be used to make you unconscious and the suggestions can be used to break your unconsciousness.

So the initial steps of what I call meditation are all hypnotic, and they are bound to be because any journey towards the self starts only from the mind. This is because you live in the mind; that is the place where you are, so the journey starts from there. But this journey can be of two kinds: either it can take you on a circular route within the mind where you will keep on going round and round like an ox at a mill who is never able to come out, or it can take you to the edge of the mind from where you can jump out. In both the cases, the initial steps will have to be taken within the mind.

So the initial form of hypnosis is the same as that of meditation, but the final form is different and so is the goal. And in both the processes one basic element is different. Hypnosis immediately requires unconsciousness, sleep; therefore, all its suggestions start with sleep, drowsiness, and then the rest follows. In meditation, the suggestion starts with wakefulness, and later the stress is on the witnessing state. The witness in you is awake, so no outside agency can affect you. And also, remember that whatsoever is happening within you, you are fully conscious of it.

Now, what is the difference between those to whom things are happening and those to whom things are not happening? The people to whom nothing is happening have a weaker willpower. They are afraid, frightened. They are even afraid that it may happen! How strange man is! They have come to meditate; they have come for meditation to take place, but now they are afraid that it may really happen. And when they see things happening to others they wonder if it is all put on.

These are their defence measures. They say, "We are not so weak as to become affected. These are weak people." This way they satisfy their egos, not knowing that this process cannot happen to a weak person. They also do not know that this happens only to intelligent people and not to the unintelligent.

An idiot cannot be hypnotised nor can he be taken into meditation. Both are impossible. Similarly, an insane person cannot be worked upon. The more of a genius the person is, the quicker he can be hypnotised. The lesser genius a person is, the longer it will take to hypnotise him.

How can people rationalise the lack of intelligence, will and genius? They will say in their defence, "It seems these people are merely acting. They are weak-minded and are influenced from the outside."

Recently in Amritsar, a person came to meet me. He is an old, learned man—a retired doctor. He came on the third day of the meditation experiment. He said, "I have come to ask your forgiveness for a sinful thought that came to my mind."

"What happened?" I asked him.

He replied, "The first day when I came for meditation, I felt you had organised your own people to dress up and put on this show, and that there were some weak-minded people who were following them blindly. Then I said, 'Let me see for a second time.' The second day I saw two or three of my friends who are also doctors, fully participating in the meditation experiment. I went to their houses to inquire. I told them, cannot be that you had been prepared for this? Was it really happening to you or were you pretending?'

"They replied, 'Where is the need to make anything up? Until yesterday we too thought the same, but today it has happened to us.'"

Then on the third day, when it happened to him, he came to apologise. He said, "Today it happened to me, and now my illusions are all gone; otherwise I would not have believed it. I had also suspected my doctor friends. You can never say these days what a person will do. Maybe they had an acting contract with you! I know them, but who can tell?—they might have come under your hypnotic spell. But today it has happened to me. Today when I reached home, my younger brother, who is also a doctor, asked, 'How was the show? Did something happen to you?' I told him, 'Forgive me, brother, I can call it a show no longer. For two days I was also making fun of the whole experiment, but today it has happened to me. And I am not angry with you, because up to yesterday I myself was critical like you.'"

This man again asked my pardon for his negative thoughts.

These are our defence measures. Those who find nothing happening to them will find ways and means of protecting their egos. But there is only a very small distance between the one to whom it happens and the one to whom it does not happen. There is only the lack of a little more resolve. If one gathers courage, makes a strong resolve and drops all inhibitions, the happening will take place.

Now today a woman came to me and told me that her friend called her up on the phone and told her that, "In these experiments some people become naked, some people do strange things. How can ladies of decent families take part in them?"

Some people have the illusion of belonging to "decent" families, and some others belong to "unvirtuous" families. These are all defence measures. The woman who thinks she belongs to a decent family will now miss this experiment and confine herself to her house. If she is troubled by another person becoming naked, then she is not from a decent family. What has she to do with him?

So our mind creates strange excuses. It says, "This is all a muddle and a mess, and it cannot happen to me. I am not a weak person—I have a powerful mind." If this were so, if you were a powerful and intelligent person, the happening would have taken place.

The sign of an intelligent person is that he makes no decisions before trying out a thing. He will not even say that what the other is doing is false. He will say, "Who am I to comment on him? To label another as false is not good. Who are you to decide that someone else is wrong? Such wrong decisions have caused a lot of difficulty.

People did not believe that anything had happened to Jesus; otherwise they would not have hung him on the cross. They said, "This man is crazy and dangerous; he says any absurd thing!" People would not have stoned Mahavira if they had not thought that he was causing a disturbance by being naked. They said that nothing has happened to Mahavira.

On what authority can we decide what is happening inwardly to another person? This is a symptom of an intelligent person—that he does not express an opinion until he has tried a thing out for himself. If nothing is happening to me, I must find out whether I am carrying out the instructions of the experiment fully. If I am not doing it fully, how will anything happen?

Recently in the Porbandar meditation camp I said that if a person has not exerted himself up to one hundred per cent, even if his effort has come up to ninety-nine per cent, he will fail.

One friend came and said, "I was going along leisurely thinking that it will take a little longer time to happen. But today I realised that it will never happen this way. So I exerted myself fully today, and it has happened."

If you have this attitude of doing the experiment slowly, then why do it at all? In this way we want to sail in two boats at a time, but he who puts each foot in a different boat finds himself in great difficulty. One boat is good; then even if it goes to hell at least you are in one boat. But we are strange people; we put one foot in a heavenward boat and another foot on the boat to hell!

In fact, the mind is confused as to where to go. It is afraid and undecided whether it will be happy in heaven or in hell. Putting one foot each in two boats you will reach nowhere; you will die still in the river. Such is the working of the mind all the time. It is schizophrenic. We will make an effort to go and then stop ourselves too. This is very harmful.

Do the experiment with your total intensity, and do not form any opinions of others. If one goes through the full experiment things will certainly happen. I am talking about very scientific things, not something belonging to religious superstition.

It is a scientific fact that with total effort the result is bound to take place. There is no other way, because God is energy and this energy is impartial. Here, prayers or worship, or the fact of having been born into a high-class family or on the soil of India, will not work. This is purely a scientific matter. If a person goes through this sincerely, even God cannot stop him from succeeding. And even if there is no God it does not matter. See that you are putting your total energy into the meditation experiment. And always make decisions according to your inner experiences, not from the outer appearance of events; otherwise you will go on the wrong track.

3

THE PATH OF KUNDALINI: AUTHENTICITY AND FREEDOM

In yesterday's talk, *You said that false experiences of kundalini can be projected which You consider to be not spiritual but psychic. In Your initial talk, however, You had said that kundalini is only psychic. This means, according to You, that there are two states of the kundalini—psychic and spiritual. Kindly explain this.*

In order for you to understand this the structure of the various subtle bodies must be fully elaborated upon.

The individual can be divided into seven bodies. The first body is the physical body which we all know. The second is the etheric body, and the third—which is beyond this second—is the astral body. The fourth—which is beyond this—is the mental or psychic body; and the fifth—which is beyond this again—is the spiritual body. The sixth is beyond the fifth, and it is called the cosmic body. Then the seventh and the last is the *nirvana sharir,* or the *nirvanic* body, the bodiless body. A little more information about these seven bodies will make it possible for you to understand the *kundalini* fully.

In the first seven years of life, the *sthul sharir*—the physical body—alone is formed. The other bodies are in seed form. They have a potential for growth but they lie dormant in the beginning of life. So the first seven years are years of limitation. There is no growth of intellect, emotion or desire during these years. Only the physical body develops within this period. Some people never grow beyond seven years; they stagnate at this stage and are no more than animals. Animals develop only in the physical body; the other bodies remain untouched within them. In the next seven years—that is from seven years to fourteen years—the *bhawa sharir,* the etheric body, develops. These seven years are years of emotional growth of the individual. This is why sexual maturity, which is the most intense form of emotion, is reached at the age of fourteen. Now some people stagnate at this stage. Their physical bodies grow but they are stuck with the first two bodies.

In the third seven-year period, between the ages of fourteen and twenty-one, the *sukshma sharir,* the astral body, develops. In the second body emotion is developed; in the third body reasoning, thinking and intellect are developed. This is why no court of law holds a child responsible for his actions up to the age of seven, because the child has only the physical body. We treat the child the same way as we would treat an animal; we cannot hold him responsible. Even if a child commits a crime it is assumed that he has committed it under the guidance of someone—that the real criminal is someone else.

After the development of the second body a person reaches adulthood. But this is the adulthood of sex. Nature's work is complete with this development, and this is why nature gives its full cooperation up to this stage. But at this stage man is not man in the full sense of the word. The third body, where reason, intellect and the thinking power develop, is an outcome of education, civilisation and culture. This is why the right to vote is granted to a person when he is twenty-one years of age. Though this is prevalent all over the world, some countries are debating whether to allow an eighteen-year-old the right to vote. This is natural, because as man is becoming more and more evolved the usual span of seven years for the growth of each body is becoming less and less.

All over the world girls reach puberty at the age of thirteen to fourteen years. Since the last thirty years the age for this is becoming less and less. Even a girl of eleven reaches puberty. The lowering of the voting age to eighteen is an indication that man now completes the work of twenty-one years in eighteen years. Normally, however, twenty-one years are required for the growth of the third body, and the majority of people do not develop further than this. Their growth stops short with the development of the third body, and there is no further development for the rest of their lives.

What I call the psyche is the fourth body—the *manas sharir*. This body has its own wonderful experiences. Now a person whose intellect is not developed may not be able to take interest in or enjoy mathematics, for instance. Mathematics has its own charm, and only Einstein can be absorbed in it as a musician is in music or a painter is in colours. For Einstein mathematics was not work but play, but the intellect must reach this peak of development in order to turn mathematics into play.

With each body that develops infinite possibilities open before us. One whose etheric body does not develop, who stagnates after the first seven years of development, does not have any interest in life beyond eating and drinking. So the cultures of those civilisations where the majority of people have developed only up to the first body revolve entirely around their taste buds. The civilisation where the majority of people have got stuck at the second body will be sex-centred. Their personalities, their literature, their music, their films and books, their poetry and paintings, even their houses and vehicles, will all be sex-centred: all these things will be completely filled with sex, with sexuality.

In the civilisation in which the third body develops fully, people will be intellectual and contemplative. Whenever the development of the third body becomes very important in a society or in a nation, many intellectual revolutions take place. In Bihar, the majority of people were of this calibre at the time of Buddha and Mahavira. This is why eight persons of the stature of Buddha and Mahavira were born in the small province of Bihar. Besides, there were thousands of others at the time who were endowed with genius. Such was the condition of Greece at the time of Socrates and Plato; such also was the condition of China at the time of Lao Tzu and Confucius. What is even more wonderful to note is the fact that all these luminous beings existed within a period of five hundred years. Within those five hundred years the development of the third body in man reached its peak. Generally man halts at the third body. The majority of people do not develop after twenty-one years.

There are unusual experiences of the fourth body. Hypnotism, telepathy, clairvoyance, are all the potential of the fourth body. Persons can have contact with one another without hindrances from time or place; they can read the thoughts of another without asking or project thoughts into another. Without any external help one can instil a seed of thought into another. A person can travel outside of his body; he can do astral projection and know himself apart from the physical body.

There are great possibilities in the fourth body, but we do not normally develop this body as there are many hazards as well as much deception. As things begin to get more and more subtle, the possibilities of deception increase. Now it is difficult to find out whether a man has actually stepped out of his body or not. He can dream that he stepped out of his body and he can actually do so too, and in both the cases there is no other witness than himself. So there is every possibility of deception.

The world that starts from the fourth body is subjective, whereas the world before that is objective. If I have a rupee in my hand, I can see it, you can see it, fifty others can also see it. This is a common reality in which we can all take part, and it can be investigated whether the rupee is or is not. But in the realm of my thoughts you cannot be a partner, nor can I be a partner in the realm of your thoughts. From here the personal world begins with all its hazards; none of our external rules of validity can be used here. So the real world of deception starts from the fourth body. All the deceptions of the preceding three can be seen through.

The greatest danger is that it is not necessarily the case that the deceiver is aware of the fact that he is deceiving. He can deceive unknowingly—himself as well as others. Things are so subtle, so rare and personal on this plane, that one has no means to test the validity of his experiences. So he cannot tell whether he is imagining things or whether they are really happening to him.

So we have always tried to save humanity from this fourth body, and those who made use of this body were always condemned and slandered. Hundreds of women were branded as witches and burnt in Europe because they used the faculties of the fourth body. Hundreds who practised *tantra* were killed in India because of the fourth body. They knew some secrets that seemed dangerous to human beings. They knew what was taking place in your mind; they knew where things were placed in your house without ever having stepped into it. So the realm of the fourth body was looked upon as "black" art all over the world, as one never knew what might happen. We have always tried our best to stop progress from going any further than the third body, because the fourth has always seemed very dangerous.

There are hazards, but together with these there are wonderful gains. So instead of stopping, research was necessary. Then we could have found ways of testing the validity of our experiences. Now there are scientific instruments, and also man's power of understanding has increased. So ways can be found just as in the case of many other new discoveries that have been made in science.

It is not known whether animals dream or not. How could this be ascertained unless an animal speaks? We know what we dream because we get up in the morning and say that we have dreamed. After great perseverance and effort, now the way has been found. One man has worked for years on monkeys in order to find out about this, and the measures he took for this experiment are worth understanding. He started by showing a film to the monkeys. As soon as the film started, the monkey being experimented upon was given an electric shock. A button was provided on the monkey's chair and he was taught to press this button whenever he felt the shock. So every day he was made to sit on the chair, and when the film began he felt the shock. Then he pressed the button to turn it off.

This went on for a few days; then he was made to sleep in this chair. Now when he began to dream he would begin feeling uncomfortable, because to him the film on the screen and the film in his dream were one and the same. He at once pressed the button. Time and again he would press the button, and this proved that he was dreaming. In this way, man is now able to penetrate into the inner dream-world of dumb animals. Meditators too have found ways of testing the experiences of the fourth body from outside, and now it can be proved whether what happens is true or false. The experiences of the *kundalini* on the fourth body can be psychic, but that does not make them false. There are authentic psychic states and false psychic states. When I say that *kundalini* could be only a mental experience, it does not necessarily mean that it is a false experience. Mental experiences can be false as well as authentic.

You see a dream at night. Now this dream is a fact because it has happened. But on waking in the morning you might recollect some dream that you did not actually dream; yet you can insist that that is what you dreamed. Then this is false. A man might get up in the morning and say he never dreams. Many people believe they do not dream. They do dream: all night long they dream, and this has been proved scientifically. But in the morning they assert they never dreamed. So what they say is absolutely false, though they are not aware of it. In fact, they do not remember the dreams. Quite the opposite also takes place: you remember dreams you never dreamed. This will also be false.

Dreams are not false; they have their own reality. But dreams can be real as well as unreal. Real dreams are those which have been actually dreamed. The trouble also is that you cannot narrate your dream precisely upon waking. For this reason, in the old days any man who could narrate his dream clearly and precisely was held in high esteem. It is very, very difficult to report a dream correctly. The sequence of the dream is one thing when you dream it and just the opposite when you remember it. It is like a film. When we see a film the story unwinds from the beginning of the film. Similarly, the reel of the dream drama winds in one direction in sleep and begins to unwind in the opposite direction in the waking state, so we remember the last part of the dream first and go backwards in recollection. What we dreamed first becomes last in recollection. This would be just like someone who tries to read a book from the wrong end; the reversed words would cause just such a chaos. So to remember a dream and give a true representation of it is a great art. Generally, when we recall a dream we recollect happenings we never dreamed of. We drop a good portion of the actual dream and later most of the rest.

Dreams are a happening of the fourth body, and the fourth body has a great potential. Whatever *siddhis* are mentioned in yoga are attained in this body. Yoga has incessantly warned the meditator not to go into them. The greatest danger is there of going astray. Even if you go into a psychic state it has no spiritual value.

So when I said that the *kundalini* is psychic, what I meant was that it is actually a happening of the fourth body. This is why physiologists cannot discover the *kundalini* within the human body. So it is only natural that they deny the existence of *kundalini* and the *chakras* and call them imaginary. They are the happenings of the fourth body. The fourth body exists, but it is very subtle; it cannot come within our grasp. Only the physical body can be grasped. Yet there are corresponding points between the first body and the fourth body.

If we were to place seven sheets of paper, one on top of the other, prick a hole through them with a pin so that all the papers are pierced, then even if the hole disappears from the first sheet it will still carry a mark that corresponds to the holes in the rest of the sheets. Then although the first paper does not have the hole, it has the point which will correspond directly with the pinholes on the other sheets when it is placed upon them. So *chakras, kundalini,* etcetera, do not belong to the first body as such, but there are corresponding points in the first body. So a physiologist is not wrong if he denies them. The *chakras* and the *kundalini* are in other bodies, but points corresponding to them can be found on the physical body.

So *kundalini* is the happening of the fourth body and it is psychic. And when I say that this psychic happening is of two kinds—one true and one false—then you will understand what I mean. It will be false when it is a product of your imagination, because imagination is also a characteristic of the fourth body. Animals do not have the power of imagination, so they have very little memory of the past and no idea of future. Animals are free from anxiety as anxiety is always of the future. Animals see many deaths taking place, but they never imagine that they can die also; therefore, they have no fear of death. Among men also there are many who are not bothered by the fear of death. Such a man always associates death with others and not with himself. The reason is that the power of imagination in the fourth body has not developed fully enough to see into the future.

This means that imagination can also be true or false. True imagination means that we are capable of seeing further ahead, that we can visualise that which has not yet come to pass. But to imagine that something will happen that cannot be, which does not exist, is false imagination. When imagination is used in its right perspective it becomes science; science is primarily only imagination.

Since thousands of years man has dreamed of flying. The men who had dreamed in this way must have been very imaginative. If man had never dreamed about flying, it would have been impossible for the Wright brothers to make the first airplane. They made man's desire to fly something concrete. This desire took some time to shape; then experiments were carried out, and finally man succeeded in flying.

Also, for thousands of years man has wanted to reach the moon. First it was only in his imagination; slowly it gained ground, and now it has been fulfilled. Now, these imaginations were authentic: that is, they were not on a false path. These imaginations were on the path of a reality which could be discovered at a later date. So a scientist also imagines, and so does a person who is mad.

If I say that science is imagination and madness is also imagination, don't think they are one and the same thing. A madman imagines things which do not exist and which have no relationship with the physical world. The scientist also imagines: he imagines things which are directly related with the physical world. And if it does not seem so at first there is a complete possibility of their being so in the future.

Among the possibilities of the fourth body there is always a chance of going wrong. Then the false world begins. This is why it is best if we do not harbour any expectations before entering this body. This fourth body is the psychic body. Now, for instance, if I want to go down to the ground floor of this house I will have to look for a lift or a staircase in order to do so. But if I want to go down in my thoughts there is no need for a lift or a staircase. I can sit right here and go down.

The hazard of imagination and thoughts is that one has to do nothing except imagine or think, and so anyone can do it. Moreover, if anyone enters this realm with preconceived ideas and expectations, then he immediately goes down only into these, because then the mind will be only too willing to cooperate. It will say, "You want to awaken the *kundalini?* All right! It is rising...it has risen." Then you will begin to imagine the *kundalini* rising, and the mind will encourage you in this false feeling until ultimately you will feel that it is fully awakened and that the *chakras* are fully activated. But there is a way of testing the validity of it, and that is that with the opening of each *chakra* there will be a distinct change in your personality. This change you cannot imagine or preconceive, because this change takes place in the world of matter.

So, for instance, when the *kundalini* awakens you cannot take intoxicants; it is impossible. The mental body gets influenced by alcohol very quickly as it is very delicate. This is why—and you will be surprised to know this—when a woman consumes alcohol she becomes more dangerous than a man who does so. This is because her mental body is even more delicate, and it gets affected so quickly that things get out of her control. This is why women have protected themselves from this hazard by certain rules in society. This is one place where women did not seek equality with men, although unfortunately of late she is trying to. The day she asserts her equality in this area and tries to outdo men in it she will cause such harm to herself as has never been caused by any action by men.

In the fourth body the awakening of the *kundalini* cannot be proved by your telling about the experience, because, as I said before, you can falsely imagine the awakening and experiencing of the *kundalini* also. It can only be judged by your physical traits: whether any radical transformation has taken place in your personality. No sooner does the energy awaken than there will be immediate signs of change in you. This is why I always say that behaviour is the outer criterion and not the inner cause. It is a criterion of what has happened within. With each attempt some things inevitably begin to happen. When the energy awakens it becomes impossible for the meditator to take any intoxicants. If he does indulge in drugs and alcohol, then know that his experiences are all imaginary, because it is absolutely impossible.

After the awakening of the *kundalini* the tendency for violence disappears completely. Not only does the meditator not commit violence, but he has no feeling of violence within himself. The urge to commit violence, the urge to harm others, can only exist when the vital energy is dormant. The moment it awakens the other ceases to be the other and so you cannot wish to harm him. Then you will not have to repress violence within yourself because then you cannot be violent.

If you find that you have to repress the feeling of violence, then know that the *kundalini* has not awakened. If after the eyes open you still feel your way about with a stick, then know that the eyes cannot see yet, no matter how much you claim otherwise—because you have not yet given up your stick. Whether an outsider can find out whether you can see or not is dependent upon your actions. Your stick, your stumblings and your unstable walk prove that the eyes have not yet opened.

So there will be a radical change in your behaviour with the awakening, and all the religious vows like those of the *mahavrata*—non-violence, not stealing, non-possession, celibacy and full awareness—will become natural and easy for you. Then know that your experience is authentic. It is psychic, however, but authentic all the same. Now you can proceed further. You can proceed ahead if your path is authentic, but not otherwise. You cannot stay forever in the fourth body because it is not the goal. There are yet other bodies that have to be crossed.

We find, as I said, that very few are able to develop the fourth body. That is why there are miracle performers in the world today. If the fourth body in everyone were developed, miracles would vanish from the earth at once. If there were a society of people whose development had stagnated after the fourteenth year of age, then the one who had developed a little further, who could add or subtract, would be thought to be performing miracles.

A thousand years ago, when a person declared the date of the eclipse of the sun, it was considered a miracle that only the very wise could perform. Today we know that even a machine can give us this information. It is a matter of calculation and does not require an astronomer or a prophet or a very learned person. A computer can give the information not of a single eclipse but of millions of eclipses. It can even forecast the day when the sun will get cold—because these are all calculations.

The machine can calculate from the date provided that the quantity of energy the sun emits per day divided by the total energy of the sun gives the number of years the sun will last.

But all this does not look like a miracle to us now, because now we are all developed up to the third body. A thousand years ago it was a great miracle if a man prophesied that next year, in this month, on this night, there would be an eclipse of the moon. He would be considered superhuman. The "miracles" that take place nowadays—the magic charms, the ash dropping from picture frames—are all ordinary happenings of the fourth body. But since we do not know it is a miracle for us.

It is just as if you are standing under a tree and I am sitting on the tree, and we two are talking. Now I see a cart coming from far away and I tell you that in an hour's time a cart will come and halt under the tree. You will say, "Are you a prophet? You talk in riddles. There is no cart anywhere around. I do not believe what you say." But in an hour's time the cart rolls up to the tree, and then of necessity you have to touch my feet and say, "Beloved Master, my respects. You are a prophet." The difference was only this, that I was sitting on a little higher level than you—on the tree—from where the cart became visible an hour before it did for you. I was not talking of the future, I was talking very much in the present. But there is a distance of one hour between your present tense and mine because I am at a higher level. For you it will become the present after one hour, but for me it is present now.

The deeper a man stands within his inner being, the greater a miracle he becomes for those who are still on the surface layers. Then all his doings will become miraculous for us because we have no way to gauge these happenings as we do not know the laws of the fourth body. This is how magic and miracles take place: they are a slight growth of the fourth body. So if we want miracles to end in this world, it will not happen by preaching to the masses. Just as we have given man the education of the third body and made him understand languages and mathematics, we must now give him training for the fourth body. Each man has to be qualified accordingly, because only then will miracles cease; otherwise, someone or other will always take advantage of this. The fourth body develops until the twenty-eighth year—that is, for seven years more. But very few people are able to develop it.

The *atma sharir*—the fifth body, which is called the spiritual body—is of great value. If growth in life continues in the proper manner, then by the age of thirty-five this body should be fully developed. But this is a faraway idea because even the fourth body is only developed in a very few people. This is why the soul and such things are only a topic of discussion for us; there is no content behind the word. When we say *atman,* it is merely a word; there is nothing behind it. When we say wall, there is not only the word but also the substance behind the word; we know what "wall" means. But there is no meaning behind the word *atman,* because we have no knowledge, no experience of the *atman*. This is our fifth body, and only if the *kundalini* awakens in the fourth body is entrance possible in the fifth; otherwise we cannot enter. We are not aware of the fourth body so the fifth also remains unknown.

Very few people have discovered the fifth body; they are those whom we call spiritualists. These people take this to be the journey's end and declare, "To attain the *atman* is to attain all." But the journey is not yet over. However, these people who stop at the fifth body deny God. They say, "There is no *brahman;* there is no *paramatman,*" just as he who stagnates on the first body would deny the existence of the *atman*. Just as the materialist says, "The body is everything; when the body dies, everything dies," so the spiritualist declares, "There is nothing beyond the *atman:* the *atman* is everything; it is the highest state of being." But this is only the fifth body.

The sixth body is the *brahma sharir*—the cosmic body. When a person evolves beyond his *atman,* when he is willing to lose it, he enters the sixth body. If mankind develops scientifically the natural development of the sixth body would take place at the age of forty-two, and that of the *nirvana sharir*—the seventh body—at the age of forty-nine. The seventh body is the *nirvanic* body which is no-body—which is a state of bodilessness, an incorporeal state. This is the ultimate state where only the void remains—not even the *brahman,* the cosmic reality, but only the emptiness. Nothing has remained; everything has disappeared.

So when anyone asked Buddha, "What happens there?" he replied, "The flame dies out." "Then what happens?" he would be asked again. "When the flame is lost, you do not ask, 'Where has it gone? Where is the flame now?' It is lost, and that is all." The word *nirvana* implies the extinction of the flame. Therefore, Buddha said, *nirvana* takes place.

The state of *moksha* is experienced in the fifth body. The limitations of the first four bodies are transcended and the soul becomes totally free. So liberation is the experience of the fifth body. Heaven and hell pertain to the fourth body, and he who stops here will experience them. For those who stop at the first, second or third body, life between birth and death becomes everything; there is no life beyond death for them. If a person goes beyond into the fourth body, after this life he experiences heaven and hell where there are infinite possibilities of happiness and misery.

If he reaches up to the fifth body there is the door of liberation, and if he reaches up to the sixth there is the possibility of the state of God-realisation. Then there is no question of liberation or no liberation; he becomes one with that which is. The declaration of *"Aham Brahmasmi"*—I am God—is of this plane. But there is yet one step more, which is the last jump—where there is no *aham* and no *Brahman,* where I and thou are totally non-existent, where there is simply nothing—where there is total and absolute void. That is *nirvana.*

These are the seven bodies which are developed within a period of forty-nine years. This is why the midpoint of fifty years was known as the point of revolution. For the first twenty-five years there was one system of life. Within this period efforts were made to develop the first four bodies; then one's education was supposed to be complete. Then one was supposed to search for his fifth, sixth and seventh bodies throughout the remainder of his life, and in the remaining twenty-five years he was expected to attain to the seventh body. Therefore, the age of fifty was looked upon as a crucial year. At this time a man became a *wanaprasth,* which only means that now he should turn his gaze towards the forest—that now he should turn his eyes away from people, society and the marketplace.

The age of seventy-five was yet another point of revolution—when a man was to become initiated into *sannyas*. To turn toward the forest means to remove oneself from crowds and people; *sannyas* means, now the time has come to look beyond the ego, to transcend the ego. In the forest the 'I' will necessarily be with him though he has renounced all else, but at the age of seventy-five this 'I' too has to be renounced.

However, the condition was that in one's life as a householder one had to pass through and develop all the seven bodies so that the rest of the journey would become spontaneous and joyful. If this is not done it is very difficult, because with every seven-year cycle a particular state of development is connected. If the physical body of a child does not grow fully in the first seven years of his life, he will always be sickly. At the most we can see to it that he does not remain ill—but healthy he will never be because his basic foundation for health that should have been formed in the first seven years has been shaken. That which should have become strong and firm was disturbed, and that was the time for its development.

It is just like laying the foundations for a house: if the foundations are weak it will be difficult—no, impossible—to repair it once the roof is reached. At the foundation stage only could it have been well laid. So in the first seven years, if proper conditions are available for the first body, the body develops properly. Now if the second body and the emotions do not develop fully over the next seven years, a number of sex perversions result. Then it is very difficult to remedy these later. So the period of development for a particular body is most crucial.

On each step of life, each body has its predetermined period of development. There may be a slight difference here and there, but that is beside the point. If a child does not develop sexually within fourteen years his whole life becomes a long ordeal. If the intellect does not develop by the time he is twenty-one there is very little chance of its developing at a later period. But so far we are in agreement: we take care of the first body, then we take care to send the child to school to develop his intellect also. But we forget that the rest of the bodies also have their apportioned time which if lost puts us in great difficulties.

A man takes fifty years to develop the body he should have developed in twenty-one years. It is obvious that he does not have as much strength at fifty as he had at twenty-one, so he has to put in a lot of effort. Then what would have been easier to accomplish at the age of twenty-one becomes long and arduous.

There is yet another difficulty which he encounters: at the age of twenty-one he was right at the door but he missed it. Now, over the following thirty years, he has been to so many places that he has lost sight of the right opening. His wandering now makes it impossible for him to locate the place where he stood at twenty-one and which then needed only a slight push to open.

Therefore, a well organised situation is required for children until they reach the age of twenty-five. It should be so well planned that it takes them to the fourth body level. After the fourth body the rest is easy. The foundation will then be well laid; now only the fruits remain to grow. The tree is formed up to the fourth body; then fruits begin to appear from the fifth which culminate in the seventh. We may have to make a little allowance here and there, but we should be very mindful of the foundations.

In this respect a few more things should be kept in mind. There is a difference between man and woman throughout the first four bodies. For instance, if the individual is a man his physical body is a male body. But his second body—the etheric body, which is behind the physical body—is female, because no negative or positive pole can exist by itself. A male body and a female body, in the terms of electricity, are positive and negative bodies.

The woman's physical body is negative; therefore, she is never aggressive in the matter of sex. She can bear the violence of man in this respect, but cannot be violent herself. She can do nothing to a man without his consent. Man's first body is positive—aggressive. He can, therefore, do something aggressive to a woman without her consent; he has an aggressive first body. But by negative is not meant zero or absent. In terms of electricity, negative means receptivity, reservoir. In the woman's body, energy lies in reserve; much energy lies in reserve. But it is not active: it is inactive.

This is why a woman does not create anything. She does not compose poetry, nor does she create a great painting, nor does she carry out any scientific research. This is because it is necessary to be aggressive for research or for some work of creation. She can only wait; that is why she can only produce children.

Man has a positive body, but wherever there is a positive body there must be a negative body behind it or else it cannot last. Both are present together; then the circle is complete. So the second body of a man is female, whereas the second body of a female is male. This is why—and this is an interesting fact—man looks and is, as far as his physical body goes, very strong. But behind this outward strength stands a weak female body. This is why he manages to show his strength only for a few moments at a time. In the long run he loses at the hands of the female, because the body behind her weak female body is a strong positive body.

This is why a woman's power of resistance, her capacity to endure, is greater than a man's. If a man and a woman suffer from the same illness the woman can endure it longer than the man. Women produce children. If men had to produce children they would realise the ordeal that has to be passed through. Then perhaps there would be no need for family planning—because man cannot bear so much pain for so long a time. For a moment or two he can freak out in anger, beat a pillow perhaps, but he cannot carry a child in his abdomen for nine months, nor bring him up patiently for years afterwards. If it cries all night long he might strangle it. He will not be able to tolerate the disturbance. He has extraordinary strength, but behind him is a frail, delicate etheric body. Because of this he cannot bear pain or discomfort.

This is why women fall sick less than men, their lifespan is longer than that of men. For this reason we should keep a difference of five years between a boy and a girl at the time of marriage, or else the world would be filled with widows. If the boy is twenty we should choose a girl of twenty-four or twenty-five for him. Man's lifespan is four or five years less, so this difference would equalise things and both synchronise each other.

A hundred and sixteen males are born to every hundred females. The difference in number at the time of birth is sixteen, but later on the number becomes equal. Sixteen males die by the time they reach the age of fourteen and so the number becomes almost equal. More boys die early than girls. This is because the latter have a great power of resistance that comes to them through the second male body.

Now the third body of the male—that is the astral body—will again be male, and the fourth or the psychic body will again be female. Just the reverse will be the case in the female. This division of male and female exists only up to the fourth body; the fifth body is beyond sex. Therefore, as soon as the *atman* is attained there is no male and no female—but not until then.

There is another thing that comes to mind in this connection. Since every male has a female body within him and every female has a male body within her, if by coincidence a woman gets a husband who is identical with the male body within her, or if a man marries a woman who is identical with the female body within him, then only is a marriage successful; otherwise not.

This is why ninety-nine per cent of marriages are failures: because the intrinsic rule of success is not known yet. As long as we are unable to ascertain the right alliance between the respective energy bodies of two persons, marriages are bound to remain a failure no matter what steps we take in other directions. Successful marriages can only be possible if absolutely clear scientific details concerning these various inner bodies are achieved. A boy or a girl who has reached up to the point of the awakening of the *kundalini* finds it very easy to choose the right partner in life. With the full knowledge of all his bodies within, one can make the right choice outwardly. Prior to this it is very difficult.

Therefore, those who knew insisted that the child should be made to develop his first four bodies in the first twenty-five years by maintaining *brahmacharya,* and then only could he marry—because whom should he marry? With whom does he want to spend the rest of his life? Whom is he seeking? What man does a woman seek? She seeks the man within her. If by coincidence the right connections are made, then both the man and woman are satisfied; otherwise, dissatisfaction remains and a thousand perversions result from this. The man then goes to a prostitute or seeks the woman next door. His distress grows day by day, and this misery is bound to increase with the growth of man's intellect.

If a person's growth stops at fourteen he will not suffer this agony, because all suffering starts from the growth of the third body. If only the first two bodies are developed the man would be satisfied by sex. So there are two ways: either in the first twenty-five years, during the period of *brahmacharya,* we should develop the child up to the fourth body, or else encourage child marriages. Child marriage means marriage before the development of intellect so that the person stagnates at sex; then there is no trouble as the relationship is entirely on the animal plane. The relationship of a child marriage is purely a sexual relationship; there is no possibility of love in it.

Now in places like America, where education has made great strides and where the third body has developed completely, marriages break. They are bound to, because the third body rebels at a wrong partnership. So divorce results, because it is not possible to drag such marriages along.

The correct form of education is that which develops the first four bodies. Right education is that which takes you up to the fourth body. There the work of education is complete. No education can help you enter the fifth; you have to go there by yourself. Right education can easily take you up to the fourth body. After this the growth of the fifth body, which is very valuable and personal, begins. *Kundalini* is the potential of the fourth body; this is why *kundalini* is a psychic phenomenon. I hope this is now clear to you.

Is there a possibility of psychic binding between the meditator and the medium in shaktipat? Can it be detrimental to the meditator or is it helpful for him?

Ties that bind can never be useful, because ties are bad in themselves. The deeper the attachment, the worse it is. Psychic binding is a very bad thing. If someone ties me in chains only my physical body is affected, but if someone ties me with the chains of love it penetrates deeper and is more difficult to break. If someone binds me with the chain of *shraddha,* faith, it goes deeper still. Then to break this chain would be "unholy." So all bonds are bad, and psychic bonds even more so.

He who acts as a medium in *shaktipat* would never want to bind you. If he does so he is not worthy of being a medium. But it is quite likely that you may get tied to him. You may catch hold of his feet and vow never to leave him because of the great blessing bestowed on you. It is necessary to be very alert at that moment. The meditator should protect himself from attachment. However, if it becomes clear to the meditator that all attachments prove to be heavy burdens on the spiritual journey, then the feeling of gratitude will not be a binding force but a liberating one. If I am thankful to you for something, where is there any question of attachment? In fact, if I do not express my gratefulness this fact will remain as a bondage within: that I did not even show my gratitude. But this thanksgiving completes the matter.

Gratitude is not a bondage. On the contrary, it is the expression of ultimate freedom. But the tendency to become bound is always within us because there is a fear within. We are never sure whether we shall be able to stand by ourselves or not; hence there is an urge to cling to someone. What to say of clinging to another—when a man passes through a dark street in the night he sings loudly because the sound of his own voice alleviates fear. If it is the voice of another person, then too it would be something to cling to, but basically he musters strength and courage from his own voice. Man is frightened, so he holds on to anything; that is why if a drowning man comes across a piece of straw he will hold fast to it even though this does not protect him from drowning. Rather, the straw also sinks with him. So out of fear the mind tends to hold on to someone, to something, whether it be a guru or anyone or anything else. By doing so we want to protect ourselves. The fear is the root of all kinds of binding.

Meditators should always be wary of security. Security is the greatest web of attachment for a meditator. If he seeks security for even a single moment, if he feels that he has the support of someone in whose protection he has nothing to fear and thus he will now not go astray, if he is thinking that he will go nowhere and be under his guru's wing forever, then he has already lost his way. For a seeker there is no security; insecurity is a blessing for a seeker. The greater the insecurity, the greater is the opportunity for his soul to expand and to become bold and fearless. The more the protection, the weaker he will become in the same proportion. To take assistance is one thing, but to keep on being dependent is quite another.

You are given support so that you can stand without support. It is given with the intention that soon you will need no more. Have you noticed that when a father is helping his child to walk he holds the child's hand and not the child? In a few days' time he learns to walk, and then the father lets go of his hand. But at first the child catches hold of the father's hand for confidence. So if the child takes hold of the father's hand it means that although he has learned to walk he will not let go of it. If the father holds the child's hand, then know that the child still does not know how to walk and it is dangerous to let him be on his own. The father wants his hand to be relieved soon; that is why he teaches the child to walk. If some father allows his child to go on holding his hand out of the sheer pleasure he gets from it he is his child's enemy.

Many fathers, many gurus, do this, but this is a mistake. The reason for which the support was given is defeated. Instead of giving rise to a strong healthy person who can walk on his own two feet he has given rise to a cripple who will depend upon crutches all his life. This, however, is the pleasure that gives satisfaction to the father or the guru—that you cannot go on your way without their support. In this way their egos are satisfied.

But such a guru is not a guru. So it is for the guru to shake off the meditator's hand and tell him firmly to walk on his own two feet. And there is no harm if he falls a couple of times: he can get up again. After all, one has to fall in order to rise, and it is necessary to fall a few times in order to get over the fear of falling.

The mind tries to catch hold of some support and so the binding starts. This should not happen. The meditator should always keep in mind the fact that he is not in search of security. He is in search of truth, not security. If he is sincere about his quest for truth he must give up all ideas of safety and security. Falseness affords a lot of protection—and very quickly too, so he who is in search of safety is quickly attracted towards it. The seeker of convenience never scales the heights of truth, because the journey is long. Then he fashions falsehoods out of fanciful ideas and begins to believe that he has attained while he remains sitting just where he was.

Therefore, any type of attachment is dangerous—and even more so the attachment to a guru, because this is a spiritual attachment. The very term spiritual attachment is contradictory. Spiritual freedom has a meaning, but spiritual slavery is meaningless. But in this world other types of slaves are considerably less enslaved than are the slaves of spirituality. There is a reason for this. The fourth body, from where the spirit of freedom arises, remains undeveloped. The majority of human beings have developed only up to the third body.

It is seen very often that a high court judge or a vice-chancellor of a university is sitting at the feet of an absolute idiot. Seeing this, others follow suit thinking that if such well-known people are sitting at this man's feet...we are nothing in comparison. They do not know that though this judge, this vice-chancellor, has developed his third body to the full, that though he has developed his intellect to a very high level, he remains ignorant so far as his fourth body is concerned. He is equally as ignorant as they are in matters of the fourth body. And his third body—that which has developed intellect and reason—is thoroughly exhausted by constant thinking and debating and is now at rest.

Now when the intellect gets tired and relaxes it indulges in very unintelligent pursuits. Anything that relaxes after extreme activity becomes opposite to its nature. This is the danger, and this is why you will invariably find high court judges in *ashrams*. They are exhausted and they are distressed by their intellects, so they wish to be rid of them. In such a condition they will do anything irrational; they will just close their eyes and put their faith in anything. Their contention is that all their learning and reasoning and discussions led them nowhere, so they drop them. And in order to sever all connection with them they promptly catch hold of something that is completely contrary. Then the rest of the crowd, which gives credence to the intellects of such high-placed people, begins to imitate them. These people may be very intellectual, but in matters of the fourth body they are just nothing. Therefore, a slight development of the fourth body in any individual will suffice to bring the greatest of intellectuals to his feet, because he has something that the intellectual lacks completely.

This sort of binding occurs when the fourth body is not developed. Then the mind wants to hold on to someone whose fourth body is developed, but this will not help you to develop your fourth body. Only by understanding such a person can your fourth body develop. However, in order to avoid the trouble of understanding him you catch hold of his person. Then you will say, "Where is the need to understand? We will hold on to your feet so that when you cross the river of hell we too will cross with you; we will cling to your boat to cross the river of heaven."

One has to suffer in order to grow into understanding. A transformation is needed for the understanding to happen. Understanding is an effort, a *sadhana*. Understanding needs endeavour, understanding is a revolution. In understanding a transformation takes place, everything changes. The old has to be changed into the new. Why go through all this bother? It is better to hold on to one who knows. But the fact is that no one can attain to truth by following someone else. One has to go alone. It is a path of total aloneness. Therefore, any kind of attachment is a hindrance.

Learn, understand, welcome the glimpse wherever you get it. But do not stop anywhere; do not make an abode out of any resting place; do not catch hold of the hand that is extended to you and take it as the destination. You will, however, find many who will say, "Go no further. Stay here; this is the other shore." As I said before, some fearful people desire to be bound and there are other fearful ones who want to bind them in order to feel fearless themselves. When a man sees a thousand people following him he is bound to feel that he is wise—or else why should these people follow him? He says to himself, "Surely, I know something, or why should these people believe in me?"

It will surprise you to know that many a time the phenomenon of gurudom is caused by an inferiority complex that seeks to gather a crowd around itself. So a guru gets busy increasing the number of followers—a thousand, ten thousand, twenty thousand. The greater the number, the more he is assured of his knowledge—or else why should these people follow him? This reasoning helps to boost his morale. If these followers are lost, everything is lost. Then he would feel that all is lost and that he does not know.

Many mind games go on and it is better to be aware of them. And this game can be played from both the sides. The disciple is bound to the guru, and he who is bound today will bind someone else tomorrow because all this is a chain reaction. He who is a disciple today will be a guru tomorrow. How long can he remain a disciple? If he has caught hold of someone today he will see that someone catches hold of him tomorrow. Slavery runs in a series, and the intrinsic reason for all this is the non-development of the fourth body. If you set about developing this body you can be independent. Then there is no bondage.

This does not mean that you become inhuman, that you will have no connection with people. Rather, the opposite will be the case: where there is bondage there is no relationship. Between a husband and wife there is bondage. Do we not use the expression "bound in holy matrimony"? We send out invitations reading that "My son or daughter is being joined by the thread of affection...." Where there is servitude there is no relationship. How can there be? Perhaps, in some distant future a father might send out an invitation saying that "My daughter is becoming free in someone's love." And it feels intelligent that somebody's love is making her free in life; now there will be no bondage; she is becoming free in love. And love should give birth to freedom. If even love enslaves then what else in this world will liberate?

Where there is bondage, there is misery, there is hell. Appearances are deceptive; inside everything is rotten. Be this the bondage of guru-disciple, father-son, husband-wife or even of two friends: where there is bondage there cannot be relationship. If a relationship is there then the bondage is not possible. And though outwardly it seems correct that where there is a bond there should be relationship, the fact is that we can have a relationship only with that person to whom we are not tied in any way. This is the reason why many times it happens that you tell a stranger things which you would never tell your son.

I was surprised to know that a woman talks more openly to a stranger whom she has met just an hour before and even tells things which she would not dream of telling her husband. It is a fact that when there is no bondage relationship becomes easier. This is why we are always so nice to strangers and not so nice to those we know. With strangers there are no bonds, and hence no relationship; otherwise there are bonds, and hence no relationship. Then even if you wish someone good morning, it seems like a task.

There can be a relationship between guru and disciple, however, and all relationships can be beautiful. But bondage cannot be beautiful. Relationship means that which liberates.

There was a beautiful custom among the zen masters. When a disciple finished his training, the master ordered him to join the campus of his antagonist and study there. He would say, "You have gained knowledge from one side, now know it from the other." Then the meditator would go from one monastery to another for years and sit to learn at the feet of his master's rivals. His master would say, "It could be possible that what my opponent says is correct. Go and hear all that he has to say; then you decide for yourself. It may also be possible that you will be able to decide things better after hearing both of us. Or perhaps what remains after discarding both of us may turn out to be the truth. Therefore, go and seek." This only happens when spiritual genius reaches its ultimate growth. Then nothing can bind.

My feeling is that when the condition of this country becomes such that masters will send their disciples out into the world without binding them, then there will be wonderful results. And who knows what the final outcome will be! Now such a man who sends you out to learn and hear others cannot be wrong, even if all that he himself has taught you turns out to be wrong. When such a man says to you, "Go, seek elsewhere; perhaps I may be wrong," then even if all his teachings prove false, you will be grateful to him. He can never be wrong, because it is he who has sent you out.

Today, what is happening is that everybody binds the meditator and stops him from going out. One guru forbids his disciple from hearing another guru. The scriptures say, "Never go to another temple. It is better to be trampled by a mad elephant than to take refuge in someone else's temple." The fear is always there that something might fall on the meditator's ears. So even if the teachings of a guru who binds you are correct, still the man is wrong and you can never be grateful to him. Such a man has only made you a slave. He has crushed your spirit and killed your soul. If this is understood, there is no question of bondage.

You have said that if shaktipat is authentic and pure, there is no bondage. Is that correct?

Correct. There will be no binding.

Is psychic exploitation possible in the name of shaktipat? How is it possible and how is the meditator to guard against it?

It is possible. Much spiritual exploitation is possible in the name of *shaktipat*. In fact, where there is a demand, a declaration, there is always exploitation. When a person declares that he will give, he will take something in return also, because giving and taking go together. Then whatsoever form it is in—in the form of wealth, in the form of reverence, in the form of trust—he will take. Where there is giving with insistence, then for sure there is taking. And he who claims to give is bound to take more in return, or else there was no need for him to shout in the marketplace.

A fisherman puts a worm on the hook of his rod because the fish does not eat the hook. Perhaps, someday the fish may be coaxed into swallowing the hook directly, but it is the worm that attracts the fish to the rod and it swallows the hook with the intention of eating the worm. It is only after swallowing it that it comes to know that the hook was the main thing and the worm was only a bait. But by then it is caught.

So whenever you come across anyone who claims to do *shaktipat,* who claims to give you wisdom and take you to *samadhi,* who makes a thousand other claims, beware. Be aware, because he that belongs to the realm of the beyond makes no claims for himself. If you tell such a person, "Because of you I experienced grace," he will say, "How can it be? I do not even know. You must be mistaken. It must have happened by the grace of God." So your thanks will not be acknowledged by such a one; he won't even acknowledge that he was a medium for the happening. He will insist that grace descended because you were worthy of it—that was God's compassion falling on you. Who is he? Where does he stand? What is his worthiness? He does not come in at all is what he will say.

Jesus was passing through a town. A sick man was brought to him. Jesus embraced him and he was cured of all his ills. This man told Jesus, "How can I thank you? You have rid me of all my woes."

Jesus replied, "Do not speak thus. Give thanks where it is due. Who am I and where do I come in?"

The man said, "But there is no one else except you here."

Jesus said, "You and I are not. You are unable to see he who is—and all happens through him. He has healed you."

Now, how can such a man exploit? The hook has to be covered with the worm in order to exploit. He is not even ready to own the worm, let alone the hook. So wherever a person claims results, be on your guard. When he claims to do this for you and that for you, he is only covering the hook with the worm. He is raising your expectations; he is inciting your hopes and desires. And when you are possessed by desire and you say, "Oh, beloved master, give...!" he will begin his demands. Very soon you will come to know that the worm was just on the top and the hook was inside.

So watch your step wherever there are miraculous claims. It is dangerous territory. Avoid the path where someone waits to be your guru. There is fear of entanglement there. So how is the seeker to guard himself? He should guard himself from those who make big claims, and thus he will save himself from all evil. He should not seek those who claim wonderful results; otherwise he will be in difficulty, because such men are also seeking. They are on the lookout for those who will fall into their trap. There are persons such as these going about everywhere. Do not ask for any spiritual gains and do not accept any spiritual claims.

What you have to do is entirely a different matter. You have to prepare yourself from within. And the day you are ready the happening is bound to take place. Then it will happen via any medium. The medium is secondary; he is like a hook. The day you acquire a coat the hook is ready to hang it by. Then the hook is not very important. If there is no hook you can hang your coat on the door. If there is no door you can hang it on the branch of a tree. Any hook will work; the main question is of the coat. But we do not have the coat, while the hook calls out: "Come here! I am the hook." You will be caught if you go. You do not have the coat so what will you do by going to the hook? There is every danger of your hanging yourself on it. You have to seek your own worthiness, your own capability. You have to make yourself ready in order to be able to receive grace when it comes.

You do not have to worry about the guru at all; that is not your concern. That is why what Krishna says to Arjuna is correct. He says, "Carry out your action and leave the fruits to the divine." You have not to worry about the result of your action; that will become a hindrance. Then all kinds of complexities will arise: concern over what your action will yield, over what will be the result. And in your anxiety about the result your performance will go off. That is why the action itself should be our main concern.

We should be concerned about our own worthiness and receptivity. The moment our effort is complete—just as when a seed has reached its point of bursting—that very moment all is achieved. The moment the bud is ready to burst and blossom into a flower the sun is always ready, but we do not have the bud that breaks into a flower. Then even if the sun shines brightly in the sky it is of no use. So don't go seeking the sun; get involved in developing your bud. The sun is there forever and is always available.

No vessel remains unfilled for even a moment in this world. Any kind of receptacle becomes filled immediately. In fact, to be receptive and to be filled are not two happenings; they are the two sides of the same happening. If we were to remove all air from this room, fresh air from outside would at once fill the vacuum. These are not two happenings, because as we remove the air in the room the outside air rushes in.

Such are also the laws of the inner world. We are hardly even ready on our side when the fulfilment of our efforts begins to descend. Our difficulty is, however, that our demands start long before our preparedness. Then there are always false supplies for false demands.

Some people really amaze me. One man comes and says, "My mind is very restless; I want peace." He talks to me for half an hour, and in the course of his talk he confesses that the cause of his unrest is that his son is jobless. If the son gets a job his mind will be at rest. Now this man came with the excuse that he wanted peace of mind, but his actual requirement was absolutely different; it has nothing to do with peace of mind. He only wanted a job for his son. Thus, he had come to the wrong man.

Now, one who has gone into the business of religion will say, "You want a job? Come here. I will get you a job and I will give you peace of mind too. Whoever comes here gets a job; whoever comes here, his wealth increases and his business runs well."

Now a few people will gather around the "shop" who will tell you, "My son got a job." Another will say, "My wife was saved from death." A third will say, "I won my lawsuit." A fourth will say, "Wealth is pouring on me." It is not that these people are telling lies or that they are hirelings; nor are they the agents for this business. It is nothing like that. When a thousand men come asking for jobs ten of them are bound to get employed in the normal course of things. Now these ten remain while the remaining nine hundred and ninety go away.

Then these ten slowly spread word of the "miracle", and the crowd around increases. This is why every such shop has salesmen and advertisers. Those who say their son got a job are not telling an untruth; nor have they been bought over by the shopkeeper. Such a man had also come seeking, and it happened that his son got a job. Those whose sons did not get a job left long ago to seek other gurus who would fulfil their desires. Those whose desires are fulfilled begin to frequent the shop often; they come on each festival every year. The crowd increases day by day, and a group forms around such a so-called guru. Then what they tell becomes his indisputable testimony. If so many people's wishes were fulfilled, why not yours? Now this is the worm; the hook which traps the man is within.

Never ask or else you are bound to be caught. Prepare yourself and leave all else to evidence. Let the grace happen when the moment is ripe for it to happen. If it does not happen we will know we are not yet ready to receive.

The fact is that you will feel the need for *shaktipat* again and again only when the happening has not yet taken place. And you will find the need to take from others only when your experience with the first has been in vain. If the first *shaktipat* is successful, the matter ends there. It is like trying many doctors because the disease has not yet been cured. Naturally, the doctors have to be changed. But the patient who is cured never raises the question of changing doctors.

The slightest experience of a glimpse due to *shaktipat* makes this question irrelevant. Besides, once this glimpse is attained from someone it makes no difference if it is attained again from another. It is the same energy coming from the same source, only the medium is different—but this does not result in any difference. Whether it comes from the sun or an electric bulb or oil-lamp, the light is the same.

It makes no difference and there is no harm, if the happening has taken place. But we do not go seeking for the happening. If it comes to you along the way, accept it and go further—but do not seek it. If you seek there are hazards, because then only the tricksters will come your way and not someone who can really give. He will appear only when you are not seeking, when you have prepared yourself. So to seek him is wrong, to ask is wrong. Let the happening take its own time and let the light come from a thousand paths. All paths will prove the authenticity of the same original source. It is the same; only it is appearing from all sides.

Someone was saying the other day that he went to a *sadhu,* a religious man, and said that wisdom should be one's own. The *sadhu* retorted that it cannot be—that wisdom "always pertains to another, and that such and such a monk gave it to such and such, then he passed it on to another."

Then I explained to this friend that Krishna's experience was his own. When he says that "so and so got it from so and so," he means that this wisdom that has revealed itself to him has not been revealed to him alone; it was revealed to so and so also, before him. Then this person had shared the happening with another person, and this happening took place in him also. But what is to be noted here is that the revelation did not take place by mere telling; it was told after the happening. So Krishna says to Arjuna, "This wisdom I am conveying to you is the same that has come to me. But my telling of it will not bring it about in you. When it happens to you, you will be able to tell others that it is like this."

Do not go begging for it, because it is not attained from anyone. Prepare yourself for it and it will begin to come from all directions. Then one day when the happening takes place you will say, "How blind I was that I could not see that which was coming to me from all sides."

A blind man may pass by a lamp or an electric light or go out in the sun, but he will never see light. Then one day if his sight is restored he will be shocked to see that he was always surrounded by light. So on the day of the happening you will see it all around you. And until the time comes when it takes place, offer your respects wherever you get the glimpse of truth. Take it from wherever you can get it, but please do not beg for it like a beggar—because truth is never obtained by a beggar. Do not beg for truth or else some businessman might lure you with lucrative suggestions. Then a spiritual exploitation will begin.

Go along your way always preparing yourself, and wherever you happen to find it, accept it. Offer your gratitude and move on; then at the moment of full attainment you will not be able to say that you got it from so and so. That moment you will say, "What a miracle I got from existence. Whosoever I approached, I received from him." Then the final thanksgiving will be to existence and not to anyone in particular.

This question had arisen because of the fact that the effect of shaktipat wears off by and by.

Yes, it will get less and less. In fact, what is attained from another is bound to diminish. Besides, it is only a glimpse and you are not to depend on it. You have to awaken it within yourself: then only will it be permanent. All influences are foreign; they belong to the outside. I pick up a stone and I throw it in the air: it will fall according to the force exerted by me. The stone has no strength of its own, but it may well think, as it flies through the air, that it has strength to cut through the air and that there is no one to stop it. But then it does not know what influence has caused this; it does not know the force of the hand behind it. It will fall—if not after ten feet then after twenty, but it will fall. Actually, any effect that comes from another is always limited and it is bound to diminish.

The only advantage of an outside influence is that in the momentary glimpse you experience you may be able to find your original source. Then it will be useful. It is as if I light a matchstick: how long will its flame last? Now you can do two things: firstly, you stay in the darkness and depend on the light of my matchstick. In a moment the light will go out and it will become pitch dark. Secondly, in the light of the matchstick you locate the door and you run out; you no longer depend on my matchstick. You are out; now it makes no difference to you whether the match is burning or not. Now you have reached where the sun is. Now something has become lasting and stable.

All these happenings have only one use: that with outside help you do something inner for yourself. But don't wait for these happenings, because the matchsticks will burn and go out again and again and you will become conditioned to them. Then you will become dependent on the matchstick and you will wait in the dark for the match to light, and when it lights you will keep on dreading the moment when it goes out, when once again you will be plunged into darkness. So this will become a vicious circle. No, you are not to stop at the matchstick. It is lit so that in its light you see the way and run out of the darkness as fast as possible.

This is all the advantage we can take from the other. It can never be a permanent gain; yet it is a gain and is not to be neglected. It is a wonder that we can get even so much from another. If the other is wise and understanding he will never tell you to stay on. He will say, "The match has been lit, now run—because soon the match will burn out." But if the medium tells you to stay on, on the ground that he and no other has lit the match, if he tells you that you should be initiated by him and take vows of being loyal to him, then this relationship will remain. If he asserts his right over you and forbids you to go elsewhere or listen to anyone else, then this is very dangerous.

It would have been much better if such a person had not lit the matchstick at all, because he has done great harm. In the dark you would have felt your way out someday and reached the light. Now you have landed yourself in difficulty by holding on to his matchstick. Now where will you go? And one thing is certain: this man has stolen this match from somewhere. It is not his own; otherwise he would have known its use. He would have known that it is meant to help a man to get out of darkness and that it is not meant to stop anyone or halt his progress.

Therefore, this is a stolen match that he is trading in. Now he proclaims that all who get a glimpse from his matches must stay with him and be devoted to him: this is the end! First darkness barred the way; now it is this guru. And darkness is better than a demanding guru, because it does not spread its hands to stop you. The obstruction of darkness is passive, it is quiet, but this guru obstructs actively. He will catch you by the hand and bar your way saying, "This is treachery, this is deceit."

Just the other day a girl came and told me that her guru objected to her coming to see me. The guru said, "Just as a husband or a wife belong to each other and not to anyone else, so also if a disciple forsakes the guru it is a great sin." He is right—but his are stolen matchsticks. There is no difficulty in stealing matches; there are many available in the scriptures.

Can stolen matches burn?

The thing is that one who has not seen the light cannot tell what has been burned in order to show him the light. When he sees the actual light, only then will he know what was what. Not only will he know what had been lit but he will even know whether anything was really lighted or whether he was only made to imagine it was.

The moment the light is seen, ninety-nine per cent of the gurus will be proved to be friends of darkness and enemies of light. Then only will we know what dangerous enemies they are: they are the agents of darkness.

4

THE MYSTERIES OF THE SEVEN BODIES AND SEVEN CHAKRAS

IN YESTERDAY'S TALK You said that the seeker should first worry about his own receptivity and should not go begging from door to door. But the very meaning of a sadhak is that there are obstacles on his path of spiritual growth. He does not know how to be receptive. Is it so difficult to meet the right guide?

To seek and to ask are two different things. Actually, only he who does not want to seek asks. To seek and to ask are not one and the same; rather, they are contradictory. He who wants to avoid seeking asks. The process of seeking and the process of begging are very different. In asking the attention is centred on the other—on the giver; in seeking the attention is centred on oneself—on the receiver. To say that there are obstacles in the path of spiritual growth means there are obstacles within the seeker himself. The path too lies within and it is not very difficult to understand one's own hindrances. It will have to be explained at length what obstacles are and how they can be removed. Yesterday I told you about the seven bodies. We shall talk in greater detail about these and it will become clear to you.

As there are seven bodies, so there are also seven *chakras,* energy centres, and each *chakra* is connected in a special way with its corresponding body. The *chakra* of the physical body is the *muladhar*. This is the first *chakra* and it has an integral connection with the physical body. The *muladhar chakra* has two possibilities. Its first potentiality is a natural one that is given to us with birth; its other possibility is obtainable by meditation.

The basic natural possibility of this *chakra* is the sex urge of the physical body. The very first question that arises in the mind of the seeker is what to do in regard to this central principle. Now there is another possibility of this *chakra,* and that is *brahmacharya,* celibacy, which is attainable through meditation. Sex is the natural possibility and *brahmacharya* is its transformation. The more the mind is focused upon and gripped by sexual desire, the more difficult it will be to reach its ultimate potential of *brahmacharya.*

Now this means that we can utilize the situation given to us by nature in two ways. We can live in the condition that nature has placed us in—but then the process of spiritual growth cannot begin—or we transform this state. The only danger in the path of transformation is that there is the possibility that we may begin to fight with our natural centre. What is the real danger in the path of a seeker? The first obstacle is that if the meditator indulges only in nature's order of things he cannot rise to the ultimate possibility of his physical body and he stagnates at the starting point. On the one hand there is a need; on the other hand there is a suppression which causes the meditator to fight the sex urge. Suppression is an obstacle on the path of meditation. This is the obstacle of the first *chakra*. Transformation cannot come about with suppression.

If suppression is an obstruction, what is the solution? Understanding will then solve the matter. Transformation takes place within as you begin to understand sex. There is a reason for this. All elements of nature lie blind and unconscious within us. If we become conscious of them, transformation begins. Awareness is the alchemy; awareness is the alchemy of changing them, of transforming them. If a person becomes awake toward his sexual desires with his total feelings and his total understanding, then *brahmacharya* will begin to take birth within him in place of sex. Unless a person reaches *brahmacharya* in his first body it is difficult to work on the potentiality of other centers.

The second body, as I said, is the emotional or the etheric body. The second body is connected to the second *chakra*—the *swadhishthan chakra*. This too has two possibilities. Basically, its natural potential is fear, hate, anger, and violence. All these are conditions obtained from the natural potential of the *swadhishthan chakra*. If a person stagnates at the second body, then the directly opposite conditions of transformation—love, compassion, fearlessness, friendliness—do not take place. The obstacle on the meditator's path in the second *chakra* is hate, anger and violence, and the question is of their transformation.

Here too the same mistake is made. One person can give vent to his anger; another can suppress his anger. One can just be fearful; another can suppress his fear and make a show of courage. But neither of these will lead to transformation. When there is fear it has to be accepted; there is no use hiding or suppressing it. If there is violence within there is no use in covering it with the mantle of non-violence. Shouting slogans of non-violence will bring no change in the state of violence within. It remains violence. It is a condition given to us by nature in the second body. It has its uses just as there is meaning to sex. Through sex alone other physical bodies can be given birth. Before one physical body falls, nature has made provisions for the birth of another.

Fear, violence, anger, are all necessary on the second plane; otherwise man cannot survive, cannot protect himself. Fear protects him, anger involves him in struggle against others and violence helps him to save himself from the violence of others. All these are qualities of the second body and are necessary for survival, but generally we stop here and do not go any further. If a person understands the nature of fear he attains fearlessness, and if he understands the nature of violence he attains non-violence. Similarly, by understanding anger we develop the quality of forgiveness.

In fact, anger is one side of the coin, forgiveness is the other. They each hide behind the other—but the coin has to be turned over. If we come to know one side of the coin perfectly we naturally become curious to know what is on the other side—and so the coin turns. If we hide the coin and pretend we have no fear, no violence within, we will never be able to know fearlessness and non-violence. He who accepts the presence of fear within himself and who has investigated it fully will soon reach a place where he will want to find out what is behind fear. His curiosity will encourage him to see the other side of the coin.

The moment he turns it over he becomes fearless. Similarly, violence will turn into compassion. These are the potentials of the second body. Thus, the meditator has to bring about a transformation in the qualities given to him by nature. And for this it is not necessary to go around asking others; one has to keep seeking and asking within oneself. We all know that anger and fear are impediments—because how can a coward seek truth? He will go begging for truth; he will wish that someone should give it to him without his having to go into unknown lands.

The third is the astral body. This also has two dimensions. Primarily, the third body revolves around doubt and thinking. If these are transformed doubt becomes trust and thinking becomes *vivek,* awareness. If doubts are repressed you never attain to *shraddha,* trust, though we are advised to suppress doubts and to believe what we hear. He who represses his doubts never attains to trust, because doubt remains present within though repressed. It will creep within like a cancer and eat up your vitality. Beliefs are implanted for fear of scepticism. We will have to understand the quality of doubt, we will have to live it and go along with it. Then one day we will reach a point where we will begin to have doubt about doubt itself. The moment we begin to doubt doubt itself, trust begins.

We cannot reach to the clarity of discrimination without going through the process of thinking. There are people who do not think and people who encourage them not to think. They say, "Do not think; leave all thoughts." He who stops thinking lands himself in ignorance and blind faith. This is not clarity. The power of discrimination is gained only after passing through the most subtle processes of thinking. What is the meaning of *vivek,* discrimination? Doubt is always present in thoughts. It is always indecisive. Therefore, those who think a great deal never come to a decision. It is only when they step out of the wheel of thoughts that they can decide. Decision comes from a state of clarity which is beyond thoughts.

Thoughts have no connection with decision. He who is always engrossed in thoughts never reaches a decision. That is why it invariably happens that those whose life is less dominated by thoughts are very resolute, whereas those who think a great deal lack determination. There is danger from both. Those who do not think go ahead and do whatever they are determined to do, for the simple reason that they have no thought process to create doubt within.

The dogmatists and the fanatics of the world are very active and energetic people; for them there is no question of doubting—they never think! If they feel that heaven is attained by killing one thousand people, they will rest only after killing one thousand people and not before. They never stop to think what they are doing, so there is never any indecision on their part. A man who thinks, on the contrary, will keep on thinking instead of making any decision.

If we close our doors for fear of thoughts we will be left with blind faith only. This is very dangerous and is a great obstacle in the path of the meditator. What is needed is an open-eyed discretion and thoughts that are clear, resolute, and which allow us to make decisions. This is the meaning of *vivek:* clarity, awareness. It means that the power of thinking is complete. It means we have passed through thoughts in such detail that all the doubts are cleared. Now only pure decision is left in its essence.

The *chakra* pertaining to the third body is manipur. Doubt and trust are its two forms. When doubt is transformed trust is the result. But, remember, trust is not opposed or contrary to doubt. Trust is the purest and most ultimate development of it. It is the ultimate extreme of doubt, where even doubt becomes lost because here doubt begins to doubt even itself and in this way commits suicide. Then trust is born.

The fourth plane is the mental body or the psyche, and the fourth *chakra,* the *anahat,* is connected with the fourth body. The natural qualities of this plane are imagination and dreaming. This is what the mind is always doing: imagining and dreaming. It dreams in the night and in the daytime it daydreams. If imagination is fully developed, that is to say if it is developed to its fullest extent, in a complete way, it becomes determination, will. If dreaming develops fully it is transformed into vision—psychic vision. If a man's ability to dream is fully developed he has only to close his eyes and he can see things. He can then see even through a wall. At first he only dreams of seeing beyond the wall; later he actually sees beyond it. Now he can only guess what you are thinking, but after the transformation he sees what you think. Vision means seeing and hearing things without the use of the usual sense organs. The limitations of time and space are no more for a person who develops vision.

In dreams you travel far. If you are in Bombay you reach Calcutta. In vision also you can travel distances, but there will be a difference: in dreams you imagine you have gone, whereas in vision you actually go. The fourth, psychic body can actually be present there. As we have no idea of the ultimate possibility of this fourth body, we have discarded the ancient concept of dreams in today's world. The ancient experience was that in dream one of the bodies of man comes out of him and goes on a journey.

There was a man, Swedenborg, whom people knew as a dreamer. He used to talk of heaven and hell and that they can only exist in dreams. But one afternoon, as he slept, he began to shout, "Help! Help! My house is on fire!" People came running, but there was no fire there. They awoke him to assure him that it was only a dream and there was no danger of fire. He insisted, however, that his house was on fire. His house was three hundred miles away and it had caught fire at that time. On the second or third day news came of this disaster. His house was burnt to ashes, and it was actually burning when he cried out in his sleep. Now this is no longer a dream but a vision. The distance of three hundred miles was no longer there. This man witnessed what was happening three hundred miles away.

Now scientists also agree that there are great psychic possibilities of the fourth body. Now that man has set out in space, research in this direction has become all the more important. The fact remains that no matter how reliable the instruments at man's disposal, these cannot be relied upon completely. If the radio communication in a spaceship ceases to function the astronauts lose contact with the world for all time. They will not be able to tell us where they are or what has happened to them. So today scientists are keen to develop telepathy and vision of the psychic body to overcome this risk. If the astronauts were able to communicate directly with the power of telepathy it would be a part of the development of the fourth body. Then space travel can be safe. A lot of work has been carried out in this direction.

Thirty years ago a man set out to explore the North Pole. He was equipped with all that was necessary for wireless communication. One more arrangement was also made which has not made known until now. A psychic person whose fourth body faculties were functioning was also made to receive the transmission from the explorer. The most surprising thing was that when there was bad weather the wireless failed, but this psychic person received the news without any difficulty. When the diaries were compared later on it was found that eighty to ninety-five per cent of the time the signals received by the psychic person were correct, whereas the news relayed by the radio was not available more than seventy-two per cent of the time, because there were many breakdowns. Now Russia and America are both very eager, and a great deal of work is going on in the field of telepathy, clairvoyance, thought projection and thought reading. All these are the possibilities of the fourth body. To dream is its natural quality; to see the truth, to see the real, is its ultimate possibility. *Anahat* is the *chakra* of this fourth body

The fifth *chakra* is the *vishuddhi chakra*. It is located in the throat. The fifth body is the spiritual body. The *vishuddhi chakra* is connected to the spiritual body. The first four bodies and their *chakras* were split into two. The duality ends with the fifth body.

As I said before, the difference between male and female lasts until the fourth body; after that it ends. If we observe very closely all duality belongs to the male and the female. Where the distance between male and female is no more, at that very point all duality ceases. The fifth body is nondual. It does not have two possibilities but only one.

This is why there is not much effort for the meditator to make: because here there is nothing contrary to develop; here one has only to enter. By the time we reach the fourth body we develop so much capability and strength that it is very easy to enter the fifth body. In that case how can we tell the difference between a person who has entered the fifth body and one who has not? The difference will be that he who has entered the fifth body is completely rid of all unconsciousness. He will not actually sleep at night. That is, he sleeps but his body alone sleeps; someone within is forever awake. If he turns in sleep he knows it; if he does not he knows it. If he has covered himself with a blanket he knows it; if he has not then also he knows it. His awareness does not slacken in sleep; he is awake all the twenty-four hours. For the one who has not entered the fifth body, his state is just the opposite. In sleep he is asleep, and in the waking hours also one layer of him will be asleep.

People appear to be working. When you come home every evening the car turns left into your gate; you apply the brake when you reach the porch. Do not be under the illusion that you are doing all this consciously. It happens unconsciously by sheer force of habit. It is only in certain moments, moments of great danger, that we really come into alertness. When the danger is so much that it will not do to go about lacking awareness, we awaken. For instance, if a man puts a knife at your chest you jump into consciousness. The point of the knife for a moment takes you right up to the fifth body. With the exception of these few moments in our lives we live like somnambulists.

Neither has the wife seen the husband's face properly nor has the husband seen the wife's face. If the husband tries to visualise the wife's face he will not be able to do so. The lines of her face will start slipping away and it will be difficult to say whether it was the same face he has seen for the last thirty years. You have never seen, because there must be an awakened person within you to see.

One who is "awake" appears to be seeing but actually he is not—because he is asleep within, dreaming, and everything is going on in this dream state. You get angry, then you say, "I do not know how I got angry; I did not want to." You say, "Forgive me! I did not want to be rude, it was a slip of the tongue." You have used an obscenity and it is you who deny the intention of its use. The criminal always says, "I did not want to kill. It happened in spite of me." This proves that we are going about like an automaton. We say what we do not want to say; we do what we do not want to do.

In the evening we vow to be up at four in the morning. When it is four o'clock and the alarm goes off we turn over saying there is no need to be up so early. Then you get up at six and are filled with remorse for having overslept. Then you again swear to keep the same vow as yesterday. It is strange that a man decides on one thing in the evening and goes back on it in the morning! Then what he decides at four in the morning changes again before it is six, and what he decides at six changes long before it is evening, and in between he changes a thousand times. These decisions, these thoughts, come to us in our sleepy state. They are like dreams: they expand and burst like bubbles. There is no wakeful person behind them—no one who is alert and conscious.

So sleep is the innate condition before the beginning of the spiritual plane. Man is a somnambulist before he enters the fifth body, and there the quality is wakefulness. Therefore, after the growth of the fourth body we can call the individual a *buddha,* an awakened one. Now such a man is awake. Buddha is not the name of Gautam Siddharth but a name given him after his attainment of the fifth plane. Gautama the Buddha means Gautam who has awakened. His name remained Gautam, but that was the name of the sleeping person, so gradually it dropped and only Buddha remained.

This difference comes with the attainment of the fifth body. Before we enter into it, whatever we do is an unconscious action which cannot be trusted. One moment a man vows to love and cherish his loved one the whole life and the next moment he is quite capable of strangling her. The alliance which he promised for a lifetime does not last long. This poor man is not to be blamed. What is the value of promises given in sleep? In a dream I may promise, "This is a lifelong relationship." What value is this promise? In the morning I will deny it because it was only a dream.

A sleeping man cannot be trusted. This world of ours is entirely a world of sleeping people; hence, so much confusion, so many conflicts, so many quarrels, so much chaos. It is all the making of sleeping men.

There is another important difference between a sleeping man and an awakened man which we should bear in mind. A sleeping man does not know who he is, so he is always striving to show others that he is this or he is that. This is his lifelong endeavour. He tries in a thousand ways to prove himself. Sometimes he climbs the ladder of politics and declares, "I am so and so." Sometimes he builds a house and displays his wealth, or he climbs a mountain and displays his strength. He tries in all ways to prove himself. And in all these efforts he is in fact unknowingly trying to find out for himself who he is. He knows not who he is.

Before crossing the fourth plane we cannot find the answer. The fifth body is called the spiritual body because there you get the answer to the quest for "Who am I?" The call of the 'I' stops once and for all on this plane; the claim to be someone special vanishes immediately. If you say to such a person, "You are so and so," he will laugh. All claims from his side will now stop, because now he knows. There is no longer any need to prove himself, because who he is is now a proven fact.

The conflicts and problems of the individual end on the fifth plane. But this plane has its own hazards. You have come to know yourself, and this knowing is so blissful and fulfilling that you may want to terminate your journey here. You may not feel like continuing on. The hazards that were up to now were all of pain and agony; now the hazards that begin are of bliss. The fifth plane is so blissful that you will not have the heart to leave it and proceed further. Therefore, the individual who enters this plane has to be very alert about clinging to bliss so that it does not hinder him from going further. Here bliss is supreme and at the peak of its glory; it is in its profoundest depths. A great transformation comes about within one who has known himself. But this is not all; there is further to go also.

It is a fact that distress and suffering do not obstruct our way as much as joy. Bliss is very obstructive. It was difficult enough to leave the crowd and confusion of the marketplace, but it is a thousand times more difficult to leave the soft music of the veena in the temple. This is why many meditators stop at *atma gyan,* self-realization, and do not go up to Brahma *gyan,* experience of the Brahman—the cosmic reality.

We shall have to be alert about this bliss. Our effort here should be not to get lost in this bliss. Bliss draws us towards itself; it drowns us; we get immersed in it completely. Do not become immersed in bliss. Know that this too is an experience. Happiness was an experience, misery was an experience; bliss too is an experience. Stand outside of it, be a witness. As long as there is experience there is an obstacle: the ultimate end has not been reached. At the ultimate state all experiences end. Joy and sorrow come to an end, so also does bliss. Our language, however, does not go beyond this point. This is why we have described God as *sat-chit-ananda*—truth-consciousness-bliss. This is not the form of the supreme self, but this is the ultimate that words can express. Bliss is the ultimate expression of man. In fact, words cannot go beyond the fifth plane. But about the fifth plane we can say, "There is bliss there; there is perfect awakening; there is realisation of the self there." All this can be described.

Therefore, there will be no mystery about those who stop at the fifth plane. Their talk will sound very scientific because the realm of mystery lies beyond this plane. Things are very clear up to the fifth plane. I believe that science will sooner or later absorb those religions that go up to the fifth body, because science will be able to reach up to the *atman*.

When a seeker sets out on this path his search is mainly for bliss and not truth. Frustrated by suffering and restlessness he sets out in search of bliss. So one who seeks bliss will definitely stop at the fifth plane; therefore, I must tell you to seek not bliss but truth. Then you will not remain long here.

Then a question arises: "There is *ananda:* this is well and good. I know myself: this too is well and good. But these are only the leaves and the flowers. Where are the roots? I know myself, I am blissful—it is good, but from where do I arise? Where are my roots? From where have I come? Where are the depths of my existence? From which ocean has this wave that I am arisen?"

If your quest is for truth you will go ahead of the fifth body. From the very beginning, therefore, your quest should be for truth and not bliss; otherwise your journey up to the fifth plane will be easy but you will stop there. If the quest is for truth, there is no question of stopping there.

So the greatest obstacle on the fifth plane is the unequalled joy we experience—and more so because we come from a world where there is nothing but pain, suffering, anxiety and tension. Then, when we reach this temple of bliss, there is an overwhelming desire to dance with ecstasy, to be drowned, to be lost in this bliss. This is not the place to be lost. That place will come, and then you will not have to lose yourself; you will simply be lost. There is a great difference between losing yourself and being lost. In other words, you will reach a place where even if you wish you cannot save yourself. You will see yourself becoming lost; there is no remedy. Yet here also in the fifth body you can lose yourself. Your effort, your endeavour, still works here—and even though the ego is intrinsically dead on the fifth plane, I-am-ness still persists. It is necessary, therefore, to understand the difference between ego and I-am-ness.

The ego, the feeling of 'I', will die, but the feeling of 'am' will not die. There are two things in "I am", the 'I' is the ego and the 'am' is *asmita*—the feeling of being. So the 'I' will die on the fifth plane, but the being, the 'am', will remain: I-am-ness will remain. Standing on this plane, a meditator will declare, "There are infinite souls and each soul is different and apart from the other." On this plane the meditator will experience the existence of infinite souls, because he still has the feeling of 'am', the feeling of being which makes him feel apart from others. If the quest for truth grips the mind the obstacle of bliss can be crossed—because incessant bliss becomes tedious. A single strain of a melody can become irksome.

Bertrand Russell once said jokingly, "I am not attracted to salvation, because I hear there is nothing but bliss there. Bliss alone would be very monotonous—bliss and bliss and nothing else. If there is not a single trace of unhappiness—no anxiety, no tension in it—how long can one bear such bliss?"

To be lost in bliss is the hazard of the fifth plane. It is very difficult to overcome. Sometimes it takes many births to do so. The first four steps are not so hard to cross, but the fifth is very difficult. Many births may be needed to be bored of bliss, to be bored of the self, to be bored of the *atman*.

So the quest up to the fifth body is to be rid of pain, hatred, violence and desires. After the fifth the search is in order to be rid of the self. So there are two things: the first is freedom from something; this is one thing and it is completed at the fifth plane. The second thing is freedom from the self, and so a completely new world starts from here.

The sixth is the *Brahma sharira,* the cosmic body, and the sixth *chakra* is the *agya chakra*. Here there is no duality. The experience of bliss becomes intense on the fifth plane and the experience of existence, of being, on the sixth. *Asmita* will now be lost—I am. The 'I' in this is lost at the fifth plane and the 'am' will go as soon as you transcend the fifth. The is-ness will be felt; *tathata,* suchness will be felt. Nowhere will there be the feeling of 'I' or of 'am'; only that which 'is' remains. So here will be the perception of reality, of being—the perception of consciousness. But here the consciousness is free of me; it is no longer my consciousness. It is only consciousness—no longer my existence, but only existence.

Some meditators stop after reaching the *Brahma sharira,* the cosmic body, because the state of "I am the Brahman" has come of *"Aham Brahmasmi"*, when I am not and only the *Brahman* is. Now what more is there to seek? What is to be sought? Nothing remains to be sought. Now everything is attained. The *Brahman* means the total. One who stands at this point says, "The *Brahman* is the ultimate truth, the *Brahman* is the cosmic reality. There is nothing beyond."

It is possible to stop here, and seekers do stop at this stage for millions of births, because there seems to be nothing ahead. So the *Brahma gyani,* the one who has attained realisation of the *Brahman,* will get stuck here; he will go no further. This is so difficult to cross because there is nothing to cross to. Everything has been covered. Does not one need a space to cross into? If I want to go outside of this room there must be some place else to go. But the room has now become so enormous, so beginningless and endless, so infinite, so boundless, that there is nowhere to go. So where will we go to search? Nothing remains to be found; everything has been covered. So the journey may halt at this stage for infinite births.

So the *Brahman* is the ultimate obstacle—the last barrier in the ultimate quest of the seeker. Now only the being remains, but non-being has yet to be realised. The being, the is-ness, is known, but the non-being has yet to be realised—that which is not still remains to be known. Therefore, the seventh plane is the *nirvana kaya, nirvanic* body, and its *chakra* is the *sahasrar*. Nothing can be said in connection with this *chakra*. We can only continue talking at the most up to the sixth—and that too with great difficulty. Most of it will turn out to be wrong.

Until the fifth body the search progresses within a very scientific method; everything can be explained. On the sixth plane the horizon begins to fade; everything seems meaningless. Hints can still be given but ultimately the pointing finger breaks and the hints too are no more because one's own being is eliminated. So the *Brahman,* the absolute being, is known from the sixth body and the sixth *chakra.*

Therefore, those who seek the *Brahman* will meditate on the *agya chakra* which is between the eyes. This *chakra* is connected to the cosmic body. Those who work completely on this *chakra* will begin to call the vast infinite expanse that they witness the third eye. This is the third eye from where they can now view the cosmic, the infinite.

One more journey yet remains—the journey to non-being, non-existence. Existence is only half the story: there is also non-existence. Light is, but on the other side there is darkness. Life is one part, but there is also death. Therefore, it is necessary also to know the remaining non-existence, the void, because the ultimate truth can only be known when both are known—existence and non-existence. Being is known in its entirety and non-being is known in its entirety: then the knowing is complete. Existence is known in entirety and non-existence is known in its entirety: then we know the whole; otherwise our experience is incomplete. There is an imperfection in *Brahma gyan,* which is that it has not been able to know the non-being. Therefore, the *Brahma gyani* denies that there is such a thing as non-existence and calls it an illusion. He says that it does not exist. He says that to be is the truth and not to be is a falsity. There simply is no such thing, so the question of knowing it does not arise.

Nirvana kaya means the *shunya kaya,* the void from where we jump from the being into the non-being. In the cosmic body something yet remains unknown. That too has to be known—what it is not to be, what it is to be completely erased. Therefore, the seventh plane in a sense is an ultimate death. *Nirvana,* as I told you previously, means the extinction of the flame. That which was 'I' is extinct; that which was 'am' is extinct. But now we have again come into being by being one with the all. Now we are the *Brahman,* and this too will have to be left. He who is ready to take the last jump knows the existence and also the non-existence.

So these are the seven bodies and the seven *chakras,* and within them lie all the means as well as the barriers. There are no barriers outside. Therefore, there is not much reason to inquire outside. If you have gone to ask someone or to understand from someone, then do not beg. To understand is one thing, to beg is another. Your search should always continue. Whatever you have heard and understood should also be made your search. Do not make it your belief or else it will be begging.

You asked me something; I gave you an answer. If you have come for alms you will put this in your bag and store it away as your treasure. Then you are not a meditator but a beggar. No, what I told you should become your quest. It should accelerate your search; it should stimulate and motivate your curiosity. It should put you into greater difficulty, make you more restless and raise new questions in you, new dimensions, so that you will set out on a new path of discovery. Then you have not taken alms from me, then you have understood what I said. And if this helps you to understand yourself, then this is not begging.

So go forth to know and understand; go forth to search. You are not the only one seeking; many others are also. Many have searched, many have attained. Try to know, to grasp, what has happened to such people and also what has not happened; try and understand all this. But while understanding this, do not stop trying to understand your own self. Do not think that understanding others has become your realisation. Do not put faith in their experiences; do not believe them blindly. Rather, turn everything into questioning. Turn them into questions and not answers; then your journey will continue. Then it will not be begging: it will be your quest.

It is your search that will take you to the last. As you penetrate within yourself you will find the two sides of each *chakra*. As I told you, one is given to you by nature and one you have to discover. Anger is given to you; forgiveness you have to find. Sex is given to you; *brahmacharya* you have to develop. Dreams you have; vision has to evolve.

Your search for the opposite will continue up to the fourth chakra. From the fifth will start your search for the indivisible, for the non-dual. Try to continue your search for that which is different from what has come to you in the fifth body. When you attain bliss try to find out what there is beyond bliss. On the sixth plane you attain the *Brahman,* but keep inquiring, "What is there beyond the *Brahman*?" Then one day you will step into the seventh body, where being and non-being, light and darkness, life and death, occur together. That is the attainment of the ultimate...and there are no means of communicating this state.

This is why our scriptures end with the fifth body, or at the most they go up to the sixth body. Those with a completely scientific turn of mind do not talk about what is after the fifth body. The cosmic reality, which is boundless and unlimited, begins from there, but mystics like the Sufis talk of the planes beyond the fifth. It is very difficult to talk of these planes because one has to contradict oneself again and again. If you go through the text of all that one Sufi has said you will say this person is mad. Sometimes he says one thing and sometimes something else. He says, "God is" and he also says, "God is not." He says, "I have seen Him" and in the same breath he says, "How can you see Him? He is not an object that the eyes can see!" These mystics raise such questions that you will wonder if they are asking others or asking themselves.

Mysticism starts with the sixth plane. Therefore, where there is no mysticism in a religion, know that it has finished on the fifth body. But mysticism also is not the final stage. The ultimate is the void—nothingness. The religion that ends with mysticism ends with the sixth body. The void is the ultimate, nihilism is the ultimate, because after it there is nothing more to be said.

So the search for *advaita,* the nondual, starts with the fifth body. All search for the opposites ends with the fourth body. All barriers are within us and they are useful, because these very obstacles when transformed become your means to go ahead.

A rock is lying on the road. As long as you do not understand it will remain an obstacle for you. The day you understand it will become a ladder for you. The rock is lying on the road: as long as you did not understand you shouted, "The rock is in my way. How can I go ahead?" When you have understood you will climb over the rock and go ahead, thanking the rock with the words, "You have blessed me very much, because after climbing over you I have found myself on a higher plane. Now I am proceeding along on a higher level. You were a means and I took you to be a barrier," you will say. The road is blocked by this boulder. What will happen? Cross over it and know. In this way, overcome anger; cross over it and reach forgiveness which is on a different level. Cross over sex and attain *brahmacharya* which is an entirely different plane. Then you will thank sex and anger for being the stepping stones.

Every rock on the path can be a barrier as well as a medium. It depends entirely on what you do with it. One thing is certain: Do not fight with the rock, because then you will only break your head and the rock will not be helpful. If you fight with the rock, the rock will bar your way, because wherever we fight we stop. We have to stop near the person or thing we fight with; we cannot possibly fight from a distance. That is why if someone fights sex he has to be involved with sex just as much as another who indulges in it. In fact, many times he is closer to sex, because the one who indulges in it can get out of it someday, can transcend it. But the one who fights cannot get out of it; he keeps going around and around.

If you fight anger you will become angry yourself. Your whole personality will be filled with anger and each fibre of your body will vibrate with it. You will emanate anger all around you. The stories we read of sages and ascetics like Durvasa being very angry happen because they fought with anger; thus, they could think of nothing but cursing. The personality of such a person turns into fire. These are people who have fought with rocks and are now in difficulty. They have become what they struggled against.

You will read of other *rishis* that celestial maidens descended from heaven and corrupted them in a moment. Strange! This is only possible if a man has fought with sex; not otherwise. He has fought and fought and thus weakened himself. Then sex is secure in its own place; it is just waiting for him to break down. This sex can now burst forth from anywhere. There is little possibility of an *apsara* actually coming down from heaven—are such maidens on contract to harass *rishis* and *munis*? When sex is suppressed with a heavy hand, an ordinary woman becomes a celestial being. The mind projects dreams at night and thoughts in the day and it becomes completely filled with these thoughts. Then a thing which is not at all fascinating becomes bewitching.

So the seeker has to beware of the tendency to fight. He should try his utmost to understand, and by trying to understand is meant understanding that which is given to him by nature. Through that which has been given to you, you will attain that which is yet to be attained. This is the starting point. If you run away from that which is the very beginning it is impossible to reach the goal. If you run away from sex in fright how will you ever reach *brahmacharya*? Sex was the opening given by nature and *brahmacharya* is the quest that has to be undertaken through this very opening. If you see in this perspective there is no need to beg from anywhere; understanding is what is required. All of existence is there for the purpose of understanding. Learn from anybody, hear everyone, and, finally, understand your own self within.

You have enlightened us about the seven bodies. Could You tell us the names of some individuals—ancient or modern—who have attained the nirvana body, the cosmic body and the spiritual body?

Do not bother about this. It serves no purpose; it is meaningless. Even if I tell you, you have no means to verify it. As much as possible, avoid comparing and evaluating individuals because it serves no purpose; it has no meaning. Drop such concerns.

Do those who reach the fifth and following bodies again assume physical forms after death?

Yes, it is true. One who attains the fifth or the sixth body before death is reborn in the highest celestial realm, and there he lives on the plane of the *devas*. He can stay in this realm as long as he likes, but to attain *nirvana* he has to come back to the human form. After attaining the fifth there is no birth in the physical body, but there are other bodies. In fact, what we call *devas* or gods signifies the kind of body that is obtained. This type of body is obtained after reaching the fifth body. After the sixth body, even these will not be there. Then we shall obtain the form of what we call *Ishwar*, the Supreme Being.

But all these are still bodies. What type is a secondary matter. After the seventh there are no bodies. From the fifth onwards the bodies become more and more subtle until they reach the bodiless state after the seventh.

In a previous talk, You said You prefer shaktipat to be as close to grace as possible—that it is better if it is so. Does this mean that there is a possibility of gradual progress and development in the process of shaktipat? In other words, is there a likelihood of qualitative progress in shaktipat?

There is every likelihood. Many things are possible. In reality, the difference between *shaktipat* and grace is great. Fundamentally, only grace is useful and without a medium it is at its purest, because there will be no one in between to make it impure. It is just like when I see you directly with my own eyes: your image will be the clearest. Then I put on a pair of spectacles: vision will not be that pure, because now a medium has come in between. Now there could be many varieties of mediums—pure, impure. A pair of spectacles could be coloured, another transparent, and the quality of the lens itself will vary.

So when we obtain grace from a medium there are bound to be impurities and they will be of the medium. Therefore, the purest grace is that which is received directly when there is no medium. Now, for instance, if we could see without the eyes it would mean purer vision, because even the eyes are a medium and are bound to cause some hindrance. Someone may have jaundice, someone may have weak eyesight, someone may have some other eye trouble—so these are the difficulties. One whose eyesight is weak will find the medium of a particular pair of glasses very helpful. It may perhaps give him a clearer vision than his unaided eyesight, and so the spectacles will have become one more medium. There are now two mediums, but the second medium compensates for the weakness of the first.

In exactly the same manner the grace that reaches a person through another gathers impurities along the way. Now if these impurities are such that they have a reverse effect upon the impurities within the seeker, these both will compensate each other. Then what will happen will be nearest to grace. But this will have to be decided separately in each case.

Therefore, my preference is for direct grace. Do not bother about a medium. If at some time it is necessary in the course of life the glimpse can come through a medium also, but the seeker should not worry or be anxious about this. Do not go begging, because as I said, then the giver is bound to turn up. Then the more dense the medium the more adulterated will be the effect. The giver should be such that he is not conscious of giving; then *shaktipat* can be pure. Even then it is not grace. You will still need to receive grace directly without a medium. There should be no one between you and God; there should be no one between the divine and you. And this should always be in your mind. This should be your longing and this should be your search. Many happenings will take place on the way, but you are not to stop anywhere; that is all that is required of you. And you will feel the difference. There are bound to be qualitative as well as quantitative differences, and the reasons will be many.

Shaktipat can take place through a medium who has attained the fifth body, but it will not be as pure as that which would come through a person of the sixth body, because his *asmita,* his am-ness is still intact. The 'I' is dead, but the 'am' still remains. Now this 'am' will still feel self-pleasure. In a person of the sixth body the 'am' also has disappeared; there is only the *Brahman*. Then the *shaktipat* will be purer. Yet some illusion remains, because the state of non-being has not yet been reached even though the state of being has been. This being is also a very subtle veil—very fragile, very transparent; all the same, it is there.

So *shaktipat* through a person of the sixth body will be better than that which comes through a person of the fifth body, and it will be very near to direct grace. However close it may be, the slightest distance is, after all, a distance. And the more priceless a thing, the more even the slightest distance becomes a great distance. So invaluable is the realm of grace that even the most subtle veil of being proves to be a barrier.

Now the *shaktipat* obtained from a person who has attained the seventh plane would be the purest—but still it will not be grace. The purest form of *shaktipat* descends through the seventh body—the purest. Here *shaktipat* will reach its ultimate state, because there is no veil as far as the medium is concerned: he is one with the void. But as far as you are concerned, there are barriers. You will consider him as a human being all your life; your veil will cause the ultimate barrier. He is one with the void; he is without any barriers—but you will look upon him as an individual.

Now suppose I reach the seventh plane: I would know that I have attained the void, but what about you? You will look upon me as a person, and this notion of an individual will become the final veil. You can only get rid of this conception when the happening occurs through the formless. In other words, then you cannot point out from where and how the happening took place. When you will be unable to find the source this notion will drop. The happening must be sourceless. If sunrays are coming you will think that the sun is a person. But when a ray comes from nowhere, when the rain falls without any cloud, then the final veil that is formed by personification falls.

As you continue on, the distances will become more and more subtle, and the final happening of grace will take place when there is no one in between. Your very thought that there is someone in between is barrier enough. As long as there are two, there is a lot of obstruction: you are there and the other is there. Even when the other is no more, you are, and because you are the other's presence is also felt. The grace which descends without any source, without any origin anywhere, will be the best. The individual in you will flow away in this grace that comes from the void. If another person is present he serves the purpose of saving your individuality despite the fact that he is working for you.

If you go to the seashore you experience greater peace, if you go to the forest you experience greater peace, because the other is not present there and so your 'I' remains firm and strong. If two men sit in a room, there are waves and counter-waves of tension there even though these two may not be fighting or quarrelling or even talking. So even when they are silent the 'I' of each is constantly working. Aggression and defence are there in full swing. These things can go on silently also and there is no need for a direct encounter. The mere presence of two people and a room is filled with tension.

If you were to gain full knowledge of all the currents that come out from you, you would see clearly that a room containing two persons has been divided into two and each individual has become a centre. The energy vibrations from both stand facing each other like armies on a battlefield. The presence of the other strengthens your 'I'. When the other leaves, the room will become a different place altogether. You relax. The 'I' that was on edge will let itself go. It now leans against the cushion and rests, it now breathes freely because the other is not there. Hence, the significance of solitude is to relax your ego and to help it to let go. It is for this reason that you are more at ease near a tree than in the company of another person.

This is why, in countries where tensions between man and man are becoming deeper, people tend to live with pets. It is easier to live with animals than with men, because they have no 'I'. Tie a collar to a dog, and he goes about happily. We cannot tie a collar to a man in this way, though we try very hard. The wife ties the husband, the husband the wife, and they both go about happily—but these collars are subtle and cannot be seen openly. Yet each tries to shake off the collar and be free—but the dog walks happily along, wagging his tail. So the pleasure the dog gives no other man can give, because another man at once brings your ego to your attention, and then the trouble starts.

Gradually man tries to break his relationship with others and establish relationships with objects because they are easier to handle. So the bulk of objects is increasing day by day. There are more articles in the house than people. People bring disorder and confusion; objects give no bother. The chair remains where I place it. If I sit on it, it creates no trouble. The presence of trees, rivers, mountains, is not troublesome; therefore, we feel at peace near them. The reason is only this: the 'I' is not standing in full strength before us; therefore, we too feel relaxed. When the other is not there, where is the need for the 'I'? Then the 'I' too is not. But the slightest inkling of the other, and the 'I' jumps to attention. It is worried about its security, about its lack of information as to what the next moment may bring; hence, it has to be ready all the time.

The ego always remains alert until the very last moment. Even if you meet a person of the seventh plane, the ego is alert. Sometimes it becomes excessively alert before such a person. You are not so much afraid of the ordinary man, because even if he hurts you the injury is not very deep. But a man who has reached the fifth body or beyond can inflict deep surgery that reaches up to the same body of yours that he has reached. Thus, your fear becomes more, because "God knows what he might do." You begin to feel something unknown as if unfamiliar forces are watching at you through him, so you become wary. You see an abyss all around him. You become alert and on guard. You begin to feel the experience of the deep valley, and you are caught by the fear that if you go within him you will fall into this abyss.

That is why when men like Jesus, Krishna and Socrates are born we kill them: their very presence causes great confusion among us. To go near them is to go willfully near danger. Then when they die we worship them because now there is no fear. Now we can cast their image into gold and stand with folded hands before them calling them our beloved master. But in their lifetime we treat them differently. Then we are very much afraid of them and this fear is of that which is unknown to us: you do not know for certain what is the matter. The deeper a man goes within himself, the more he becomes like an abyss to us. Then it is just like when someone is afraid to look down into a valley because it makes his head reel. Similarly, to look into the eyes of such a person will also create fear: our heads are sure to reel.

There is a beautiful story about Moses. After Hazrat Moses had the vision of God he never kept his face uncovered. All his life he went about with a veil drawn over his face, because to look at his face became dangerous. Whosoever did so escaped. There was an infinite abyss in his eyes. So Moses moved about with his face covered because people were frightened of his eyes. His eyes seemed to draw them like a magnet towards that unknown abyss within. They became struck with fear because they did not know where his eyes would take them and what would happen to them.

The man who has reached the seventh and the last plane also exists so far as you are concerned, but you will try to protect yourself from him and a barrier will remain in between. Therefore, *shaktipat* in this case also cannot be pure. It can be pure if you give up the thought of such a one being a person—but this can only happen when your 'I' is lost. When you reach the stage where you are completely unaware of the ego you will be able to obtain *shaktipat* from anywhere, because then there is no question of its coming from anybody; it will have become sourceless, it will have become grace.

The greater the crowd, the harder and more condensed is your ego. Therefore, it has long been a practice to get out of the crowd and try to drop the ego in solitude. But man is strange: if he stays under a tree for long he will begin to talk to it and address it as 'you'. If he stays near the ocean he will do the same. The 'I' in us will go to any length to keep itself alive. It will create the other no matter where you go, and it will establish sentimental relationship even with inanimate objects and will begin to look upon them as individuals.

When a person approaches the last stage he makes God the other so that he can save his 'I'. Therefore, the devotee always says, "How can we be one with God? He is He and we are we. We are at His feet, and He is God." The devotee is saying nothing but this, that if you want to be one with Him you will have to lose your ego. So he keeps God at a distance and he begins to rationalise. He says, "How can we be one with Him? He is great, He is absolute. We are wretched outcastes so how can we be one with Him?" The devotee is saving the 'thou' in order to save his 'I'. Therefore, the *bhakta,* the devotee, never rises above the fourth plane. He does not even go up to the fifth plane: he gets stuck at the fourth. Instead of imagination, on the fourth plane visions come to him. He discovers all the best possibilities of the fourth body. So many happenings take place in a devotee's life that are miraculous, but the *bhakta* remains on the fourth plane all the same.

The *atma sadhak*—one who is searching for the self—the *hatha yogi*—the *yogi* who goes through austerities—and many others who undergo similar practices, reaches the fifth plane at the most. Such a *sadhak's* intrinsic desire is to attain bliss, to attain liberation and freedom from suffering. Behind all of these desires stands the 'I': he says, "I want liberation"—not liberation from the 'I', but liberation of the 'I'. He says, "I want to be free, I want beatitude." His 'I' stands condensed, so he only reaches to the fifth plane.

The *raja yogi* reaches up to the sixth plane. He says, "What is there in the 'I'? I am nothing; he alone is—not I, but he, the *Brahman,* is everything." He is ready to lose the ego but he is not prepared to lose his being. He says, "I shall remain as part of the *Brahman;* I am one with him. I am the *Brahman*. I shall let myself go, but my inner being within me will remain merged in him." Such a seeker can go up to the sixth body.

A meditator like Buddha reaches the seventh plane because he is ready to give up all—even the *Brahman*. He is ready to lose himself and lose everything. He says, "Let what is remain. On my part I do not desire anything to remain: I am ready to lose my all." He who is prepared to lose everything is entitled to gain all.

The *nirvanic* body is attained only when we are prepared to be nothing. Then there is a readiness to know even death. For knowing life many are ready. Therefore, he who wants to know life will stop at the sixth plane. But he who is ready to investigate death also will be able to know the seventh plane.

Why has the meditator who has gained the capacity for vision and subtle sight on the fourth plane—and many have attained this stage—not been able to reveal the knowledge of the moon, the sun, the earth and their movements, as the scientists have done?

Three or four things have to be understood in connection with this. The first thing is that many of these facts have been revealed by persons such as these, of the fourth plane. For instance, there is very little difference between the age of the earth as shown by these men and as shown by the scientists, and as yet it cannot be said that science is correct. Scientists do not themselves claim to be absolutely correct.

Secondly, there is even less difference in the information given by each of these two categories about the shape and measurement of the earth. Besides, even in connection with this matter it is not necessarily the case that those who have reached the fourth plane are wrong in their estimate. The shape of the earth is forever changing. The distance between the earth and the sun is not the same as it was in ancient times, and the same is the situation between the moon and the earth. Africa is not where it used to be; once upon a time it was joined with India. Thousands of changes have occurred and are still occurring, and many changes take place constantly. Keeping in mind these constant changes you will be surprised to know that people of the fourth plane have long ago revealed many of the discoveries that science is making today.

It should also be understood that there is a fundamental difference between the language of expression of the man of the fourth plane and the scientist. This is a very great difficulty. The man of the fourth plane has no mathematical language. He has the language of vision, images and symbols. He has the language of signs. As there is no language in dreams, in vision too there is no language. If we understand thoroughly we will know that if we were to dream at night what we did throughout the day we would have to choose the medium of symbols and signs, because there is no language there. If I am an ambitious person who wants to be above everybody else, I will dream I am a bird flying high in the skies over and above other birds. In dreams I will not be able to express verbally that I am ambitious, so the whole language changes in dreams. In the same manner, the language of vision is not of words but of pictures.

Dream interpretation began to develop after Freud, Jung and Adler. Now we can find out the meaning of a dream. In the same manner, whatever persons of the fourth plane have said still awaits interpretation. As yet we have not even been able to explain the phenomenon of dreams thoroughly; explanation of psychic visions is an altogether different matter. We must know the meaning of what has been seen in visions and of what people of the fourth plane are saying.

For example, when Darwin said that man has evolved from the animal he spoke in a scientific language. But if we were to read the story of the Hindu incarnations we would find that this is nothing but the same story told thousands of years ago in symbolic form. The first incarnation was not a man, he was a fish. Darwin also says that man's first form was that of a fish. Now, when we say that the first incarnation was *matsya avatar*—a fish, this is symbolic. This is not the language of science: an incarnation and a fish! We denied this statement. But when Darwin said that the first element of life came in the form of the fish and then other forms followed, we readily agreed because it seemed reasonable to us. Darwin's method and search is scientific.

Now those who saw visions saw the divine first taking birth as a fish. The visionary speaks the language of parables. Then the second incarnation is a tortoise. This creature belongs both to the land and water. Obviously, the transition of life from water to land could not be sudden. There had to be an intermediary state. So whatever creature evolved must have belonged both to land and water. Then gradually the descendants of the tortoise began to live on land, and then there must have been a marked separation from life in the water.

If you read through this story of the Hindu incarnations you will be surprised to note that we had discovered long ago what Darwin discovered thousands of years later, and in the right chronological order. Then, before the final metamorphosis, there is the half-man, half-animal *avatar*—*narsimha avatar*. After all, animals did not become human at one stroke; they too must have had to pass through the intermediate phase where there were half men and half animals. It is impossible that an animal gave birth to a human being. There is a missing link between animal and man which could be narsimha—half-man and half-animal.

If we understand all these stories we will know that what Darwin said in scientific terms people of the fourth plane said long ago in the language of the *Puranas*. But up to now these Hindu mythological scriptures have not been properly explained. The reason for this is that the *Puranas* have fallen into the hands of ignorant, illiterate people. They are not in the hands of scientists.

Another difficulty is that we have lost the key to decipher the code of the *Puranas*. We do not have the deciphering code; hence, the difficulty. Now science says that man can exist on earth at the most for another four thousand years. The forecast in many *Puranas* is that this world cannot last for more than five thousand years. Science speaks a different language. It says the sun will cool down, its rays will diminish, its heat will diffuse, and in four thousand years it will get cold. Then life on earth will cease together with it.

The *Puranas* speak a different language. And if the *Puranas* give a time of five thousand years and not four thousand as the scientists say, it should be kept in mind that it is yet not decided whether science is absolutely correct. It can be five thousand—and I believe that it will be, because there can be a mistake in the calculation of science but there is never a mistake in vision. Science, therefore, improves upon itself day by day. It says one thing today and another tomorrow and yet another the day after. It has to change every day. Newton says one thing, Einstein says something else.

Every five years science changes its theories because it comes upon better solutions. It cannot be decided whether the ultimate in science will be different from the visions of the fourth plane. And if these do not coincide with each other it is not necessary to make hasty decisions on the grounds of what we know now through science and through what is told by the visionaries. Life is so profound that only an unscientific mind makes a hasty decision. If we examine the discoveries of science over the last hundred years we will find that all discoveries that are a hundred years old read like *Puranic* tales: no one is ready to believe them anymore because other and better things are discovered in the course of time.

The code that revealed the truth in the *Puranas* is lost. Now, for example, if there is a Third World War, the first outcome of it will be that all of the educated, civilised class of people will be destroyed. It is strange that only the uneducated, uncultured people will remain. Some primitive tribes in India in the faraway mountains and jungles will go unscathed. No one will be spared in Bombay or New York. Whenever there is a world war it is always the best communities that are destroyed, because it is they who are attacked. Some aboriginal in Bastar, India, might survive. He might tell his children of the planes in the skies though he will not be able to explain them. He had seen them flying and that is a truth, but he cannot explain the how and why of it as he does not have the code. The code was with the people of Bombay, but now they are dead.

For a generation or two the children might believe in their elders, but later on they will ask in doubt, "You have seen them?" And the elders will reply, "So we have heard, so our fathers said—and they in turn were told by their fathers—that planes flew in the skies. Then came the big war and everything was destroyed." By and by the children will question, "Where are the planes? Show us some indication, some sign." After two thousand years the children will say, "This is all the imagination of our forefathers. No one ever flew in the skies."

Such events have taken place. In this country the knowledge that was obtained by the psychic mind was destroyed in the battle of the *Mahabharata*. It is now only a story. Now we are suspicious of whether Rama could have flown in a plane from Sri Lanka. It is all a matter of doubt because when not even a bicycle remains from that age, then the airplane seems to be an impossibility. And there is no mention of it in any book. In fact, the entire knowledge that existed before the *Mahabharata* was destroyed in this war. That which could be retained in the memory was all that could be saved. Therefore, the names of the ancient branches of knowledge were *smriti*—traditionally remembered and written down later; and *shruti*—traditionally heard and then written down. These are collections of knowledge which were remembered and which were told; they are not an account of proven and tested facts. Someone told someone, then he told someone else, and all these things we have gathered and kept in the form of these scriptures. But now we cannot claim to prove anything from them.

Remember also that the intelligentsia of the world consists of a very small number of people. If an Einstein dies it will be difficult to find another to explain the theory of relativity. He himself said that there were not more than ten to twelve people who understood this theory. If these twelve died we would have books on relativity but not a single man who understands it. Similarly, the *Mahabharata* destroyed all the proficient people of those times. Then what remained became just stories. Now, however, investigations are going on for their verification, but we in India are unfortunate because we ourselves are doing nothing in this direction.

Recently, a place has been discovered that is about four to five thousand years old and which seems to have been an airport. There is no other possible reason for such a place. Such constructions have been found which could not have been possible without machines. Really, the stones that were lifted up the pyramids are as yet beyond the capacity of our largest cranes. These stones have been placed there—that much is clear—and they have been lifted by men. Either these people had elaborate machinery at their disposal or they made use of the fourth body.

For example, I shall tell you an experiment which you may try. Let one man lie down on the ground. Now four others should gather around him. Two should place their fingers on his knees one on each side, and the other two similarly under his shoulders. Let them put only one finger each. Then each should make a firm resolve to lift him only with his finger. They should breathe hard for five minutes, then hold the breath and lift the man. They can succeed in lifting this man with their fingers only. So the boulders of the pyramids were either lifted by giant cranes or by some psychic force. The ancient Egyptians might have utilised some such method; there is no other way. The rocks are there and they have been placed there: this cannot be denied.

Another thing to note is that psychic force has infinite dimensions. It is not absolutely necessary that a person who has attained the fourth plane should know about the moon. It is possible he is not interested to know; he may not consider it worth knowing. Such persons were interested in knowing other things—things which were more valuable according to them—and they have completed their search in these directions. For instance, they were eager to know if spirits were an actuality or not—and they have known. Now science has discovered that spirits are there. Those who had reached the fourth body were eager to know where people go after death and how.

Those who reached the fourth plane had hardly any interest in the material world. They did not care about the diameter of the earth. To expect them to be interested in such matters is like children telling a grown-up, "We do not consider you wise because you cannot tell us how a doll is made. The boy next door knows all about it. He is all-knowing." They are right in their own way, because they are interested in knowing what is inside the doll, whereas the elders cannot be.

The inquiry of a man of the fourth plane changes dimensions. He wants to know other things. He wants to know about the journey of the soul after death: where a man goes when he dies, what paths he travels, what the principles of the journey are, how he is born again, and whether his birth and birthplace could be foretold. This man is not interested in man going to the moon: that is irrelevant for him. He is eager to find ways for man's enlightenment, because that alone is meaningful for him. Such a man was always anxious to know how the *atman* entered the womb when a child was conceived, whether an *atman* could be helped to choose the right womb, and how long it takes for an *atman* to enter the embryo.

There is a Tibetan book called *The Tibetan Book of the Dead*. Everyone in Tibet who attained the fourth body has worked on one project: how a person can best be assisted after death. Suppose you are dead: I love you, but I cannot help you after death. But in Tibet there is a full arrangement to guide and assist a man and to encourage him to take a special birth and enter a special womb. Science will still take time to discover this, but it will discover it, there is no difficulty. And the Tibetans have found ways and means to test the validity of these happenings also.

In Tibet, when the Dalai Lama dies he tells beforehand where he will take birth next and how the others should recognise him. He leaves symbols behind for his recognition. Then after he dies the search starts all over the country. The child that tells the secret of the symbol is taken to be the incarnation of the dead lama, because he alone knows the secret. The present Dalai Lama was discovered in this manner. The Dalai Lama preceding him had left a symbol. A special saying was proclaimed in every village, and the child who could explain it was understood to be the one in whom the former lama's soul had taken entry. The search took long, but finally the child was discovered who could explain the code. It was a very secret formula, and only the authentic Dalai Lama could know its meaning.

So the curiosity of a man of the fourth plane is entirely different. Infinite is the universe and infinite are its mysteries and secrets. Do not think that we have discovered all that is to be discovered by present-day scientific research. A thousand new sciences will come to light because there are thousands of different directions and dimensions. And when new sciences develop people will call us non-scientific people, because we will not have known what they will know. But we should not call the ancient people non-scientific; it is only that their curiosity was of a different nature. The possible dimensions for inquiry are so diverse and so many.

We can very well ask that as we have found cures to many illnesses, why did these people of the fourth plane not find them? You will be shocked to know the number of herbal remedies prescribed in the Ayurvedic and Yunanic branches of medicine. How could these people, without the aid of research in laboratories, discover the proper cures for every illness? There is every possibility that this was brought about by the use of the fourth body.

There is a well known story about Vaidya Lukman which tells that he would go up to each plant and ask what were its uses. Now, this story has become meaningless in the world of today. It seems to be a failure of logic to expect plants to talk. It is also a fact that until the last fifty years plants were not supposed to have life. But now science admits there is life in plants. Thirty years ago we did not believe that plants also breathe; now we admit that they do. Fifteen years ago we did not believe that plants could feel, but in the last fifteen years we have had to admit that they do. When you approach a plant in anger its psychic state changes, and when you approach it in love then again it changes. So it will not be out of place if we discover in the next fifty years that we can talk to plants also—but this will be a gradual development.

However, Lukman proved it long ago. But this mode of conversation could not have been the same as ours. To become one with plants is a quality of the fourth body. Then they can be questioned. I believe this story, because there is no mention of any laboratory huge enough in those days where Lukman could have carried out his research on the millions of varieties of herbs he brought into use. It is improbable, because each herb would require a lifetime to reveal its secret if done scientifically, whereas this man talked of unlimited herbs. Now science admits the efficiency of many of these herbal cures in illness and they are still used. All of the research of the past is the research of the men of the fourth plane.

Now we treat thousands of illnesses, which is very unscientific. The man of the fourth plane will say, "There are no illnesses at all. Why are you treating them?" Now science understands this and allopathy is using new methods of treatment. In some hospitals in America they are working on new methods. Suppose there are ten patients suffering from the same ailment. Five are given water injections and the other five are given the regular medicinal treatment. Then the findings show that the patients of each group respond to their treatment equally. This proves that those treated with water were not really ill but had an illusion of illness. If these people were given the regular treatment for this illness it would have poisoned their systems and brought about contrary results. They required no treatment.

Many illnesses are born out of unnecessary treatment and then they are difficult to cure. If you have no real illness—only a phantom illness—the medicine for that illness will have to act in some way even though the necessary conditions of the illness are not within you. It will create poisons within for which you will have to undergo new treatments. The phantom illness will go on giving way to some actual malady. According to science, ninety per cent of illnesses are psychosomatic. Fifty years ago modern science refused to believe this, but now allopathy admits it as fifty per cent. I say they will have to admit to forty per cent more, because that is the reality.

There is now no one to define what the man on the fourth plane knew; no one has tried to interpret him. There is no man who can put his knowledge in the right perspective in today's scientific terms; this is the only difficulty. Once this can be done there will be no problem. But the language of parables is very different.

Today science says that the sun's rays pass through a prism and break into seven parts, and in this way they become distributed into seven colours. The *rishis* of the *Vedas* say, "The sun god has seven horses of seven colours." Now this is the language of parables. "The sun has seven horses of different colours and he rides them" means that the sun's rays break into seven parts. The latter is a parable and the former is the scientific version. We will have to understand the language of parables just as we understand the language of science today. There should not be any difficulty.

People with parapsychic faculties predict things much earlier and science understands them much later. But then predictions are all in a symbolic language. It is only when science proves the same facts that they are put down in the normal day-to-day language. Before that there is no language. You will be surprised to know, if you investigate in all directions, that science is just a recent arrival and language and mathematics came much earlier. Those who discovered language and mathematics, what statistics could they have used? What means could they have had—what measure? How did they come to know that the earth goes around the sun once a year? It is this one revolution of the earth around the sun that has been taken as one year. Now, this is a very old discovery—very much before science; the same is the case with the fact that there are three hundred and sixty-five days in a year. But there does not seem to have been any scientific means behind the ancient seers. Therefore, psychic vision is the only alternative answer.

A very strange fact came to light. A man in Arabia has in his possession a map of the world which is seven hundred years old. This is an aerial view of the world which could not possibly have been conceived of on land. There are only two solutions: either there were airplanes seven hundred years ago—and this does not seem possible—or some person lifted himself that high in his fourth body and then drew the map. One thing is certain: there were no airplanes then. But this aerial map of the world was made seven hundred years ago. What does this mean?

If we were to study Charak and Sushrut, two ancient masters of the science of herbs, we would be shocked to know that they have described everything about the human body which scientists came to know by dissection. There could be only two means of knowing. One possibility is that surgery had become so subtle that there could be no evidence of surgery being carried out—because no surgical instruments or books on surgery have been discovered. But there are descriptions of very minute parts of the human body—parts so minute that science could discover them only much later, parts which only twenty-five years ago scientists refused to accept as being present. But these have been described by these ancient physicians. There is a second possible way by which they could have known: a person in a state of vision may have entered the human body and seen these things.

Today we know that x-rays can enter the human body. If a man said that he could photograph our bones a hundred years ago we would not have believed him. Today we have to believe because it is so. But do you know: the eyes of a man in the fourth body can see even more deeply than an x-ray, and that a picture of your body can be made which is more complete than that which is made as a result of dissection? Surgery developed in the West because there they bury their dead. In a place like India where the body is burned this was not possible. And you will be surprised to know that this research came about with the help of thieves, so they would steal the dead bodies and sell them to the physicians for research and studying.

The custom of cremation was also the idea of psychic persons, because they believed that the soul had difficulty in taking a new birth if the body of the previous life still remained. It then hovered around the old body. If the body is burned to ashes the soul will be rid of this encumbrance—because once it sees the body turning to ashes, in the next body it will perhaps realise that what it considered to be its own was after all only a destructible thing.

So there was cremation in India, and hence no way of dissecting the human body. In the West thieves had stolen the bodies from burial grounds and sold them to scientists for their research. There were court cases and many other difficulties for these people, because stealing a corpse and dissecting it were both considered crimes.

So what we have come to know by countless dissections, books three thousand years old reveal without any dissection. This only proves that there is another method by which things can be known besides scientific experimentation. Sometime I shall talk in detail on this subject so that you may understand better.

5

THE OCCULT MYSTERIES OF RELIGION

***In yesterday's talk** You said that it is possible for science to enter the fifth or spiritual body. Then You talked of the possibilities of science in the fourth body. Kindly tell us about the possibilities of science in the fifth body.*

What we call the physical body and what we call the soul are not two things that are different and apart. There is no break between them; there are links. We have always thought that the body is separate and the soul is separate, and that there is nothing to connect them. Also, we have been thinking not only that they are apart but that they are the opposite of each other. This idea separated religion from science. Religion was supposed to search for that which is other than the body, whereas science was that which discovered everything about the body - all except the *atman,* the soul. So it is only natural that each should deny the other.

Science was engrossed in the physical body and so it asked, "The body is true, but where is the soul?" Religion searched for the inner and called it the soul. It said, "The spirit is real but the physical is an illusion." Therefore, when religion reached its peak it described the body as an illusion, a fantasy, *maya,* and said that in actuality it did not exist. It proclaimed the *atman* as truth and the body as illusion. When science reached its heights it disclaimed the *atman*. It said, "The concept of the soul is false; it is a lie. The body is everything." This error is the cause behind the concept that the body and the *atman* are two opposite things.

I have talked about the seven bodies. If the first body is the physical and the last is the spiritual, then if we do not consider the five bodies in between there will be no bridge between these two. It would be just as if you were to climb a ladder and then discard all the intervening rungs between the last and the first. Then there is no connection between the first and the last steps.

If you see the full ladder you will find that the first rung is connected with the last. And if you examine it more closely you will find that the last rung is the last part of the first rung, and the first rung is the first part of the last one. Similarly, if we take all the seven bodies together we will find a connection between the first and the second bodies. The first body is the physical body; the second is the etheric body - the emotional body. It is only the subtle form of the physical and it is not non-material. It is just that it is so subtle that it has not yet been fully grasped by physical means. But now the physicists do not deny the fact that physical matter becomes more and more rarified and non-physical in its subtle form.

For instance, modern science says that matter, when analysed, is ultimately reduced to electrons which are not matter but which are particles of electricity. Nothing like substance remains in the end — only energy. So science has made a wonderful discovery in the last thirty years. Though it had considered matter to be a reality, it has now come to the conclusion that matter does not exist whereas energy is a fact. Science now says that matter is an illusion brought about by the movement of energy at a high speed.

When a fan is made to rotate at high speed we cannot see the three blades separately. What we see is a circle going around and around. Also, the spaces between the blades appear filled. Actually, the blades move so fast that before the reflection of one blade passes our eyes the second blade is already there. Then the third blade comes just as swiftly, with the result that they follow one after the other so that we cannot see the vacant spaces between them. The fan can be made to revolve at such a speed that you can sit on it and never know that anything is moving underneath you. The space between two blades can be filled so swiftly that after one blade passes under you the second will immediately replace it; then you will not feel the empty space at all. It is entirely a matter of speed.

When energy revolves at a high speed it looks like matter. The atomic energy on which our entire modern scientific research is based has never been perceived visually; only its effects are visible. The fundamental energy is invisible and the question of seeing it does not arise, but we can observe its effects.

So if we look upon the etheric body as the atomic body it will not be wrong, because in this case also we only see the effects and not the etheric body itself. Because of the effects we have to admit its existence. This second body is the subtle form of the first; hence, there is no difficulty in connecting the two. They are, in a way, joined to each other. One is gross and so it can be seen; the other is subtle and hence it cannot be seen.

Beyond the etheric is the astral body. It is a subtler form of ether. Science has not yet reached there, but it has reached a conclusion that if we analyse matter, what ultimately remains is energy. This energy can be called ether. If ether is further broken up into more subtle components, what will remain is the astral, and this is subtler than the subtle.

Science has not yet reached the astral but it will. Until recently science only accepted matter and denied the existence of the atom. Until yesterday, almost, it said that matter is solid. Today it says that there is nothing like solid substance and everything is non-solid. Now they have proved that even a wall, which appears solid, is not so solid. It is porous and things can pass back and forth through its holes. We may be inclined to say that at least that which is around the pores must be solid, but this too is not solid: each atom is porous.

If we magnify an atom to the same size as the earth we will find that there is as much distance between two components of an atom as there is between the earth and the moon or the sun and the stars. Then we might say that at least the two components at the two ends are solid, but science says that these too are not solid; they are particles of electricity. Now science is not even ready to accept the word particle, because with that is joined the concept of matter. Particle means a portion of matter, but the atom's components are not matter, because matter is solid and keeps its shape whereas these components are continuously changing shape. They are like waves, not particles. When a wave arises in water, before you even say to yourself, "This is a wave," it has changed, because a wave is that which comes and goes continuously.

But a wave is also a material happening, so science has coined a new word which was not there thirty years ago. The word is quanta. It is difficult to find a Hindi equivalent just as many Hindi words have no equivalents in English: for instance, the word *Brahman* — the cosmic reality. Words are formed because there is a necessity of expression on the part of those who have experienced. When the *Brahman* was experienced it was necessary for those who experienced to coin a word to express it, so the word *Brahman* was coined in the East. The West has not reached this stage yet; hence they do not have any equivalent word, because they did not require it.

This is why many religious terms do not have any equivalents in English. For example, the word *aum* — this word cannot be translated into any language of the world. It is an expression of a deep spiritual experience. The West has no parallel word by which it can be expressed. In the same manner, quanta is a word coined to express the peak of scientific heights and it has no parallel word in any other language. If we try to understand the meaning of quanta, it means a particle and a wave together. It will be difficult to conceive of it however. It is something which behaves sometimes like a particle, sometimes like a wave, and whose behaviour is very unpredictable.

Until now matter was most reliable; there was a certainty about matter. But the ultimate part of matter, the atomic energy that has been discovered, is very uncertain. Its behaviour cannot be foretold. First science stood firmly by the certainty of matter. It said that everything is precise and definite. Now the scientist does not press this claim, because he knows that from where he has reached in research today this certainty is very superficial. There is a deep uncertainty within, and it would be interesting to know what this uncertainty means.

Where there is uncertainty there is bound to be consciousness; otherwise uncertainty cannot be. Uncertainty is a part of consciousness, certainty is a part of matter. If we leave a chair in a certain place in a room we will find it exactly there upon our return, but if we leave a child in the room we will never find it where we left it. There will always be a doubt, an uncertainty, where he will be and what he will be doing. We can be sure about matter, but never about consciousness. Therefore, when science accepted the uncertainty in behaviour on the part of the ultimate portion of the atom, it also accepted the possibility of consciousness in the ultimate part of matter.

Uncertainty is the quality of consciousness, but matter cannot be unpredictable. It is not that fire may burn when it chooses and not burn when it does not choose to, nor can water flow in whatever direction it pleases or boil at any temperature it fancies. The functions of matter are determined, but when we go within matter we find that ultimately it is undetermined.

You can take it this way: if we want to find out how many people die in Bombay, this is possible. If there are ten million people we can take the number of deaths in one year and find out approximately how many die per day, and this would be almost correct. If we calculate the mortality rate for this whole country of nine hundred million in the same way, the figure would be closer to the exact number. If we calculate the mortality rate for the whole world, the certainty of the figure will be even greater. But if we want to find out when a single person will die our calculations will be most uncertain.

The greater the crowd, the more material things become. The more individual the phenomenon, the more we find consciousness. In fact, a single piece of matter is a crowd of millions of atoms; therefore, we can predict about it. But if we penetrate within the atom and catch hold of the electron we find that it is individual: we cannot determine its course and it seems as if it decides that on its own. So about a solid rock we can be certain: we will find it in a particular place. But the structure of the individual atoms within will not be the same. By the time we return again to the rock, all the atoms within will have changed their positions and travelled from one place to another.

Uncertainty begins by going deep within matter. This is why science has changed its language from certainty to probability. No longer does it say, "This is how this or that will be." Rather, it says, "It is more probable this way than that." It no longer says emphatically, "This is it." In the past all the claims of science were in the language of certainty: whatever it said was bound to be. But when the search of science went deeper all its former concepts began to break down. The reason was that science had unknowingly stepped from the physical realm into the etheric, about which it has no understanding. Until it accepts the fact of stepping from the physical to the etheric plane, it cannot have any understanding. It has reached the second dimension of matter, the etheric dimension, and this has its own possibilities. There is no gap between the first and the second body.

The third or the astral body is even more subtle. It is the subtlest of the subtle. If we break the ether into atoms - which still seems improbable, because we have barely unfolded the physical atom—so to experiment with ether will still take a long time. When the ether atoms are known we will find that they are the particles of the body that comes next, namely, the astral body. When we broke the physical atom its most subtle particles were found to be etheric. Similarly, if we break the etheric atom the most subtle particles will be that of the astral body. So we shall find a connection between them. These three bodies are clearly joined to one another and it is for this reason that photographs of ghosts have been taken.

A ghost does not have a physical body. Its veiling starts with the etheric body. It has been possible to photograph ghosts, because when the etheric body condenses a sensitive camera can catch its reflection. Another thing about ether is that it is so subtle, that it is easily influenced by the psyche. If the spirit of a dead person wishes to appear it can condense its form so that the atoms that are spread out come closer and form an outline. This can be caught by a camera.

Thus, our second body that is etheric is much more influenced by the mind than the physical body. The latter too comes under the influence of the mind, but not to that extent. The more subtle the body, the more it is affected by the mind and the nearer it will be to the mind. The astral body is even more influenced by the mind. This is why astral travelling is possible. A man can be asleep in this room but he can reach any part of the world with his astral body. You must have heard stories of a man being seen in two or three places at the same time. This is possible. His physical body will be in one place and his astral body in another. It is a matter of a little practice and this can be brought about.

The powers of the mind develop more and more as we go inward and they dissipate as we go outward. Going outward is just like burning a lamp and then putting a glass shade over the flame. After putting it the flame will not appear very bright. Then we put another and yet another. In this way we place seven covers over it. After the seventh covering the light of the flame will be extremely dull and dim because it has to pass through seven layers.

In this way our life energy becomes very dim by the time it reaches the physical body. This is why we do not seem to have much control over the physical body. But if someone begins to travel within, his control over his physical body becomes more and more, exactly in proportion to the depth of his inner journey. The subtle form of the physical is the etheric and the still more subtle part of the etheric is the astral. Then comes the fourth body — the mental body.

Until now we were under the impression that mind is one thing and matter another. Mind and matter were considered as two separate things. In fact, there was no way of defining them. If we were to ask, "What is mind?" we would be told, "That which is not matter," and vice versa. If we were to ask, "What is matter?" there was no other definition. And this is how we have always been thinking about them — as being different and apart. Now, however, we know that mind also is a more subtle form of matter. Conversely, we can say that matter is the condensed form of mind.

When atoms of the astral are broken they become thought waves. There is a close proximity between quanta and thought waves; it was not taken into consideration. So far, thoughts were not considered to have a physical existence, but it is a fact that when you think a particular kind of thought the vibrations around you change accordingly. It is interesting to note that not only thoughts but even words have their own vibrations. If you spread sand particles on a glass top and chant *Aum* loudly, under the glass the pattern caused by the vibration of the sound will be different from the pattern caused by chanting Rama. If you were to utter an abuse the pattern would again change.

You will be surprised to know that the more foul an abuse, the more ugly is the pattern formed, and the more beautiful a word, the more beautiful will be the pattern of its vibration. The abuse will form a chaotic pattern, whereas the lines of the beautiful words will be well formed and well balanced.

Therefore, for thousands of years research was carried out to find words that produced beautiful vibrations, and it was considered whether their intensity was enough to affect the heart. Words are thoughts that are manifested. However, unmanifested words also carry a resonance and we call them thoughts. When you think about something a particular kind of resonance is created around you, a particular kind of vibration surrounds you. This is why you find sometimes that when you go near a particular person you feel sad for no apparent reason. It could be that the person has not uttered a single negative word, and perhaps he is even laughing and happy to meet you. Yet a sadness takes hold of you from within. On the other hand, in the company of someone else you may suddenly feel cheerful.

You enter a room and you may feel a sudden change inside yourself. Something holy or unholy takes hold of you. In some moments you are surrounded by peace and tranquillity, and in others by restlessness. You cannot understand and you wonder, "I was feeling very peaceful. Why has this restlessness suddenly arisen in my mind?" All around you there are thought waves, and they keep on entering within you all the twenty-four hours.

Recently, a French scientist developed an instrument which has succeeded in catching thought waves. As soon as a man approaches this instrument it begins to show what thoughts are within him. The instrument begins to catch the thought waves. If an idiot is made to stand before it there will be very few waves reported, because such a person hardly thinks. If an intellectual is made to stand before it the machine takes over all the vibrations of his thoughts.

So what we know as the mind is the subtle form of the astral. As we go more and more within the layers get more and more subtle. Science has reached the etheric body but even now it insists on calling it the atomic plane or the plane of atomic energy. But science has reached down to the second body of matter. It will not take long to reach the third plane, because now it has become necessary to do so.

Work is being done on the fourth plane also but from a different dimension. As mind was considered to be apart from the body, some scientists are working only upon mind; they have left the body completely out. They have experienced a lot of things about the fourth body. For instance, we are all, in a way, transmitters. Our thoughts spread all around us. Even when I am not talking to you my thoughts reach you.

A lot of work is in progress in Russia in the field of telepathy. One scientist, Fayadev, has been successful in transmitting thoughts to a person at a distance of a thousand miles just as is done in radio transmission. If we concentrate our attention with full will-power in a particular direction and transmit a thought, it reaches that particular destination. If the mind at the other end is equally open and ready to receive at that moment and is concentrated in the same direction, the thought is received.

You can try a simple experiment at home. Small children catch thought waves very quickly because their receptivity is very sharp. Seat a child in a dark room in one corner and tell him to concentrate on you for five minutes. Tell him that you will tell him something in silence and he should try and listen. If he hears it he should repeat what he heard. Then you choose a word, say Rama. Now concentrate on the child and repeat this word within yourself until it resounds in you. Do not say it aloud. In two to three days' time, you will find that the child has caught the word.

The reverse can also take place. Once the experiment succeeds it will be easy to carry out further tests. Now you may tell the child to concentrate on you. He should think of a word and throw it in your direction in the same way. With the first part of the experiment your doubt was cleared when the child caught your word. So now you will be receptive and catch the child's word. When the experiment is successful you will stop doubting, and your receptivity will increase accordingly.

Between you and the child there is the physical world. This thought should be intrinsically physical in its content or it will not be able to cross the physical medium. You will be surprised to know that Mahavira has even defined *karmas* as material. If you are angry and you kill someone it is an action of anger and of murder. Mahavira says that the subtle atoms of these actions cling to you as the scum of *karmas* and actions. So actions too are physical, and they also hold onto you like matter.

Mahavira calls becoming free of this accumulated conditioning of *karmas, nirjara* — deconditioning. All the atoms of these *karmas* that have collected around you should fall off. The day you are rid of them all, what remains of you will be absolutely pure. *Nirjara* means the falling off of the atoms of actions. When you are angry it is an action, then this anger remains with you always in its atomic form. That is why when the physical body falls these atoms do not disintegrate - because they are very subtle. They come along with you in the next birth.

So the mental body is the subtle form of the astral body. Thus, as you can see, there is no gap between these four bodies. Each is a more subtle form of the preceding body. A lot of work is being done on the mental body. Scientists are working in the field of psychology and especially parapsychology, and the strange and wonderful rules of mental energy are slowly coming within their grasp. Religion grasped them a long time ago, but now many things have become clear to science as well.

There are many people in Monte Carlo who cannot be defeated in the game of dice. Whatever dice they throw brings about the numbers they want. At first it was thought that perhaps the dice were specially designed to throw the number they desired. Then the dice were changed but the result was the same: the dice fell exactly where these people wanted them. Several changes of dice yielded the same result. Even when blindfolded these people managed to throw the right number. This made others sit up and take note. Investigations were begun to find the reason. Actually, the very determination of their thought influenced the dice. They threw the dice with a determination to get the number they wanted. Their thought waves then brought the dice to that same number. What does this mean? If thought waves are capable of changing the direction of dice, they must also be material or else this would not be possible.

Carry out a small experiment and you will understand. Since you talk of science, I talk of experiments. Take a glass filled with water. Add a little glycerine or any other greasy liquid so as to form a thin film on the surface of the water. Place a straight pin lightly over this film so that it floats on the surface. Close the room from all sides. With your palms flat on the ground, concentrate your attention fully on the pin. For five minutes look straight at the pin. Then tell the pin to turn to the left and it will turn to the left. Then tell it to turn to the right and it will turn to the right. Tell it to stop and it will stop; tell it to move and it will move. If your thought can move a pin, it can move a mountain also; it is only a matter of proportion. Fundamentally, the principle is the same. If you have the ability to move a pin the fundamentals are proven. It is a different matter that the mountain may be too huge a structure to move - but it can move.

Our thought waves touch matter and transform it. There are people who when given your handkerchief will be able to tell approximately as much about you as can be told by seeing you. This is because your handkerchief absorbs your thought waves. These waves are so subtle that a handkerchief which belonged to Alexander the Great will still carry the facts about his personality. The waves are so subtle that it takes them millions of years to come out of the object. This is why graves and *samadhis* came to be constructed.

Yesterday I told you that in India we have the custom of burning our dead, but not our dead *sannyasins*. An ordinary man's body is burned so that his soul does not go on hovering around him. But the *sannyasin* is not cremated because his soul had already stopped hovering around his body while he was still alive. Now there need be no fear of his soul having any attachment to his body. We wish to conserve his body, because the body of a man who has spent years in experiencing the divine will diffuse the same thought waves for thousands of years. His burial spot will be meaningful; it will yield results. The body is dead, but this body has been so close to this soul that it absorbed a great deal of the vibrations that had spread from it.

Thoughts have infinite possibilities, but they are physical all the same. Therefore, be very careful what you think, because the subtle thought waves will remain with you even after the body falls. Your physical age is quite short compared to the age of these subtle waves. Scientists have now come to the conclusion that if there have been people like Jesus and Krishna, in the near future they will be able to catch hold of the thought waves of these people. Then we shall be able to tell whether Krishna ever really spoke the *Gita* — because the thought waves that emanated from Krishna are still present in the universe, rebounding from some planet, some asteroid.

It is just like when we throw a stone into the sea: when it falls it forms a small circle. The stone will sink because it cannot stay long on the surface of the water: it begins to sink as soon as it touches the water. The ripples caused by its impact on the water begin to increase. They become larger and larger and their extension is endless. They may go beyond the horizon of your vision, and who knows what distant shores they have reached.

So thoughts, no matter when they were born — not only those that were spoken but also those that were in the mind — also spread in the universe, and they go on spreading. And they can be caught hold of. Someday, when the momentum of science increases and man progresses further, we will be able to hear them once again. Now the radio news relayed from Delhi to Bombay takes some time to reach Bombay because sound takes time to travel. By the time it reaches Bombay it is no more in Delhi: the waves have left Delhi though the distance is only of a few moments' duration. There is a time gap.

Now suppose in India we are seeing a man in New York on television. When his image is formed in New York it is not at once visible to us; there is a gap between its formation and the time when it reaches us. It could be that in that interval the man may have died, but he will appear alive to us.

Thought waves from the earth, as well as the ripples of other happenings, go out to the infinite number of planets. If we were to go ahead of them and catch them they would still be alive in a sense. Man dies but his thoughts do not die that quickly. Man's life is very short; the life of thoughts is very long. Remember also, the thoughts we do not express live longer than those we express because they are more subtle. The more subtle a thing, the longer is its life; the more gross, the shorter is the life.

Thoughts influence the physical world in many ways. We have no idea of their effect. Biologists have now experienced that if a loving type of music is played beside a plant it begins to flower soon — even out of season. If noisy, chaotic music is played close by it then it does not flower — not even in season. The vibrations of the music touch the plant. Cows give more milk under the influence of a different type of music. Thoughts produce a more subtle ether that produces an aura of ripples. Each man carries around him his own world of thoughts from which ripples go on spreading out continuously.

These thought waves are also physical. What we know as the mind is a very subtle form of physical energy. Therefore, it is not difficult for science to reach them, because these waves can be caught and investigated. For instance, we did not know until recently how deeply a man sleeps — at what depth his mind goes. Now we know; we have instruments to find out. As we have instruments to measure the pulse rate, so we have instruments to measure sleep. A device is fixed to the head all night long, and from the graph formed on it we can tell exactly when the person's sleep became deep, how long he slept, how long he dreamt, what was the duration of good dreams, what was the duration of bad dreams, how long were the dreams, and whether they were sexual or non-sexual. All this the graph shows. There are about ten laboratories in America where thousands of people are paid to come and sleep and their sleep is closely examined. It is a matter of great concern that we remain unacquainted with sleep.

One-third of a man's life passes in sleep. Sleep is not a small matter. If a man lives for sixty years he sleeps for twenty of them. If this period of twenty years remains unknown a third of his life will remain unknown to him. Now the interesting fact is that if he does not sleep for these twenty years, he will not live for forty years. Therefore, sleep is a basic necessity. A man can sleep without awakening for sixty years, but he cannot live without sleeping. Thus, sleep is a basic requirement.

In sleep we are somewhere else; the mind is somewhere else. But this mind can be measured. Now it can be known how deep one goes in sleep. There are many people who insist they do not dream. This is an absolute falsehood, and they say this because they do not know. It is very difficult to find a man who does not dream. It is very difficult! Dreams occur all night long. You think that you only have a dream or two, but that is wrong. The machine says that dreams occur throughout the night but we do not remember them. You are asleep so remembrance is absent. The dream you remember is the very last that takes place when sleep is almost finishing. When you come back from sleep the last dream remains in your thoughts. Its faint echo still lingers within as you wake up. But you do not at all remember all the dreams of deep sleep.

Now it has become necessary to investigate what dreams occur in deep sleep, because that which a man dreams in the depths of sleep reveals his authentic personality. Really we become unauthentic upon awakening. Ordinarily we say, "What is there in dreams?" But dreams reveal more truth about ourselves than our waking state. In our conscious period we cover ourselves with false mantles. If some day we should succeed in making a window in man's head from where we can observe all his dreams, his last freedom will be gone. Then he will not be free even to dream. He will be afraid to dream, because there also morality with its laws and regulations will set up its policemen. It will say, "This dream is not proper; you are not dreaming right." At present however we do not have this freedom. Man is free in his sleep — but his freedom will not be for long, because encroachment on sleep has already begun. For instance, now Russia has started education in sleep.

A lot of work is going on in sleep teaching. In the waking hours more effort has to be made because the child resists. It is difficult to teach a child something, because basically he refuses to be taught. In fact, every man refuses to learn, because each man starts off with the basic thought that he knows already. The child also refuses saying, "What are you teaching?" In no way is he ready to learn. Then we have to bribe him by giving prizes after examinations, gold medals, etcetera. We have to kindle the spirit of ambition within him; we have to go on pushing him in order to educate him. This conflict takes too long a time. What the child can be made to learn in two hours we get through to him in two months.

So the method of sleep teaching has been evolved, and it has become as clear as day that a child can be taught very well in sleep. The reason is simple: there is no resistance in sleep. A recorded tape is played near the sleeping child which imparts whatever has to be put into the child. "Two plus two is four; two plus two is four," the tape will go on repeating. Ask the child in the morning and he will say, "Two plus two is four."

Now this thought that was imparted in sleep can also be made to penetrate the mind by means of thought waves, because now we know about thought waves. In the past we did not know; but now we know that words themselves are not imprinted on a gramophone record. Rather, the imprints of the sound waves are recorded on the disc. When the needle touches the grooves that have been created it repeats the same waves that caused the grooves to be imprinted.

As I said before, if you chant *aum* a pattern will be formed on the sand. The pattern itself is not *aum* - but if you know that this particular pattern is formed by *aum,* then someday you will be able to convert this pattern back into *aum*. Upon the formation of the pattern the sound of *aum* should occur. The pattern and *aum* can be looked upon as the same thing. In the gramophone record there are no words - only the grooves created by the impact of the sound of words. When those grooves come in contact with the needle they are converted into the corresponding sounds.

In the very near future we shall be able to make thought records. As the impact of thoughts has been realised it will not take long for man to be able to record it. Then a wonderful thing will happen. It will be possible that even though Einstein is dead his full thought process will be recorded. Then what Einstein would have thought in the future, had he remained alive, will also be supplied by the machine, because the machine will catch the impact of his entire thought waves.

Sleep, dreams and unconsciousness have been fully investigated. Thus, all the scientific possibilities of the mind are now known to man. Therefore, it is well to understand them. For instance, take a man who is angry. According to our old calculations we will advise him, "Do not give in to anger; you will go to hell." We have no other way. But if this man says he is willing to go to hell, then we are helpless; we cannot do a thing to him. And if the man further declares that he is eager to go to hell, all our morality becomes useless. We can have control over a man only if he is afraid of hell. This is why no sooner did the fear of hell leave the world than our morality went with it also. Now no one is afraid of hell. "Where is hell?" everyone wants to know.

So morality is completely finished, because the fear on which it was based is gone. But science says there is no need for morality as it has developed another formula based on stopping certain bodily secretions. When we are in anger a particular chemical process takes place within the body, because anger is a physical happening. When there is anger within it is absolutely necessary for certain chemical substances to be secreted within the body. Thus, the formula of science is this: these secretions can be stopped from forming and then there will not be any anger. Then there is no need to stop anger directly. If these fluids are stopped man will find it impossible to be angry. If we try to advise young boys or girls to abstain from sex, to practise celibacy, they never listen. Science says, "Stop all this! If we restrict the growth of certain glands sexual maturity will not come before the age of twenty-five."

This is very dangerous. The moment the mind comes fully within the grip of science man will begin to misuse its knowledge. Science says that the chemical composition of a man who has a rebellious mind is different from that of a man with an orthodox mind. This finding contains dangerous possibilities. If the composition of these chemicals becomes known to man we can make a rebellious man passive and an orthodox man rebellious. Once the compositions of the chemicals that bring about the urge to steal or kill are known there will no longer be any need for jails and executions. All that will be required then is the necessary surgery or treatment to rid the person of these. The chemicals in question can be removed or other chemicals can be introduced to neutralise them or antidotes can be given. All this work is presently under investigation.

All this shows that there are no longer many difficulties in the path of science to reaching the fourth body. The only problem is that a very large part of science is engaged in research for war purposes. That is why this kind of research is not given primary consideration; it remains a secondary matter. Yet there has been great progress and unusual results have been obtained.

Aldous Huxley has claimed that that which had happened to Meera or Kabir can be brought about by injections. It is a very heady claim, though true to some extent. Mahavira would fast for a month and his mind would become tranquil. Fasting is a physical act, and if the mind can become peaceful by a physical act then the mind too is physical. With a month's fasting the whole chemical composition of the body changes; that is all there is to it. The nutrition that the body should have had is denied to it and all of the body's reserve is used up. Fat melts and the non-essential elements undergo destruction while the essential ones are saved. In this way the whole chemical arrangement of the body undergoes a complete change.

Science says, "Where is the need to undergo such hardship for one long month? The chemical ratio can be changed according to specifications here and now." If this chemical change is brought about by science you will experience the same peace that Mahavira experienced after a month's long fast in no time at all; a month's fasting will not be necessary.

So I tell you during meditation to breathe hard and fast. But what is going to happen after a half hour of hard breathing? It is only that the ratio of carbon and oxygen within you will change - but this can be brought about by external means also. There is no need to make you labour for half an hour. The ratio of oxygen and carbon dioxide in this room can be changed and all those sitting here will experience peace and calm and will feel joyous. Thus, science has entered the fourth body from all sorts of directions, and it is still penetrating into it further.

In meditation various experiences happen to you. You smell all kinds of fragrances, you see colours. All this can now be brought about without meditation also, because science has found out which part of your brain becomes active during these experiences. If the back part of my brain is stimulated when I see beautiful colours, scientific investigation will show exactly the portion that becomes active and the length of the waves produced. You need not go into meditation. The same vibrations can be brought about within you with the help of electricity and you will begin to see colours. These are all parallel happenings, because no matter which polarity we take hold of the other end at once becomes activated.

There are hazards in this, however. The more new research by man penetrates within, the more its hazards increase. For example, we can now increase the age of man as much as we like. It is no longer in the hands of nature; it is in the hands of science. So in Europe and America there are thousands of old people clamouring for the right to die of their own free will, but they are kept lingering on their deathbeds. They are given oxygen and can be made to live for long periods. A ninety-year-old man begs to die, but the doctors say, "We cannot be a party to it; it is against the law." Even if an old man's son feels that his father is suffering too much and he should now be allowed to die, he cannot say so openly. There are machines to keep a dying man alive and the nearly dead are made to live on. Now this, in a way, is dangerous.

Our old laws were made when there were no means of keeping a person alive and when we could also kill a person. Now the laws need to be revised, because we can keep a dying person alive and lingering on for so long that he feels, "This is violence, this is an atrocity! I do not want to live any longer. What are you doing to me?" There was a time when we punished a man for his crime by hanging him. It will not be surprising if fifty years hence we punish a man by not allowing him to die. And this punishment will be worse than the first, because dying is a matter of a few seconds whereas living on can be for decades.

So whenever there is a new discovery in the inner world of man there are two results: either mankind can suffer because of it or it can benefit. Whenever power comes, it is always two-sided.

Science has reached the fourth plane within man. Within the next fifty years - rather, within the next thirty years - it will penetrate deeper into the fourth body. Perhaps, you may not know that whatever has been undertaken during a particular century reaches its climax at the end of the century. Every century completes its work by the time it comes to its end. This century has taken very many works upon itself which will be completed in thirty years' time. Its greatest task is the entrance into man's psyche, and this will be completed.

The fifth - the spiritual body - is even more subtle than the fourth. Here there are not only vibrations of thought but also vibrations of the being. If I sit absolutely silent without a single thought within, even then my being creates vibrations. If you come near me and there is no thought in me you will still be within the field of my vibrations. And the most interesting thing is that the vibrations of my thoughts are not as strong or penetrating as the vibrations of my being. Therefore, the one who reaches the no-mind state becomes very powerful. It is difficult to gauge the effect of his power because the vibrations of existence begin to arise within him. The energy vibration of the fifth body is the subtlest form of energy in the whole knowledge of man.

So it has happened in many cases, as in the case of Mahavira, that he did not speak. That is, he either spoke very little or he did not speak at all; he just sat. People came, sat before him, understood him and went back. This was possible in his time, but not so now. It is very difficult now because you will only experience the deep waves of the spiritual body if you are ready to be in the no-thought state yourself, and not otherwise. If you are filled with the noise of your own thoughts you will miss these subtle vibrations. They will just pass through you and you will not be able to grasp them.

If the vibrations of existence come within one's grasp, if there is a no-thought state on both sides, then there is no need to talk. Then communication takes place on a very intimate level, and this communication goes straight to the heart. Then there is no explaining because there is no way to explain. Then you also will not waver over whether this or that will be or will not be. Your being will directly know what has happened.

It is not necessarily the case that only human beings are reached by the vibrations of the fifth body. There is a wonderful phenomenon in the life of Mahavira: it is said that even animals attended his gatherings. Jaina monks have been unable to explain this phenomenon and they never will. Now an animal does not understand human language but it understands the language of being very well. If I sit in a no-thought condition near a cat, the cat is already in the state of no-thought. With you, however, I will have to talk. To take you to the cat's state of no-thought is a very long journey. Animals, plants and even stones understand the vibrations that begin from the spiritual body; there is no difficulty in that. So this body is also accessible, but only after the fourth body. The fourth body has been penetrated from many fronts, and science will accept the spiritual state readily. But after this there is some difficulty.

So when I said that things can be made very scientifically clear up to the fifth body but after the fifth body difficulties begin, there are reasons for this. If we understand science well it is a specialisation in a particular direction; it is a particular selection. So science can only go deeper when it restricts its search to as few things as possible and tries to know as much as possible only about them. The aim of science is to know more and more about less and less. Its work is twofold: it tries to know more about as small a thing as possible. It makes the subject of its inquiry as small as possible and increases its knowledge about it.

The doctors of old were knowledgeable about the whole body, but the doctor of today is not. The old type of general practitioner is now hardly to be seen. In the world of today he has become a relic; he is no longer reliable. He knows about too many things; hence he cannot know about any one thing well enough to be trusted. Now there are eye specialists and ear specialists, and they can be relied upon because they have acquired the maximum knowledge in a specialised field.

For instance, all the literature available about the eye is so vast that one lifetime is not enough to go through it. It is quite probable that in the near future there might be one eye specialist for the right eye and another for the left eye, or perhaps one specialist for the pupil and one for the retina. As knowledge increases the eye will be divided into many parts for special study, because each part is an important case in itself. The aim of science is to concentrate its focus of attention to such a pinpoint that it can penetrate to the greatest depth. This is how science can come to know a great deal.

So, as I said before, science will reach up to the fifth body, because up to the fifth the individual still exists; hence he can come within its focus. From the sixth the cosmic starts, and this is beyond the focus of science. The cosmic body means the total: science cannot enter there, because science goes from the small to the smallest. So it can only grasp the individual; it will find it very difficult to grasp the cosmic. Religion alone can grasp the cosmic. Hence, up to the *atman,* the self, science will have no trouble. Difficulties start with the *Brahman* - the cosmic self. I do not think science will ever be able to grasp the *Brahman,* because then it will have to leave its specialisation. And the moment it leaves its specialisation it no longer remains science. It will then be as generalised and vague as religion. So with the help of science we can travel along to the fifth body. At the sixth science will be lost, and the seventh is impossible for it because all of its search is focused only upon life.

Actually, our centre of existence is life. We want to be less ill and more healthy; we want to live longer, more happily, more comfortably. The aim of science is to make life more deeply happy, satisfying, healthy and enjoyable. But the seventh body is the acceptance of death: it is the ultimate death. Here, the meditator goes beyond the search for life. He says, "I want to know death also. I have known existence and the mystery of being; now I want to know non-existence, the non-being."

Science has no meaning in this area. Scientists like Freud will call this the death wish and say that this is not a healthy condition of the mind - that it is suicidal. According to Freud liberation and *nirvana* are not conducive to life and these concepts are a proof of your wish to die. He says that you wish to die, that's why you are ill. The scientist is against the desire for death, because science is based on the will to live and on an expansion of life. The man who wishes to live is a healthy man, but a moment comes when the wish to die is equally healthy. If someone wishes to die before this moment comes it is definitely unhealthy. However, a moment does come in life when a person wishes to die for the sake of death.

One may say it is healthy to be awake and unhealthy to sleep, and gradually we are giving more place to day than to night. At first night started at six o'clock, now it begins at two a.m. We have given the night's time to the day. There are some modern thinkers who go so far as to feel that if night can be completely removed from man's life, a sizeable part of his life can be rescued from going to waste. Where is the need to sleep? It should be done away with, they argue. But as there is a joy in waking, there is a joy in sleeping also. Just as the desire to awaken is natural and healthy, so also is the desire to sleep. If a man keeps alive his eagerness to live even up to his last breath he is not healthy, and if a man nurtures the desire to die from his very birth that too is unnatural and unhealthy. If a child longs for death he is ill, abnormal, and he should be treated. If an old man longs for life, he too should be treated because he is ill also.

Life and death are the two limbs of existence. If you accept only one you are bound to be crippled. Until the time comes when you accept the other this disability will remain. Both limbs are important — being and non-being. He who embraces and accepts both being and non-being equally can be called perfectly healthy. He who says, "I have known what it is to be; now I wish to know what it is not to be," is not afraid of non-being.

The seventh plane is only for people of courage - who having known life are eager to know death, who are keen to explore death, the state of extinction. They are keen to know what it is not to be, what extinction is like, what is non-being. They have tasted life; now they want to taste death.

At this point you should know that death descends from the seventh plane. What we normally know as death comes from the seventh plane and what we know as life comes from the first plane. Birth starts with the physical; birth means the beginning of the physical. This is why the physical body first comes into being in the mother's womb and the other bodies follow later. So the first body is the beginning of life and the last body, the *nirvanic* body, is from where death comes. So he who clings onto the physical body is very much afraid of death, and he who is afraid of death will never ever know the seventh body.

Thus, as we gradually become more and more detached from the physical body, a time comes when we accept death also. Then only do we know. And he who knows death is liberated in the true sense of the word, because then life and death become two parts of the same thing and one is beyond both. So there is no hope of science reaching to the seventh body, though there is a possibility of its going up to the sixth.

The doors of the fourth body have opened to science, and now there is actually no difficulty for it to go up to the fifth body. But such persons are required who have scientific minds and religious hearts. Once they appear, entry into the fifth will not be difficult. This combination is very difficult though, because the training of the scientist bars him from becoming religious from several directions. Also, in the same way, religious training prevents a man from becoming scientific. Nowhere do these two branches of training overlap, and this is the great difficulty.

It happens sometimes, and whenever this happens in the world a new peak of knowledge comes into being. For example, take Patanjali: he was a man with a scientific mind, but he entered into religion. He brought yoga to a height which has been difficult to surpass up to now. It is now a long time since Patanjali died and a great deal more work could have been carried out in this field, but no man was found who had the intelligence of a scientist and an inner world of spiritual practice. There has been no one to climb to higher peaks of yoga. Sri Aurobindo tried but he did not succeed.

Sri Aurobindo had a scientific mind - perhaps more scientific than Patanjali, because he was educated in the West. His education was superb. When he was about six years old his father sent him out of India and forbade him to return until he was fully matured. Even on his deathbed, when others in the family talked of calling Aurobindo back, his father would not allow it. He said, "It is all right if I do not see him before my death. He must imbibe the Western culture completely. Let not the shadow of the East fall upon him. Do not even let him know that I am dead." He must have been a very courageous father. Thus, Aurobindo drank deeply of the Western culture. If there ever was a man who was Western in the real sense of the word it was Aurobindo. He had to relearn his mother-tongue after returning to India.

So the knowledge of science was complete in him, but religion was a later implantation and so it could not be expressed deeply; otherwise this man would have scaled greater heights than Patanjali. But this was not to be. In a deep way the training of the West became a barrier, because his thinking was entirely like that of a scientist. He brought the whole evolution theory of Darwin into religion. He introduced into religion thoughts that he brought from the West. But he had no insight into religion which he could introduce to science. As a result, he created a voluminous scientific literature in which religion is very superficial, because any effort to explain about the mysteries of the sixth and seventh plane is bound to be a failure as it cannot be expressed in scientific and logical terms.

Whenever a balance has been reached between a scientific intellect and a religious mind, great heights have been attained. But there is very little possibility of this coming about in the East, because the East has lost its religion and science it never had. There is more of a possibility in the West, because there science has become too much.

Whenever there is an excess the pendulum tends to swing toward the other extreme. That is why the super intellectuals in the West read the *Gita* with a relish that is not seen anywhere in India.

The first time Schopenhauer read the *Gita* he put it on his head and danced with joy. When people asked him what was the matter, what was the cause of this mad behaviour, he said, "The book is not only worth reading but is worthy of being put upon the head and danced to! I never knew that there were once people on this earth who spoke this way. What I thought could never be put into words has been expressed in this book." Now we will not find a single man here in India who would put the *Gita* on his head and dance. We will only find people who will place the *Gita* on the seat of a train and ride sitting upon it - but this is meaningless.

By the end of this century a new height will be touched, because when the need arises many forces are activated in the world. Einstein became a religious man before he died. During his life he remained a scientist, but as his life drew to an end he became religious. That is why those who were essentially scientific said, "We should not take Einstein's last statements seriously. He was out of his mind."

Einstein's last words were meaningful. He said, "I thought I would know everything there is to know about the world, but the more I knew the more I found this to be impossible, because there was a vast infinity still left to be known. I thought that one day I would solve the mystery of the world of science and reduce it to a mathematical equation and that then it would be a mystery no longer. But the mathematical problem became bigger and bigger, and instead of solving the mystery of the world it became a mystery in itself. It is now impossible to solve this problem."

A few topmost scientists of modern times are hovering around the periphery of religion. Such possibilities now occur in science because it has crossed the second body and is approaching the third, and as it nears the third body the echoes of religion become unavoidable. It is of its own accord entering into the unknown world of uncertainties and probabilities. Sometime, somewhere, it will have to admit the unknown. It will have to agree that there is more besides that which can be seen with the naked eye. What cannot be seen exists; what cannot be heard also exists. A hundred years ago we said that what cannot be heard or seen or touched does not exist. Now science says differently. It says that the range of touch is very small but the range of the untouchable is very vast. The range of sound is very little but that which cannot be heard is limitless. What is seen is but infinitesimal compared to the limitlessness of the unseen.

Actually, what our eyes behold is a very small part of what is. Our eyes catch a particular wavelength, our ears hear at a particular wavelength. Above and below these wavelengths there is an infinity of other wavelengths. Sometimes, by accident, these wavelengths are also caught by our senses.

Once a man fell from a mountain and his ear was hurt. Now his ear began to catch the radio waves of the radio station of his town. When he was in the hospital he was in a great difficulty; in the beginning he could not understand what was happening. He thought, 'Either I am going crazy or I cannot grasp the meaning of what is happening.'

Then things began to seem clear and he complained to the doctor. He asked the doctor, "Where is the radio kept in the hospital?"

The doctor said, "Are you hearing things? There is no radio."

Still he insisted that he was hearing the news and he related what he heard. The doctor ran to the office and put on the radio. To his surprise, he found exactly the same news being relayed. Then things became clear. It was discovered that his ears had become available to strange new wavelengths; they had changed with his fall from the mountain.

It is quite possible that in the near future we shall be able to catch wavelengths directly by fixing a small gadget to the ear. Infinite sounds are passing by us and around us, but we cannot hear them because our field of hearing is very limited. Even many loud sounds cannot be heard. We cannot hear sounds above or below the hearing capacity of our ears. When a star falls the tremendous sound of its falling spreads out all around us but we cannot hear it. If the situation were otherwise we would become deaf. Similarly, the range of our body heat is approximately between ninety-eight degrees and one hundred and ten degrees. If it falls under ninety-eight degrees or goes over one hundred and ten degrees we die. Our life flickers between ten to twelve degrees. Heat has a tremendous range. It can be lower than this twelve degree range, but we are not related to this.

In the same way we have our limitations in everything. But we can know about things outside these limits because they too exist. Science has begun to accept their existence. Once there is acceptance the quest for where and what these things are begins. All this can be known, all this can be recognised, and it is for this reason I said it is possible for science to reach up to the fifth body.

Who knows non-being and on what basis can it be known?

The question itself is wrong. This question cannot arise and cannot be formed, because when we ask, "Who knows non-being?" we take it that someone remains behind. Then it is not non-being.

How is the knowledge of it reported?

There is no reporting. For instance, when you sleep at night. You are conscious only of that which occurs in your waking hours. Once asleep you are oblivious of your surroundings. So you can only report about your waking hours—of the situation that existed up to the point when you slept. But as a rule you do the opposite. You say, "I went to sleep at eight o'clock." This is wrong. You should have said, "I was awake until eight o'clock." You cannot report sleep, because when you sleep who is to report? Reporting is possible from the other side: "I was awake until eight o'clock, or until eight o'clock I knew I was awake, but I do not know anything after eight. Then I know of having awakened at six. There is a gap between eight and six during which time I was asleep."

This is by way of example. You will know what is until the sixth body. When you plunge into the seventh body and come out again into the sixth you will be able to say, "Aha! I have been elsewhere. I have experienced non-being." This account is given only in the sixth body, and so many did not speak after reaching the seventh plane. There was a reason: why say that which cannot be said?

Recently there was a man named Wittgenstein, and he has made some rare statements. One of them is: "That which cannot be said must not be said." Many persons have said what cannot be said and have thus put us into difficulty because they have also told us that it cannot be said. So this becomes negative reporting. This is the news flashed from the last boundary where it is said, "I was up to that point, but thereafter I was not. After this point there was nothing left to know and no one there to know. There was no report and no reporter. But this happened after a particular boundary before which I was." That line of boundary is the boundary of the sixth body.

The *Vedas,* the *Bible,* the *Upanishads,* the *Gita,* go up to the sixth body. The seventh is that which is inexpressible and cannot, in fact, be expressed. Up to the sixth there is not much difficulty and up to the fifth it is very easy to express. But at the seventh plane, neither the knower remains nor the knowledge. In fact, that which we imply to be the remainder does not remain. If we talk of this empty gap we will have to use the language of negation. Therefore, the *Vedas* and the *Upanishads* have to say, "Neither this, nor that." They say, "Do not ask what there is. We can only tell you what was not there; we can only say that what was, is not. There was no father there, no wife, no matter, no experience, no knowledge. And the 'I' too was not: the ego was not. Nor was there the world or its maker. There was nothing there." This is the boundary line of the sixth body. What was there? You will remain silent, because it is inexpressible.

News about the *Brahman* has been reported, but what is conveyed beyond it is bound to be negative—as was that which was told by Buddha. Buddha tried his hardest to express the seventh plane. Therefore, all that he conveys is denial, all that he conveys is negation, and so it did not come within the understanding of the people of his land. The experience of the *Brahman,* being positive, was well understood by the people. The *Brahman* was said to be *sat-chit-ananda*—truth, consciousness, bliss—and these positive assertions were well understood. One could say about it that this is, that is, but Buddha talked about that which is not. Perhaps, he is the only one who worked hard to make the seventh plane known.

Buddha was not accepted in this country because the place he talked of is without roots, forms or shapes. People heard and thought it was useless. "What will we do there where there is nothing?" they said. "At least show us a place where we will be." But Buddha said, "You will not be." So people of this country withdrew from him, because they wanted to save themselves to the very last.

Buddha and Mahavira were contemporaries, but people understood Mahavira better because Mahavira talked of phenomena up to the fifth plane. But he did not even mention the sixth plane. This was because Mahavira had a scientific mind, and whenever he tried to explain about the sixth he felt that words seemed to become ambiguous, hazy and illogical. Up to the fifth everything is stable and it is possible to give an account that this is so or that is so, because up to the fifth plane we find things similar to our experience.

Suppose there is a very small island in the middle of an ocean and only one kind of flower grows on this island. There are a few people inhabiting it and they have never stepped off the island. Then one day a passing ship takes one of them aboard and takes him to its land. Here he sees flowers of different kinds. For him "flower" meant one particular type of flower that grew on his island. Now, for the first time, the meaning of flower has expanded, and he realises that the word flower does not pertain just to one flower but to thousands of them. He sees there are roses, lilies, lotuses and jasmine. Now he is worried. How will he go and explain to his people that flower does not stand for just one type of flower? How will he explain that flowers have names, because on his island the flower, being just one, has no other name: it is merely "flower." Now he wonders how he will speak to the others about the lilies and the jasmine flowers.

He returns to his island, and in spite of his difficulty there is a way out for him. There is at least one flower to go by. Now he can elaborate on this one flower and try and explain the varieties of colours and shapes and scents of the others in order to convey some idea of his discovery. He can say, "Just as this one is white there are others that are red, pink, yellow, and many other colours. Just as this one is small there are big flowers also like the lotus." In this way he can communicate, because one flower is already there to indicate something about the others.

But suppose that this man does not go to another land but instead he goes to the moon where there are no flowers, no plants, where the atmosphere is unusual for him and the atmospheric pressure is different. When he goes back to his island and they ask him what he saw on the moon, it will be very difficult to explain, because there is nothing equivalent to his experience to explain by. There are no words or symbols in his language to convey the report.

This is exactly the situation. Until the fifth we find words to express, but it is the same as trying to express the difference between one flower and a thousand flowers. From the sixth plane language becomes confusing. There we reach a point where even the difference between the one and a thousand is not enough for explaining. It is very difficult. Even then, with the use of negation or totality some idea can be conveyed. We can say there is no limit; it is boundless. We are familiar with boundaries, so with the help of this knowledge we can convey that there is no boundary there. This will give some idea, and though it is still vague we can assume that we understand. But it is not so.

So there is a lot of confusion. We feel we have followed what is told—that there are no boundaries there. But what is meant by "no boundaries"? Our experience is that of the boundary. It is just as if those people of the island would say, "Yes, we have understood. It is a flower that you are talking about." Then the man will say, "No, no! Do not go by that flower. It has nothing to do with those flowers; such a flower is not found there at all." Then the people will say, "Why do you call them flowers if they are not like this? This alone is a flower."

We too are under the illusion that we understand. When we are told, "God is infinite, limitless," we say, "Yes, we understand." But our experience is only of boundaries. We understand nothing; we only know the word boundary. We add the word "-less" to it and we feel that we know that there is no boundary there and we are sure that we have understood. But once you begin to conceive of that which has no limits, then it will be frightening. No matter how much you visualise, the boundary remains. You go further and further—even millions and billions of miles beyond where light-years end—but wherever you stop the boundary will appear.

The meaning of boundless in our minds can at the most be the boundary of that which is very very far away; it is so far that it is beyond our grasp, but still it exists. Then again we will have missed. So something can be said about the sixth plane and we might think we have understood, but we have not.

Now with the seventh we will not even do so much as to say that we understand. The seventh cannot even be talked about. If someone tries we will immediately say, "What absurd things you are saying!" Therefore, an absurd word was used to indicate the seventh plane—a word which has no meaning, which would mean nothing.

Take, for instance, the word *aum:* it has no meaning; it is a meaningless word, and we have used it in connection with the seventh body. Until the fifth body we can talk, but when someone insists on talking about the seventh we say, *aum*. Therefore, when a scripture was completed the words *aum shanti* were written. Do you know what it means? It means that the seventh has come; there is nothing further to be said.

The scriptures end as soon as the seventh appears; the beginning of the seventh is the end of the scriptures. Therefore, at the end of each scripture we do not write "The end"; we write *Aum Shanti*. The *aum* is the symbol of the seventh and it is meant to convey that there cannot be any further discussion. It urges us to be tranquil and at peace thereafter.

We have conceived an absurd word which has no meaning, no motive behind it. And if there is any motive behind it, it is rendered useless because we have created this word for that world where all motives end. It is a motiveless word and therefore it does not exist in any other language of the world. Experiments have been carried out, but there is no meaning to *aum*. A Christian will pray and at the end of his prayer he will say "Amen." He is saying, "Enough! Finished! Peace thereafter. Now no more words." But this is not equivalent to *aum*. *Aum* cannot be translated. It is the symbol we have chosen for the seventh.

It was carved in temples to remind us not to halt at the sixth because there is also a seventh plane. It is placed in between the images of Rama and Krishna to suggest that *aum* is greater than they are. Krishna gazes out of it—but *aum* is much greater, *aum* is very vast. Everything appears out of it, everything merges into it. Therefore, we have not evaluated *aum* with anything else in the world. It is the holiest of the holy in the sense that it is the ultimate, the beyond, where everything loses its identity.

So nothing can be reported about the seventh plane. It can only be described in the language of negation: "It is not this; it cannot be that, etcetera." But this also holds meaning only up to the sixth plane. Therefore, many seers have remained silent about the seventh. Those who tried to talk about it raised many difficulties for themselves, because even while talking about it they had to repeat again and again that it is inexpressible. Again and again they had to warn their listeners: "We speak about it, but indeed it cannot be spoken about." Then we are puzzled. Why do they speak of things which cannot be spoken of? They should not tell about it. But they say, "The seventh definitely is, but we have no words worthy to describe it."

There is nothing in the world comparable to it; it is inexpressible. There is a lot that can be told about it, a lot that can be expressed, but the difficulty is that there is no means of conveying it in words. It can be known but it cannot be expressed.

That is why those who were once very talkative, those who were great orators, those who could explain everything under the sun, became suddenly dumb when they returned from the seventh plane. When they are suddenly struck mute in this way their muteness conveys a message: their silent eyes speak of the unspoken. For example, in reference to what you are asking now, Buddha had made a rule that certain questions should not be put to him. He said, "Do not ask these questions. It is not proper to ask them; it is not proper that they should be known." He would say that a certain subject was indefinable and hence should not be discussed. It would be improper to discuss it.

Lao Tzu said, "Please do not ask me to write, because whatever I write will become false. I will never be able to convey what I want to convey; I can only write that which I do not want to convey. But what is the use of that?" So he did not write until the very end. When his countrymen forced him, he wrote a small booklet. The very first sentence he wrote was: "As soon as truth is expressed it becomes a falsehood." But this is the truth of the seventh plane. At the sixth plane it becomes not false, but ambiguous. At the fifth the truth expressed is indisputable. At the seventh only its expression is impossible. Where we ourselves are no more, how can our speech and language remain? They too end with us.

What are the distinctive characteristics of aum for which it has been chosen to represent the seventh plane?

There are two reasons for choosing *aum*. One is that a word was sought which had no meaning, which cannot be given any meaning—because if it conveys any meaning it is reduced to the fifth plane. So a word was required which was, in a sense, meaningless. All of our words are meaningful; we make words so that they will convey meaning. If they do not convey any meaning why should they be used? We use them to speak, and the purpose of speaking is to convey some thought.

When I utter a word it should strike a certain meaning within you. So when people returned from the seventh plane they felt that if they made any words to express the seventh plane which conveyed a meaning, they would at once be reverting to the fifth plane. Then those words would be added to the dictionary where people will read them and think that they have understood. But the seventh has no meaning. You can say either that it is meaningless or that it is beyond meaning—both of these mean the same thing.

So in the context that all meaning is lost, no meaning remains, what sort of a word could be found for this and how was it to be formed? This word was made with the help of great vision and foresight, and in a very scientific way. A root word was to be constructed, a basic word, which was to be made the foundation. So how was this word that should convey no meaning to be found? In what manner was it to be formed? In a deep way it would become a symbol for the original source.

The three basic sounds of our speech are *a-u-m*. All our developments of words are an expansion of these three sounds. They are the root sounds. Now the sounds of *a-u-m* in themselves carry no meaning, because it is their relationships that decide the meaning. When 'a' becomes a word it carries a meaning; when 'm' becomes a word it carries a meaning. But by themselves they are meaningless. Yet they are the roots, and all our speech developments are extensions and combinations of these three sounds.

So these three root sounds were taken and were joined to make the word *aum*. Now *aum* could be written, but by writing it one could begin to think that it might have a meaning like any other written words. People would think that *aum* means that which is in the seventh plane. So no word was coined but a picture of *aum* was made: no letters were used for it. The three letters *a-u-m* are only sounds and not letters or words. So *aum* came into being in a pictorial form in order that it would not be relegated to a dictionary and would instead strike the eye and become a question mark. It came into being in this way so that one would become eager to find out what it means.

Whenever a man reads Sanskrit or comes to study the ancient books, this word becomes difficult to explain. Words come within their grasp because they have a meaning—but

[*Aum* symbol] is beyond comprehension. They always ask, "What does *aum* mean? What is its significance? What does it mean and why is it not written in letters like *a-u-m*? Why this pictorial form? If you look at its picture carefully, you will see that it is made up of three parts which are the symbols a, u and m.

This picture requires deep research; it is not an ordinary picture. Research upon it has been carried out from the fourth body and not from the physical plane. Actually, when a person enters the fourth body and is in the no-thought state, the notes of *a-u-m* begin to resound within him and their combination makes up the word *aum*. When there is perfect stillness within, when thoughts are completely lost, then the hum of *aum* begins to resound within. This sound has been caught from the fourth plane where thought is no more and language is no more. Then what remains is the sound of *aum*. So in this way the sound was caught.

Now as I said before, each word has a pattern of its own. When we use a certain word a particular pattern forms within the mind. If someone meditates on *aum,* when it resounds on the fourth plane the corresponding picture will begin to manifest within. This is how all seed *mantras* were discovered. When the resonance of a particular *chakra* is caught by a meditator in meditation, the seed *mantra* of that *chakra* is revealed. This is how these seed *mantras* have been formed, and *aum* is the ultimate seed. It is not the seed of any particular *chakra;* rather, it is the symbol of the seventh which is the infinite or the eternal.

So in this way the word *aum* was hit upon. And when it tallied with the experiences of thousands of seekers who gave it their approval, this word was accepted. It did not come into existence with the approval of a single man or even a group of men. When the same word reverberated in a number of meditators, when millions of them testified to its authenticity, then only was it chosen. Therefore, the word *aum* is not the ancestral property of any religion or organisation. Hence, the Buddhists and the Jainas make use of it freely without any fear. It is not the property of the Hindu religion. The reason is that it has been attained by all sorts of meditators from various paths. Whatever equivalents we find in other countries are also, in a way, fragments of this very word.

Now if we examine the findings of Roman or Arabic seekers, we find that the note 'm' is invariably mentioned. Some carry 'a' along with 'm', but 'm' is certain. This is because 'a' and 'u' are very subtle, and thus they are difficult to catch. So the first part of the word slips from our attention and only the latter part is heard. Therefore, when the sound of *aum* begins to resound within, the 'm' in it is easily caught. If you sit in a closed room and chant *aum* the preceding sounds will give way to the sound of 'm'. Thus, 'a' and 'u' become completely inaudible, and it is the 'm' that resounds everywhere. So meditators then came to the conclusion that the note 'm' is certain, while that which precedes was not quite clear. The difference is only one of hearing, but wherever a search has been made in this direction something or other of this word has been grasped by meditators. When an extensive research is carried out—for example, if a thousand scientists carry out the same experiment and get the same result—then its validity is proved.

This country is fortunate in that thousands of years have been spent here in the journey towards the self. Nowhere in the world have people of any country carried out this experiment on such a large scale and in such great numbers. Ten thousand meditators sat around Buddha; forty thousand, both male and female, sat around Mahavira and they carried out mass experimentation. In a small place like Bihar forty thousand disciples of Mahavira were experimenting. Nowhere else in the world has such an event taken place. Jesus, poor fellow, was all alone, and Mohammed had to spend his time futilely battling with ignorant people.

In this country a special situation had developed in which people were aware of the fact that these are not matters to fight over. Here things were clear. Mahavira would sit and forty thousand people would practise meditation in front of him. This afforded a great opportunity to observe and verify the experiences of different meditators on different planes. There could be some error where there are only one or two practising, but when there are forty thousand there cannot be any error. Forty thousand persons were occupied in different meditation techniques. Everything was properly thought out, everything was verified, everything was properly grasped.

Therefore, this country has made many more discoveries in the spiritual field than other countries, because in other countries the seeker was all alone. Just as the West is today carrying out scientific experiments on a large scale employing thousands of scientists, in the same way this country had at one time employed thousands of its geniuses, intellectuals, in the science of the soul. The discoveries which they brought back from their journey into the soul are very useful, but on their journeys to other lands this knowledge became fragmented and distorted.

For instance, the cross of Jesus: it is a remnant of the swastika. On its long journey to distant lands this is what has remained of the swastika. The swastika was a symbol like *aum*. *Aum* is the symbol of the seventh, the swastika is the symbol of the first. Therefore, the picture of the swastika is dynamic. Its branches spread out and give the effect of motion; it is rotating all the time. The ordinary world means that which is moving all the time. So the swastika was made the symbol of the first body, and *aum* that of the last. There is no movement in *aum*. It is absolutely still; there is total silence; everything is at a standstill. With the swastika there is movement.

In its journey the swastika became a cross by the time it reached Christianity. There is every possibility of Jesus having come to Egypt as well as India. He was in Nalanda, the ancient Buddhist university, as well as Egypt, and so he gathered a great deal of knowledge. One thing was the knowledge of the swastika. But this knowledge turned out to be like the news brought back by a man who had seen many flowers to a place where only one flower existed. The message of Jesus was destroyed and only the cross remained.

The upper portion of the *aum* sign reached Islam. The half moon that they revere is the upper fragment of *aum* which was separated from the main part during its travel to Arabia. Words and symbols get badly distorted in their journey, and after thousands of years they get so worn out that it is difficult to recognise their original form. New sounds, new words, are added to them as they travel from place to place, and different people with different languages use them. All kinds of changes take place, and then, when something separates from its original source, it is difficult to discern its place of origin, how it came to be and what happened to it.

The spiritual flow of the whole world is intrinsically connected with this country, because the basic, original source of spirituality was born here and it is from here that news of it spread far and wide. But the messengers who took the message to other lands and the people who received the message spoke a different language. Therefore, clarity was lacking in the delivering and receiving of the message. Now no Christian wearing the cross around his neck could ever think that it is part of the swastika; no Mohammedan can dream that the half moon he reveres is a fragment of *aum*.

According to some Catholic scholars, amen is only a far deviated form of *aum*. At the end of all Christian prayers the word amen is used to offer obeisance to the divine. It is also the belief of researchers that in *The Bible,* where it says, "In the beginning there was the word and the word was with God," *aum* is the word implied. Amen is referred to as the alpha and the omega—the beginning and the end. It is also said that Jesus has told the apostle John, "I am Amen." In other places amen has been used to mean absolute truth or "So be it."

Many Latin words are utilised in the Catholic mode of worship, and in all of them a deviated form of *aum* is present. For instance, *Per omni secula seculorum,* etcetera. It is also in the English words omnipresent, omniscient and omnipotent.

Nowadays, many churches in India have begun to use the word *aum* in their prayers, and they have also carved it on their main doors. For instance, St. Mary's College in Darjeeling has the symbol ॐ carved on the entrance of the main altar of its temple of worship.

6

SHAKTIPAT: THE MYSTERIES OF BODY-ELECTRICITY

In the context of the seventh body, You talked about aum *yesterday. There is still a small question on the same subject. Which* chakras *do* a, u *and* m *influence, and how is this helpful to the meditator?*

Yesterday, I told you a few things about *aum*. There are a few more things worth knowing in the same context. In the first place, *aum* is the symbol of the seventh body, an indication of the seventh plane. It is a symbol of the seventh state which cannot be explained by any word. No word can be associated or utilised in connection with it. Thus, a meaningless word was found—a word which has no meaning. This I told you yesterday. The search for this word had been carried out through the experiencing of the fourth body.

This was not an ordinary search. Actually, when the mind is totally empty, without any clamour of words, without even a ripple of thought, even then the sound of the void remains. The void also speaks; the void has its own sounds. Go and stand in a very secluded place where there is not a single sound and you will find that emptiness has its own music. Seclusion has its own kind of sound, and in this silence only the basic notes remain—*a-u-m*. All our melodies and tunes are developed by permutations and combinations of these basic notes. When all words, all sounds are lost, these basic notes remain.

So *aum* is the symbol of the seventh state, the seventh body, but this sound has been grasped in the fourth plane. In the emptiness of the mental body the resonance of *aum* is captured. If the meditator makes use of this *aum* there can be two results. As I told you before, all planes have two possibilities. The repetition of *aum* can bring about a state of sleepiness, a state of sleepy trance, and this state can be brought about by repetition of any word. The modulated repetition of any word has the same impact on the mind as gentle strokes on the head that produce drowsiness and sleep.

If this state is brought about by repetition of *aum* you become lost in a world of dreams and imagery which is the natural potential of the fourth body. It will then be a hypnotic sleep in which you can see whatever you want to see. You can travel to heaven and to hell or have a vision of God, but all this will be in dreams. You can experience bliss, you can experience peace, but all in a dream; nothing will be real.

This usage of *aum* happens more often, because this is easy. To produce the sound of *aum* loudly and be lost in it is very easy and enjoyable like pleasant dreams. The quality of the mental plane, as given by nature, is that of imagination and dreams. If the mind wishes to dream it can dream; this enjoyment is possible for it. The other possibility is that of will-power and visions of the divine.

If *aum* is used only as repetition upon the mind, its impact brings hypnotic sleep. What is called *yoga tandra* is brought about by the repetition of *aum*. But if *aum* is pronounced with the witness well established within; if you are fully awake and are listening to the sound without drowning in it, without getting lost in it; if the sound is on one plane and you are standing on another as the listener, the observer, the witness; if you are fully awake to the sound—then only can work on the second possibility of the fourth plane begin. Then you will not go into *yoga tandra,* but into *yoga jagriti,* wakefulness.

I strive constantly to keep you away from using *mantras*. I always advise you not to use any *mantra* or any word, because the chances are ninety-nine out of a hundred that you will go into an imaginary trance. There are reasons for this. The fourth plane is vulnerable to sleep; it knows only sleep. Its dream track is already there. It dreams every day. It is just as if we were to throw water into this room. After some time the water will dry up, but it will leave a mark on the floor. Then if we throw water again on the floor, this water will flow along the same tracks as previously.

The greater possibility with chantings and *mantras* is that your mind with its tendency to dream will at once, by its very mechanical process, fall into dreaming. But if you are fully awake and witnessing inside, observing the sound of *aum* without merging into it, without losing yourself in it, then it could do the same work as repeating "Who am I?"—which I advocate. Now if you ask "Who am I?" in a sleepy state and are not a witness, the same error can take place here and you will merely be dreaming. But the possibility of this happening with "Who am I?" is less than with the repetition of *aum,* and there is a reason for it.

With *aum* there is no question asked; it is only a gentle touch. With "Who am I?" there is a question, not a mere pat. There is a question mark after "Who am I?" and this will keep you awake. It is an interesting fact that when there is a question in the mind it is impossible to sleep. If a difficult question revolves in your mind during the day, it spoils your sleep at night also. The question will not let you sleep. The question mark is a helpmate of sleeplessness. If there is any question, any anxiety, any curiosity in the mind, it is difficult to sleep.

I suggest "Who am I?" in place of *aum* because basically it is a question, and since it is a question it is an intrinsic search for an answer. Besides, you will have to keep awake for the answer. In *aum* there is no question; it has no sharp corners and hence it does not strike you. It is absolutely round and there is no question. Its continuous gentle strokes generally lead only to imaginary trance.

Besides, there is no melody in "Who am I?" whereas *aum* is full of melody. The greater the melody, the more it will hasten you to sleep. "Who am I?" is disproportionate like the masculine form; *aum* is well proportioned like the feminine form: its gentle strokes quickly make you sleep. Words have forms and their impacts are different, their resonance is different. "Who am I?" has no melody; it is difficult to sleep with it. If we repeat "Who am I? Who am I?" near a sleeping man, he will awaken. If however we repeat *"aum, aum"* beside a man who is asleep, his sleep will become deeper because the impact is different. This does not mean that *aum* is not workable. The possibility is there for someone who stands behind the repetition as an observer, a witness. But I do not advocate the use of *aum* for meditation. There are many reasons for this.

If you utilise *aum* for meditation, then it will inevitably become associated with the fourth body. *Aum* is the symbol of the seventh plane but its resonance is experienced on the fourth plane. Once you start the meditation of *aum* this inevitable relationship of *aum* with the fourth plane will come about which will prove a barrier to further progress. So there is this difficulty with the word. It is experienced on the fourth plane but it is used for the seventh plane. We have no other word for the seventh body. Our experience of words ends after the fourth plane.

We use the last word of the fourth plane as the symbol for the seventh plane. There is no other remedy, because from the fifth starts the wordless state; then the sixth is absolutely wordless and the seventh is the ultimate void. On the last boundary line of words in the fourth state, where we leave all words, the last word heard will be *aum*. So *aum* is the last word in the realm of speech and the primal word in the realm of no-word. It is at the boundary line between the realm of words and the no-word state. This word is primarily of the fourth plane, but we have no other word nearer to the seventh plane; all others are far behind. Therefore, this word is used for the seventh.

So I prefer that you do not associate it with the fourth body. It will be experienced in the fourth, but it should be kept as a symbol of the seventh. Therefore, there is no need to use it for meditation. For meditation we should use such devices which will fall away with the fourth plane. For example, "Who am I?"—this can be used in the fourth and can be discarded also.

The meaning of *aum* should remain symbolic. There is yet another reason for not using it as a device. That which is the symbol of the ultimate should not be made a means: it should remain the end. The symbol of the absolute should remain only for the attainment. *Aum* is that which we have to attain, so I am against using it in any way as a means of meditation. It has been used in the past with detrimental results.

The meditator who practices the sound of *aum* takes the fourth for the seventh plane, because the symbol of the seventh is experienced in the fourth. When it is experienced in the fourth the meditator becomes confident that he has reached the seventh plane. He takes this to be the journey's end; thus, great harm is done on the psychic plane. The meditator then stops here.

There are many meditators who take visions, colours and inner sounds to be the attainment. This is only natural, because the symbol of the ultimate is felt on the boundary of this plane. Then they feel that they have reached the destination. So I am not in favour of prescribing the practice of *aum* for persons in the fourth body, as this technique will have no effect on the first, second and third bodies. Its effect will be felt only in the fourth. This is why other words are used to cause the necessary impact on the first, second and third bodies.

It is necessary to take one more point into consideration regarding the basic notes of *a-u-m*. Just as an example, The *Bible* does not say that God made the world; He did not perform the act of creation. It says, "God said, 'Let there be light,' and there was light." God pronounced the word. *The Bible* also says, "In the beginning there was the word"—and many old scriptures testify to the same. At the very beginning there was the word and all else followed afterwards. Now even in India we say, "The word is the *Brahman,*" although this causes a great deal of misunderstanding. Many people tend to believe that the word is enough for the attainment of the *Brahman*. The *Brahman* is attained only in the wordless state. "The word is the *Brahman*" means only this, that from all the sounds we know the most subtle of sounds is that of ॐ.

If we go back, back and back toward the source of the universe until we come to the void from where the world must have started, there also we will hear the resonance of *aum*. As we reach nearer to the void by entering the fourth plane the sound of *aum* is heard. From here we begin to fall into that world which must have been in the beginning. From the fourth we go to the spiritual body; from there to the cosmic body, and finally to the *nirvanic* body. The last resonance, which is heard between the last two, is also that of *aum*.

On one side is our individuality of four bodies which we call the corporeal world, and on the other side is our non-individuality which we may call the *Brahman*. The resonance that vibrates on the boundary line of these two is *aum*. From this experience we come to understand that when the world of matter took form from the *Brahman,* the resonance of *aum* must have been ringing continuously. Hence, there was the word. So the belief is that everything came into being through the word. If the word is broken into its basic components we find the three basic notes of *a-u-m* in it. This combination is *aum*.

So for this reason it is said that there was *aum* in the beginning and there will be *aum* in the end. The end means to revert to the beginning, and thus the circle is completed. Yet I always feel that *aum* should be used only as a symbol and not as a meditation technique. Other things can be employed as devices. A pure sound like *aum* should not be made impure by using it as a technique.

Many people fail to understand me. They come to me and say, "Why do you forbid the repetition of *aum*?" Perhaps they think that I am an enemy of *aum,* but the fact is that they themselves are. Such a pure word should not be used as a means of spiritual growth. In fact, our tongues are unworthy of pronouncing it; it is too pure to be uttered by the physical body. It is a word that begins where the tongue becomes meaningless, where the body becomes useless. Therein lies its resonance and this resonance vibrates on its own. It can be experienced; it cannot be created. Therefore, *aum* has to be experienced and not pronounced.

There is another danger. If you use *aum* as a technique you will never know the basic sound of the word as it arises from the existence, because your own articulation will be imposed upon it. So you will never witness its purest manifestation. Whoever uses the sound of *aum* as a technique never experiences *aum* in reality. By continued practice they will superimpose their own nuances on the actual resonance when it comes. Then they will be unable to hear the pure reverberation of *aum*. They fail to hear the direct resonance of the void because they are filled with their own sound. This is natural, because that with which we are familiar becomes implanted in us. Therefore, I say that it is better not to be familiar with *aum*; it is better not to make use of *aum* Someday it will appear in the fourth body and then it will have some meaning.

Its appearance in the fourth body will mean that you have reached the limits of the fourth body. Now you are about to step out of the psyche, out of the realm of words. The last word has come and you now stand at the place where the word started; you stand where the whole world stood at the beginning; you stand at the threshold of creation. And then, when its own melody begins to flow, its charm is inexpressible. There is no way of describing it. Our best music cannot compare with its smallest echo. No matter how hard we try we can never hear this music of silence with the outside ear. Therefore, it is better that we do not have any preconceived ideas about it. Let us not give any form or colour to it or else we will be caught by our imagery and this will be an obstacle.

The bioelectrical difference between man and woman persists until the fourth body. Does this mean that the effect of a male medium or a female medium is different on male and female meditators? Also, please explain why.

Many things will have to be clarified in this context. As I said before, the difference between male and female exists until the fourth body. After the fourth there is no difference. The fifth is beyond any difference in gender. But the difference is very fundamental up to the fourth body, and this basic dissimilarity will bring many kinds of results. Let us first understand the male body, then we shall go on to the female.

The first body of the man is male, the second is female, the third again is male, and the fourth female. In the female it is the opposite: her first body is female, the second male, the third is again female, and the fourth is male. There are radical differences because of this. It is these differences that have deeply influenced the whole history and religion of mankind and which have given man's culture a particular type of order.

There are some characteristics unique to the male body and some characteristics and specialities unique to the female body. These complement each other. In fact, the female body is incomplete and so is the male body; therefore, in the act of creation they have to unite. This union is of two kinds. If male a unites with female b externally, creation of a child takes place. If male a unites with female b within himself, a creation takes place which is toward the *Brahman*. This is the journey toward God, whereas the external union is the journey towards nature. However, sex is involved in both: if the male body unites externally with a female body, coitus takes place; if the male body unites with its own inner female body, then also sex takes place. In the first the energy is diffused outwardly, whereas in the second the energy begins to move inwardly. This is what is known as the rising of the sex energy: it is a union with the woman within.

The energy always flows from the male to the female regardless of whether it happens outside the body or inside the body. If the sex energy of the physical body of a male flows toward the etheric female within him it is not diffused. Then happens what is known as *brahmacharya*. Then the energy flows upwards continually; it reaches up to the fourth body. After the fourth body *brahmacharya* has no meaning, because there is nothing like male and female there.

That is why after crossing the fourth plane the meditator is neither a male nor a female. The concept of *ardhanarishwar*—Shiva as half man, half woman—came into being with the first and the second body in mind. But this merely remained a symbol and we never understood it. Shiva is incomplete and so is Parvati. Together they become one. So we drew a picture of Shiva as being half man, half woman, but in actual life this other half is not visible outwardly. It hides behind each of us. One side of you is male and the other female, and this is why very amusing incidents take place sometimes.

No matter how fearless and strong a man is in the outside world, no matter how influential—whether he is Alexander the Great or Napoleon or Hitler, whether in the office, in the store or in the market, he lives like a lion the whole day, but by evening all his swagger is lost before a simple woman in his house. This is very strange. What is the reason behind this? The fact is that he uses his male body twelve or fourteen hours and after that time his first body becomes tired. When he reaches home the first body demands rest. Then the second body which is the female comes to the forefront and the male body becomes secondary.

Now the wife has made use of her first body the whole day long, so by evening the male body behind her has the upper hand. Then the woman begins to behave like a man and the man like a woman.

It should be remembered that the intercourse with one's own inner female body is the method for the upward flow of the life energy. This process has more inner details, but we shall not talk about that at present.

Another thing: the energy always flows from the male to the female. The most important quality of the male body is that it is not receptive; it is always aggressive. The male can give but he cannot take. No current flows from the female to the male; it is always from the male to the female. The female is receptive. She can take but she cannot give.

There are two results of this and both are worth knowing about. The first result is that since the female is receptive she can never become the giver of *shaktipat; shaktipat* cannot take place through her. This is the reason why there are so few female masters in the world, nor are there any female gurus of the stature of Buddha and Mahavira. The reason is that no energy can be imparted to anyone through her. It is a fact though that women gathered in great numbers around Buddha, Mahavira and Krishna, but not a single woman of the stature of Krishna was ever born around whom millions of men would gather. The reason for this lies in the fact that women can only be recipients.

It is also an interesting fact that around a person like Krishna there will be very few men but very many women. The same was the case with Mahavira: there were ten thousand male ascetics, monks, and forty thousand nuns. The ratio is four to one always. If there is one man there are always four women around him. Men could not be as affected by Mahavira as women could be, because both they and Mahavira are men. What was transmitted by Mahavira the women could absorb. But men are non-absorbent; their receptivity is very limited. Therefore, though it is man who is the herald of religion it is woman who always protects and preserves it; it is woman who saves religion on earth. Men only pioneer religion.

Woman is receptive; the quality of her body is receptivity. She has this quality biologically also. She has to carry a child for nine months, and after that she also has to bring it up; thus, she has to be receptive. No such work is assigned to man by nature. He becomes a father for a moment and then he is out of the picture. The woman receives the semen and then retains it. This fact works in *shaktipat* also. Therefore, in *shaktipat* a man cannot receive from a woman. This is speaking generally; there can be exceptions. Of these rare cases I shall talk later. Sometimes this can happen, but the reasons are different.

Ordinarily, *shaktipat* does not take place through a female body. You can call this a weakness of the female body. But she has a complementary quality—the strength and power to take *shaktipat* quickly. Man can conduct *shaktipat* but he is unable to receive it. Therefore, *shaktipat* is also difficult from man to man because the male meditator is not receptive; such is his personality. At the very first step, there where he has to begin, stands the male in him who is not receptive. There are cults in which a man performs his spiritual practice taking himself to be a woman. This is a method of making him receptive. Still man does not become receptive. Woman becomes receptive without any difficulty because she is receptive by nature. Therefore, in *shaktipat* a woman is always in need of a medium. Why she is not able to get grace directly, please understand well.

Shaktipat happens from the first body. If I conduct *shaktipat* it happens to your first body. The energy will emerge from my first body and strike at your first body. If you are a woman this will happen quickly. If you are a man, then it will require more effort; it will be difficult. Somewhere deep within, somehow, you will have to acquire the state of complete surrender. Then only is it possible; otherwise not. Man does not surrender; no matter how hard he tries he cannot surrender. Even if he says "I surrender," it will be in an aggressive manner. In other words, it is the ego that is proclaiming the act of surrender. It says, "Look! I surrender." The 'I' standing behind does not leave him.

A woman does not have to surrender: she is already surrendered; it is in her nature. To yield is the quality of her first body. She is very receptive. Therefore, *shaktipat* from a man takes place easily within her. From man to man it is very difficult and from woman to man nearly impossible. From man to man, though difficult, it is possible. If there is a powerful man he can reduce the other man to a near-female condition. *Shaktipat* through a woman is practically impossible, because in the moment of the happening she tends to absorb the vital energy herself. Her first body is like a sponge and sucks everything in.

Until now we talked of *shaktipat*. In the case of grace the conditions are the same. Grace comes from the fourth body. The fourth body of the male is female so he receives grace very readily. Now the woman's fourth body is male so she experiences the same difficulty with regard to grace: she cannot receive grace directly. The fourth body of the male is female; therefore, Mohammed, Moses, Jesus, established relationships with God instantaneously. As the fourth body was feminine in them, they were able to drink in the grace as soon as it descended upon them.

The female has the fourth body of the male. At this extreme is her male body, and this makes it impossible for her ever to receive grace. Therefore, the female has no direct message; that is, no woman has been able to claim that she has known the *Brahman*. At her fourth body is the male that causes the hindrances. She cannot receive grace from that end.

Man receives grace directly. It is difficult for him to take it from someone, as happens in *shaktipat,* because he himself is the barrier there. But it is not so for the woman. She can receive *shaktipat* from any medium. Even very weak people are capable of performing *shaktipat* on women. This is why even very ordinary mediums are successful in this. *Shaktipat* depends less on the medium himself and more on the receptivity of the recipient. But women always require a medium. It is very difficult for them without a medium, because then no happening can take place.

We have been talking of the ordinary state of things. Extraordinary conditions can also be created. It is because of the ordinary course of things that there have been fewer women meditators. This does not mean that women have not experienced God; they have experienced God but there was always a medium in between. However negligible, the medium has always been present; they had their experience through a medium. Another thing: there can be differences caused by unusual conditions. For example, it is more difficult for grace to happen in a young woman; it is a little easier in an older woman.

It is an interesting fact that throughout life our sex remains flexible; we do not remain in the same male-female ratio throughout life. There is a continuous change; the ratio keeps on changing. So it happens that a woman develops hair on the upper lip and chin in later years. Even her voice changes by the time she is fifty and it becomes deeper, more like a man's. The feminine voice will have gone. Her ratio changes: the male factors emerge and the female factors recede. Actually, her work as a woman is over. There was a biological binding up to the age of forty-five which now is no more. She is no more bound to the female in her, so the possibility of grace is more in an older woman. This is so because the male element increases in her first body and the female element decreases in her second body. Also, the male element in her fourth body decreases and the male element in her third body increases. So grace is possible in an older woman.

A very old woman under certain conditions can act as a medium for a young woman. A very old woman, nearabout one hundred years old, and who has no trace left in her mind that she is a woman, can act as a medium for men also. But this will be a different thing altogether. It is the same for men: as a man gets older his female traits go on increasing. Old men generally behave like women. Many masculine traits fall from their personalities and feminine traits develop.

In this connection it is necessary to know that the personality of whoever receives grace in the fourth body develops feminine traits. For instance, if we were to examine the body or the personality of Mahavira or Buddha, they appear more feminine than masculine. The softness and beauty of a woman combined with the feminine receptivity is increased in them. The quality of aggression leaves them, and so they become full of non-violence, compassion and love; violence and anger are banished forever.

Nietzsche has accused Jesus and Buddha of being feminine, and he says that for that reason they should not be counted among men. They have no manly qualities and they have succeeded in making the whole world effeminate. There is some truth in his complaint. You will be surprised to know that we have depicted Buddha, Mahavira, Krishna and Rama without a beard or moustache. It is not that they did not have moustaches and beards, but by the time we made their pictures their personalities had become filled with feminine qualities; thus, the beard and moustache would have looked out of place. We dropped them because they no longer suited their effeminate manner.

Such an incident had taken place in the case of Ramakrishna. His condition could have become a unique case for scientists. It was a very strange happening. Later on his followers tried to hide the facts— because how were they to talk about it? He developed breasts and began to menstruate. This was such a strange happening—a miracle we might say. His individuality became so effeminate that he walked like a woman and talked like a woman, and in such an exceptional case many other changes can occur. For instance, in such circumstances one cannot perform *shaktipat* on anyone. His personality had become completely feminine.

With the help of the meditation techniques of Buddha and Mahavira, hundreds of thousands of people attained to the fourth body. As soon as they reached the fourth plane their personalities became feminine. By this I mean that the passive side of their nature developed. Violence and anger vanished as aggression left them; affection, love, compassion and non-violence increased. Femininity took hold as the inherent nature of this whole country, and my feeling is that this was the cause of the great amount of aggression that occurred here. All the neighbouring masculine countries succeeded in subduing the feminine personality of India.

In one way a very valuable thing took place—that we experienced wonderful things on the fourth plane. But on the plane of the first body we found ourselves in difficulty. Everything has to be compensated for. Those who were prepared to leave the treasures of the fourth plane attained the wealth and kingdoms of the first plane. Those who were not prepared to leave the pleasures of the fourth plane had to give up many things on the first.

After Buddha and Mahavira, India lost its aggressive instinct and became receptive. So with whoever came we made it a point to become receptive; whoever came we absorbed them within us. The question of segregating them never occurred to us, let alone attacking them. That question was lost forever because our personality had become feminine. India became one large womb that harboured all who came to her. We denied no one; we never tried to remove any of these aggressors from among us, because the warlike quality that was required in order to fight was no longer within us. With the great men it became lost, and the ordinary masses followed the great men. And the masses had to remain dominated by them. The ordinary man heard the great men talk on non-violence, compassion, and saw them living accordingly, so he accepted their word and remained silent. He could have fought but he had no leader.

If the history of the world is ever written from a spiritual point of view—when we no longer will consider only physical happenings as history but instead will begin to consider the happenings on the plane of consciousness as history, that is the real history—then we shall understand that whenever a country turns spiritual it becomes feminine. And whenever it becomes feminine, lesser cultures, most ordinary cultures, will defeat it. It is a surprising fact that those who conquered India belonged to very backward cultures. In many ways they were wild barbarians, whether they were Turks or Mongols or the Mughals. They had no culture, but in a sense they were men—though barbarious—and we were feminine, passive. We had no other way than to absorb them within us.

So the female body can absorb. Therefore, a woman needs a medium while the male body can transfer energy as well as receive grace. That is why men like Mahavira had to say that women will have to be reborn as men for the final attainment. This was one reason among many others. She cannot receive grace directly. It is not necessary that she should die to become a man. There are methods in which a transformation of personality can be brought about. The second body can become your first body and the first body can be made to take the position of the second. For this there are techniques of profound will-power by which in this very life physical transformation is brought about.

There is an interesting story about one of the Jaina tirthankaras. who was a woman by the name of Mallibai. The Swetambara sect calls her Mallibai while the Digambara sect calls her Mallinath; they take her to be a man because the Digambara Jainas feel that women are not entitled to *moksha*—liberation. Therefore, a tirthankara cannot be a woman, and so they call Mallibai, Mallinath. Now, nowhere else in the history of mankind is there such a controversy about a person. There have been all kinds of other controversies: over whether a man was five feet six inches or five-five, over when he was born, over when he died, but never was there a controversy where the sex of the individual became a matter of dispute. One sect believes Mallibai to be a man and the other a woman.

What I feel is that when Mallibai began her spiritual search she must have been a woman. But there are such methods by which the first body can be changed into a masculine body, and it was after this took place that she became a tirthankara. So the first sect, who take her to be a woman, revere her first state; and the second sect, who take her to be a man, worship her second state. Both are correct. She was a woman but she must have turned into a man. Mahavira's path is such that any woman who goes through it is bound to become a man. His path is not of devotion but of knowledge, and so it is completely aggressive. His path is not one of receptivity.

If any man begins to sing and dance like Meera for years on end, sleeping with the image of Krishna on his chest and considering himself his beloved, he will remain a man in name only. His consciousness will undergo a complete transformation. The first body will change and become female, and the second body will change and become male. If the transformation is very deep there will be physical changes in his body also; if not, the body will remain the same. But the mind will not be the same: he will develop a feminine consciousness. So in these special cases things can happen: the happening of *shaktipat* can take place; there is no difficulty. But this cannot be a general rule.

Shaktipat can happen through man and he can receive grace directly also, but it is difficult for a woman to attain direct grace. The door to grace can only open for her through *shaktipat*. This is a fact and not an evaluation. There is no question of high and low, above or below: such is the fact. It is as much so as the fact that man ejaculates semen and woman receives it. If someone asks whether a woman can ejaculate semen into a man we will have to say no, because there is no natural law for this. There is no question of either one being above or below. But all manner of evaluation arose out of this fact. Woman came to be looked upon as inferior because she is the recipient. Then the value of the giver went up.

The difference in status between man and woman all over the world arose from the fact that man considers himself the giver, the provider, whereas woman considers herself the recipient. But who said that the receiver must necessarily be inferior? And if there were no one to receive, what use will there be for the giver? And vice versa: if there is no giver, of what use will be the receiver? There is nothing superior and inferior in it. In fact, these two are complementary to each other and neither is independent of the other. They are interdependent; they are tied to each other. These are not two separate entities, but rather two sides of the same coin in which one gives and the other receives.

Normally, however, the very concept of the giver raises a picture of superiority within our minds. There is no reason why the receiver should be inferior. Many things are connected with this, however, and the status of women has been accepted as second to men. Not only men but even women have accepted this position. In fact, both are first in their respective places—he as a man and she as a woman. There is no second place; both are complementary.

Now this concept has had extensive consequences in many areas and it has permeated our entire civilisation and culture. That is why man went hunting—because he was aggressive. And the woman sat at home waiting for him; she accepted him naturally. He went to the fields, he harvested the crop, he worked in his shop, he flew airplanes, he went to the moon, he went out to do all these things because he was aggressive. The woman sat at home waiting for him. She also did a great many things but was not aggressive; it was receptive. She set up his house, she gathered things together, she kept everything in place. In all cultures the principle of stability is due to women.

If the woman was not there man would have been a wanderer, a vagabond; he could never set up a house. The woman acts as a peg. He wanders here and there but has to return to the peg. If the situation were otherwise he would never have settled down. Then there would have been no towns and cities. City culture came into being because woman wanted to stabilise her living in one place. She always pleads to the man, "Enough! Let us stop; let us halt. A little difficulty may come, but let us not go any further." She catches hold of the soil and grows roots into it. Then man has to make a world around her. That is how towns and cities came into being. This is how all cultures, civilisations and homes, which woman beautified and sanctified, were made. No matter what the man earned or gathered in the outside world, she saved.

Man is never interested in saving. He earns, and there the matter ends; he is no longer interested. He is eager and anxious as long as he is fighting with the world, challenging the world; his attention is always turning to other places for conquest. Whatever he brings there is someone else looking after it all, saving it all, and this individual has her own place, her own value. She is a complementary part of the whole situation, but as she does not go out to earn, as she does not accumulate, as she does not create, it seemed to her that she was lagging behind. This feeling entered even into very small things, and everywhere she began to feel a sense of inferiority which is absolutely unfounded.

This inferiority brought evil results. As long as woman was uneducated she tolerated this inferiority, but now she will not. In order to break this sense of inferiority she has gone about doing exactly what men do. This will prove very detrimental to her. She can violate her basic personality, and this can have destructive results deep within her psyche. Now she wants to be on a level with man, but she cannot be like a man completely. She will only succeed in making herself a second-rate man; she cannot be a first-rate man. She can, if she chooses, make herself first rate in her womanhood.

There is no evaluation in this, but these are the facts about these four bodies; that is what I mean to say.

In that case there must be a difference in the spiritual practices of man and woman.

There will be a difference, and it will not be in spiritual practice so much as in the state of mind. For instance, when the method is one and the same, even then a man will go about it aggressively, whereas a woman will go about it in a passive way. The man will attack, the woman will surrender. The method will be the same but the attitudes will be different. When a man enters into spiritual practice he catches it by the neck, so to speak, but when a woman starts a spiritual practice she will place her head at its feet.

This difference in attitude is natural and there is no more difference between the two than this. The woman's attitude will be that of surrender: when she reaches she will not say that she has attained God; rather, she will say that she is fortunate that God has taken her unto himself. When man reaches the ultimate he will not say that God has taken him in; he feels that he has attained God. The difference is in their comprehension. This difference is bound to be, but only up to the fourth body. After that there is no question of male and female.

You have said that the practice of chanting aum also brings about the nada, the inner sound. Does it come about spontaneously also? Which is the proper nada?

If it comes spontaneously it is more valuable. If it comes with the repetition of *aum* it can be imaginary. That which comes of its own accord is authentic, valuable. If the *nada* begins you should become a witness. Do not be merged into it, because that is the state of the seventh plane. If you tend to get lost in the *nada* before reaching the seventh you will halt there; it will act as a brake.

As these inner sounds become more and more subtle, our witnessing too will have to become more and more subtle. We will have to go on observing to the end, when the sound is completely lost.

On which plane does shaktipat take place in the meditator and on which plane does grace take place? If the meditator's first, second and third bodies are not fully developed, what effect will shaktipat and awakening of kundalini have on him?

I have already told you that *shaktipat* takes place in the first body and grace in the fourth. If *shaktipat* takes place in the first body and the *kundalini* is not awakened, it will awaken—

and with great speed. Then we will have to be very careful, because with shaktipat what ordinarily happens in the course of months happens in a few seconds. Therefore, before *shaktipat* there should be a deep preparation of the first three bodies. A sudden *shaktipat* on a person who is not at all prepared, on any Tom, Dick or Harry, can be harmful. Therefore, a little preparation is necessary before *shaktipat*. No elaborate preparation is necessary; only enough to bring the three bodies in focus. That is the first thing.

The next is that there should be a line of connection between the three so that the energy does not become blocked anywhere. If *shaktipat* gets caught on the first plane it can be dangerous. If it spreads to all the three planes it will not be harmful. If it stops at the first it is very harmful.

It is just as if you receive an electric shock while you are standing on the ground: this is then harmful. But if you are standing on a wooden frame it will be quite safe: the current of electricity then passes through your body and makes a circuit. If the circuit is formed there is no danger. It is only dangerous if the circuit breaks. All energies follow the same rule: they go around in a circle. If the circuit breaks in between you receive a shock. So if you stand on wood you cannot receive any shock.

You will be surprised to know that the use of wooden platforms for meditation had no other purpose than the fact that they were non-conductors. Deerskins and leopard skins were used for the same reason: so that the energy that is released by meditation should not give a shock. So these non-conductors were used as seats. A man can be killed by this electric shock. Therefore, the meditator put on wooden sandals and slept on a wooden platform. He may not have known why he did all this; he merely followed the rules laid down by the scriptures. Perhaps, the meditator who practised this thought that he was torturing his body so that the body should not have any comfort. This was not the reason. The danger was quite different. Any moment the happening might take place within the meditator from any unknown source. He must be fully prepared.

If his preparations for the first three bodies are completed, the energy he receives will form a circuit within him. If he is not ready and the energy is obstructed at the very first body, it is harmful. Therefore, this minimal preparation is necessary so that the meditator is able to make a circuit. This preparation is easy and does not take long. It is not at all difficult.

So *shaktipat* can be useful to a certain extent to have a glimpse of the divine; but a preliminary preparation is needed, otherwise it is harmful for an unprepared layman.

Kundalini rises with great intensity through *shaktipat,* but it can go only up to the fourth body. However, this much of a glimpse is more than sufficient. The journey after that is entirely individual. If a flash of lightning on a dark night reveals a little of the path to you, it is more than enough. Once the road is seen everything changes. Then you will no longer be the same person you were before. Thus, *shaktipat* can be used to see a little of the distance that lies ahead. The initial preparation, however, is necessary. If given to the masses directly it can be harmful.

And the most surprising thing is that it is the masses who are always looking for *shaktipat* and such things. The ordinary man wants to get something for free—but nothing is ever obtained free. Many times we come to know afterwards how expensive the free gift turned out to be. Never try to obtain anything for free. We should always be ready to pay the price. In fact, the more we show our readiness to pay the price, the more worthy we become. The greatest price we pay is by our efforts for spiritual growth.

Two days ago a lady came to me and said, "I am well advanced in years and am nearing death. When will I attain enlightenment? Please hurry and do something lest I die." I told her to come for meditation for a few days; then we would see what is to be done.

She said, "I do not want to be bothered with meditation. Do something so that I may attain enlightenment."

Now this lady is searching to get something without paying for it. Such a search is dangerous. You gain nothing by it; on the contrary you lose. The meditator should not harbour any such expectations. One receives what one is ready for. You should trust that this is so.

In fact, a man never gets less than he deserves. This is a law of existence, it is the universal law. You get as much as you are prepared for, and if you do not get then know that it is not an injustice; rather, you are lacking preparation. But our minds always lull us into the belief that injustice is being done to us. We are always very sure of our own worthiness and complain against existence.

We always receive according to our own worthiness. Worthiness and attainment are two names of the same thing. But the mind expects a great deal and strives for very little. There is a great gap between our expectations and our effort. This gap is very self-defeating. It can be very harmful. Because of this we wander here and there in the hope of getting something somewhere. Then, when the number of such persons has increased, it is certain that some clever person will come forward to exploit them. He will offer to give them what they seek for free. Such a person hardly knows anything. He comes upon some formula from somewhere which he can work upon them, and though its effect will not be very deep it can still be harmful.

For instance, take a man who has no knowledge of *shaktipat:* he too can practise a little bit of *shaktipat* with the help of body magnetism. But he has no knowledge of the other six bodies within. The body has its own magnetic force. If arrangements are made through some situation you can be made to receive shocks through it. This is why the meditator in ancient times was careful about which direction to keep the head when sleeping. He would not put his head in a certain direction or his feet in a certain direction.

The earth has its magnetic force and the meditator is always mindful to be properly aligned with it so that he is constantly magnetised by it. If you sleep at an angle to this force your body magnetism becomes less. If you lie in the direction of the current, the force which gives the earth its magnetism and which forms the earth's axis will also magnetise your own body magnet. It fills your body with the magnetic force in the same way that a piece of iron is magnetised by placing it in front of a magnet. After becoming magnetised it will begin to draw smaller objects like pins and needles.

So the body has its own magnetic force. If it can be properly aligned with the magnetic force of the earth it is very beneficial. The stars too have magnetic forces. On special occasions certain stars are particularly magnetic. This can be verified; we have all the necessary information. So if you are in a particular state seated in a particular posture at a certain special moment, a particular star will cause your body to become especially magnetised. Then you can give magnetic shocks to anyone and they can take it for *shaktipat*. But it is not *shaktipat*. The body has its own electricity. If this is produced in a proper way you can light a bulb of five to ten watts by merely holding it in your hand. These experiments have been successful. There are people who just hold the bulb in the palm of their hand and it is lighted. But the energy within the body is infinitely more.

Twenty years ago a woman in Belgium became unexpectedly electrically charged. No one could touch her; anyone who did got a shock. Her husband divorced her, and the reason given was that he got an electric shock whenever he touched her. The divorce created a sensation all over the world. After many tests it was discovered that her body had started producing surplus electricity. The body has many batteries. If they are working in order we do not feel anything. If the order is disturbed a great deal of energy is produced—released.

You take energy from the food you eat and this energy charges the batteries in your body. Therefore, many times you feel the necessity to recharge the batteries. A man is tired and spent by the evening. A good night's rest recharges him. However, he does not know what it is that recharges him in sleep. During sleep some influences are at work upon him. Much psychic research has been done and we know what kind of forces work on him in sleep. If a man wishes he can take advantage of these influences in the waking state. Then he is capable of giving you energy shocks that are not even magnetic but which are of the body electricity. You can mistake this for *shaktipat*.

There are many other ways of pseudo *shaktipat* that are equally false. They are in no way connected with the actual transmission of divine energy. If a person has no knowledge of body magnetism, of body electricity, but he knows the secret of breaking the electric circuit of your body, he can give you energy shocks then too. There are many ways of breaking your body's electrical circuit, and when this is disturbed you receive a shock. Nothing comes from the other person toward you but you feel the shock. It is the shock of your own body electricity which has been disturbed.

I cannot tell you everything in detail because it is not proper to do so. All that I say is incomplete. Even the false methods I talk of are not completely described, because it is very dangerous to speak extensively and completely about them as then there is the temptation to try them out. Our curiosities are very shallow. One mystic has referred to curiosity as sin: there is only one sin in man—the sin of curiosity. He has no other sin. Man commits so many sins entirely out of curiosity. We are not aware of this, but it is curiosity which makes him commit many crimes.

There is a story in *The Bible* that God told Adam to eat the fruits of all trees but one. This one curiosity put him into difficulties. The original sin was the sin of curiosity—and he found himself in trouble. What was the secret? In such a large forest filled with trees of delicious fruits what could be so special about the fruit of this ordinary looking tree? But this one tree began to have a meaning to him and all the rest became meaningless. His mind was hovering round this one tree until he could no longer remain without tasting the forbidden fruit. Curiosity got the better of him, and Christianity says that this was the original sin that man committed. Now, what sin could there be in tasting a certain fruit? The original sin was his curiosity.

Our mind is filled with curiosity—but it rarely inquires into it. Inquiry happens in one who has grown beyond curiosity. Remember, there is a fundamental difference between curiosity and inquiry. A curious man never inquires; he is only filled with curiosity about everything and does not see one thing in its entirety. He hardly glances at one thing when ten others draw his attention. Then he is never able to investigate.

The false methods I have talked about are not complete. Some important parts of these methods have been purposely dropped. It is necessary to do so because our minds coax us with the curiosity to try them out. There is no difficulty in performing these experiments. When false seekers go in search of power, in search of God, they come across false givers of power also. Then it is like the blind leading the blind. The blind leader is bound to fall and also the long line of blind people that is behind him. Then the harm done is not only of a lifetime but of many lives. It is easy to break a thing but very difficult to set it right again.

So do not try in this respect to investigate out of curiosity. Prepare yourself in the right direction. Then what is necessary for you will come your way; it certainly comes.

7

KUNDALINI: THE DISCIPLINE OF TRANSCENDENCE

***Yesterday you talked** to us about the effect of shaktipat and kundalini awakening on persons whose first three bodies are not prepared for it. Please explain further what kind of effect will take place if the second and third bodies are not prepared. Also, how should a meditator prepare his physical, etheric and astral bodies for the event?*

The very first thing to be understood in this connection is that complete harmony in the first, second and third bodies is absolutely essential. If there is no harmonious connection between these three bodies *kundalini* awakening can prove harmful. There are a few things which are very necessary in order to bring about this harmony, this relationship.

Firstly, as long as we are unaware and insensitive towards the physical body, this body cannot establish harmony with other bodies. By insensitiveness I mean we are not fully aware of the body. When we walk we are hardly conscious of the fact that we are walking. When we stand we are hardly conscious of the fact that we are standing. When we eat we are hardly conscious of the fact that we are eating. Whatever activity we do with the body we do in unawareness, like a somnambulist. If we are unaware about this body we must be doubly unaware towards the other inner bodies, because they are more subtle. If we are unaware of this gross body which is visible to the eye, the question of being aware of the invisible subtle bodies does not arise. It is impossible to be aware of them. Harmony cannot be without awareness. Harmony is possible only in a state of awareness. In a state of unawareness all harmony is broken.

So the first thing is to be aware of the body. With whatever small action the body performs remembering is absolutely necessary. There should be mindfulness with all that we do. As Buddha used to say. "When you walk along the road be aware that you are walking. When you lift the right leg your mind should be conscious of the fact that the right leg has been lifted. When you sleep in the night you should know when you change sides."

There is an incident in the life of Buddha from when he was still only a seeker. He was passing through a village with a companion. They were both talking when a fly sat on Buddha's neck. He was in the midst of discussion when he lifted his hand to drive the fly away. It flew away — but Buddha stopped suddenly. "I have committed a serious error," Buddha told his companion. Then he lifted his hand again in the act of driving away the fly.

The fellow seeker exclaimed in surprise. "What is this you are doing? The fly is no longer there."

Buddha replied, "Now I am driving the fly away as I should have. Now I am fully aware of what I am doing. Now as the hand lifts, I am fully aware that it is being lifted and that it is going in the direction of my neck to drive the fly away. That time I was talking to you; hence my action was mechanical. I committed a sin against my body."

If we begin to do all our physical acts with full awareness, then the identification with the physical becomes broken. If you lift one hand upward with full attention you will feel yourself apart from the hand — because the one who lifts is different from that which is lifted. The feeling of being apart from the physical body is the beginning of the awareness of the etheric body. Then, as I said before, you should be fully aware towards this second body also.

Suppose there is an orchestra playing. Many types of instruments are played in an orchestra. If there is a man in the audience who has never heard music he will only hear the drums because this is the instrument that makes the loudest sound; he will not be able to catch the softer notes of other instruments. But if he begins to become aware of the music he will slowly catch the softer notes. As his awareness increases he will begin to catch the most delicate subtle notes. Then as his awareness increases further he will not only catch the notes but he will become aware of the gap between two notes —

the silence between two notes. Then he will have grasped the music completely. The interval, the gap, is the last thing to grasp. Then it can be said that his grasp of music is complete.

The interval, the silence between the two notes, has its own meaning. In fact, the notes are meant only to accentuate this silence. How much this silence is brought into function is the real thing in music.

If you have seen Japanese or Chinese paintings you must have been surprised to note that the painting is always in one corner; the rest of the canvas is left empty. Nowhere else in the world do we find this method of painting, because nowhere else has the artist painted with such meditativeness. In fact, nowhere except in China and Japan have meditators taken up painting. If you ask this artist why he has wasted such a big canvas for such a small painting when he could have easily used a canvas one-eighth of its size, he will reply that in order to bring out the empty space of seven-eighths of the canvas he specifically worked on the remaining part. In reality, this is the ratio.

Ordinarily when a tree standing in an open space is painted the whole canvas is taken up. Actually the tree should be in one little corner, as in comparison to the vast skies the tree is very insignificant. This is the actual ratio. When the tree stands in its right spatial proportion on the canvas, then only can it be alive. Thus, all your paintings are out of proportion. If a meditator produces music there will be less sound and more silence in it — because the notes are very small compared to the silence that joins them. The sounds have only one use — to give a hint of the emptiness, the silence, and then to depart. The deeper you move in music, the deeper will become your sense of silence.

The purpose of our physical body is only that it gives us a perception of our more subtle bodies, but we never use it to this end. We remain fixed only at the physical body because of our sleepy identification with it. We are asleep; and thus we live in the body in a very unconscious manner. If you become aware of each and every action of this body you will begin to feel the presence of the second body. The second body too has its own activity, but you will not know the etheric until you have become fully aware of the activities of the physical body, as the etheric is more subtle. If you are fully aware of the activities of the physical body you will begin to feel the movements of the second body. Then you will be surprised that there are etheric vibrations within you that are active all the time.

A man becomes angry. Anger is born in the etheric body but it manifests in the first body. Basically, anger is the activity of the second body; the first body is used as a medium for expression. Therefore, you can stop anger from reaching the first body if you wish. This is what is done in repression. Suppose I am filled with anger: I feel like beating you with a stick but I can stop myself. Beating is an activity of the first plane. Basically, there is anger but now there is no manifestation of anger. I can withhold myself from the act of beating; I can even smile at you if I wish. But within anger has spread throughout my second body. So in repression what happens is that we hold back on the plane of manifestation, but it is already present at its original source.

When you begin to be aware of the processes of the physical body you will begin to understand the movements of love, anger and hatred within you; you will become aware of their presence. Until you grasp the movements of these emotions that rise from the second body, all you can do is repress them. You cannot be free from them because you only become aware of them when they have reached the first body — and not even then many times: often you only become aware of them when they have reached another person's body. We are so insensitive that not until your slap reaches someone's cheek do you realise what you have done. After the slap you come to know that something has happened.

All emotions rise from the etheric body. Therefore, I also call the second, etheric body the emotional body. It has its own momentum; it has its own movements for anger, love, hatred, restlessness. You will come to know these vibrations.

In fear the etheric body shrinks. The process of shrinking we feel in fear does not belong to the first body. The first body remains just the same; there is no change in it whatsoever. But the effect of this contraction of the etheric body becomes evident in the person's walk, in the way he sits. He looks subdued all the time. He will not stand straight. When he speaks he will stammer. His legs will shake when he walks; his hands will tremble when he writes.

Now anyone can recognise the difference between the handwriting of a man and a woman; it is not at all difficult. A woman's handwriting will never be straight. No matter how symmetrical and well formed, there will always be signs of trembling in it. This is a very feminine characteristic and it comes from a woman's body. A woman is fearful all the time; her personality has become stricken with fear. So without any difficulty one can recognise the handwriting of a woman from a man's. Also, we can find out how fearful a man is from his handwriting. There is no difference between the fingers of a man or a woman, nor in the way they hold the pen. As far as the first body goes there is no difference between the two, but on the plane of the second body the woman is fearful.

Even the contemporary woman has not been able to be fearless within. Still our society, our culture and the state of our thinking is such that we have not been able to make the woman fearless. She is fearful all the time and the vibrations of her fear spread throughout her personality. The degree of fearlessness or fearfulness in men can also be gauged from their handwriting. The state of fear is on the plane of the etheric.

I have told you to be aware of each happening in the gross body, but you should likewise be aware of the processes of the etheric body. When you are in love you feel as if you have expanded. The freedom experienced in love is because of this expansion. Now there is someone before whom you need not be fearful. There is no cause for fear near a person you love. Really speaking, to love means to be free of fear in the presence of a person before whom one can blossom to one's full capacity, no matter what one is. Therefore, a feeling of expansion is experienced in moments of love. The physical body remains the same, but the etheric body within flowers and expands.

In meditation there are always experiences of etheric body. One meditator may feel that his body has expanded - so much so that it has filled the room. However, his physical body remains the same. When he opens his eyes he is shocked: the body is just the same. But the feeling of the experience follows him and makes him realise that what he had felt was not false. The experience was clear — that he had filled the whole room. This is a happening of the etheric body; the possibilities of its expansion are limitless. It also expands and contracts according to the emotions. It can expand so that it can fill the earth; it can contract so that there is enough place for it in an atom.

So you will start noticing the movements of the etheric body — its expansions and contractions, in which situations it contracts and in which situations it expands. If the meditator begins to live in those processes in which it expands a harmony will be created. If he begins to live in the conditions that make it shrink harmony will not be established between the two bodies. Expansion is its innate nature. When it has expanded to its full capacity, when it blossoms fully, it is connected to the first body by a bridge. When it becomes fearful and shrinks, all its contacts with the first body break and it lies separate in a corner.

There are other processes of the second body which can be known by other methods. For instance, you see a man perfectly healthy, perfectly normal. Now if someone tells him he has been given a death sentence he will turn pale at once. No change has taken place in his first body but there is an immediate change in his etheric body. His etheric body is ready to leave the physical body. If the owner of a house comes to know that he has to vacate the house immediately all joyfulness and lightness will disappear; everything will be disturbed. The second body has broken its connections with the first, in a sense. The execution is to take place after some time or maybe not at all, but his connection with the first body is broken.

A man attacks you with a gun or a lion attacks you in the jungle: even though nothing has yet happened to the physical body, the etheric body promptly makes arrangements to leave it and a great distance is created between the two. So you can observe the workings of the second body in a subtle way, and this can be done without difficulty. The difficulty lies in this, that we fail to observe the processes of the physical also. If we do so we will start feeling the movements of the second body. When you have a clear knowledge of the working of both, this very fact will create a harmony between the two.

Then there is the third body — the astral body. Its movements are definitely more subtle — more subtle than fear, anger, love and hatred. It is difficult to grasp its movements unless the knowledge of the second body is complete. It is difficult even to understand the third body from the first body because the gap is now greater; we are unconscious on the first plane. The second body is nearer the first so we can understand a few things about it. It is just as if the second body is our neighbour: sometimes we hear the clatter of pots or the crying of a child next door. But the third body is the neighbour's neighbour from whose house we do not hear any sound.

The phenomenon of the third body is yet more subtle. It can only be grasped if we begin to grasp the emotions fully.

When emotions get condensed they become action. And astral vibes are subtler than the waves of emotions. That is why I will not know that you are angry with me unless you show your anger, because I can only see it when it becomes an action. But you can see it well in advance. You can feel it rising in your etheric body. Now this anger that has risen has its own atoms that come from the etheric body. If these atoms do not arise you cannot be angry.

You can call the astral body a collection of vibrations. You will be able to understand the different conditions of this body better with an example. We can see water and we can see hydrogen and oxygen separately: there is no trace of water in oxygen; there is no trace of oxygen in water. Neither oxygen nor hydrogen has any property of water, but these two combine to form water: each has a hidden quality that manifests when they combine. Anger and love are not seen in the astral body; nor are hatred or fear. But they have vibrations which become manifested when combined with the second body. So when you are completely aware of the second body, when you are completely alert about your anger, then you will know that some reactions have taken place before the advent of anger. In other words, anger is not the beginning. It is the next part of a happening that has already taken place elsewhere.

A bubble rises from the bottom of a lake and begins to travel upwards. When it rises from the sand at the bottom of the lake we cannot see it. When it reaches half the depth of the lake it is still invisible. When it is a short distance from the surface it begins to be visible although it is very small. Then it begins to get bigger and bigger as it reaches the surface, because the weight and pressure of water decreases as it comes up. Also it becomes more clear to our view. At the lower depths the pressure of water kept it small, but as it travels upwards the pressure becomes less and less until it reaches its full size at the surface. But where it reaches its full dimension it also bursts.

So it has travelled a long way. There were places where we could not see it, but it was there all the same hidden under the sand. Then it arose from there, but it was still invisible because the water pressed it down. Then it came nearer the surface from where we could see it although it was still very small. Then it swam to the surface where we could see its totality - but then it burst.

So the bubble of anger develops fully and bursts by the time it reaches the first body. When it comes to the surface it reveals itself. You can stop it at the second body if you so desire but that would be suppression. If you look into your etheric body you will be surprised to find that it has already travelled some distance. But in its place of origin it is in the form of energy vibrations.

As I told you before there are no different types of matter; rather, there are different combinations of the same energy particles. Coal and diamond are the same: the difference is only in the combination of energy particles. If you break any matter into its components, ultimately what remains is electrical energy. The different combinations of these energy vibes bring about formations of different substances. All these substances are different on the surface; deep down they are all one.

If you wake up to the etheric body and follow the emotions to their origin you will suddenly find yourself in the astral body. There you will find that anger is not anger, forgiveness is not forgiveness; the same energy vibrates in them both. The energy in the vibrations of love and hatred are the same. The difference is only in the nature of the vibrations.

When love changes into hatred and hatred changes into love, we wonder how two directly opposite feelings change into one another. For example, a man whom I called my friend until yesterday has become my enemy today. Then I console myself that perhaps I was mistaken — that he was never my friend, because how can a friend turn into an enemy? The energy vibrating in friendship and enmity is the same; the difference is only in the nature of vibrations. The difference is in the structure of the waves. What we call love is love in the morning and hatred in the evening. At noon there is love, and this changes into hatred by evening. It is a difficult situation. The one we love in the morning we hate by evening.

Freud was under the impression that we love those we hate and we hate those we love. The reason he put forward was correct to some extent, but since he had no knowledge of the other bodies of man he could not go further with his investigations. The reason he puts forward is very superficial. He says that the relationship with the mother is the first relationship the child experiences: the mother is the first object he loves. When the mother gives him all her care and attention he loves her, and he hates the same mother when she scolds or punishes him. So two feelings fill his mind towards the same object — the mother: he hates her as well as loves her. Sometimes he feels like murdering her and at other times he feels that he cannot live without her — that she is his every breath. This dual thinking makes the mother his first object of love and hate. Thus, later in life, because of this association in his mind, whomsoever he loves he will also hate.

This is a very superficial finding. The bubble has been caught on the surface where it is about to burst. If a child can love and hate his mother also, it means that the difference between love and hate is quantitative and not qualitative. Love and hatred cannot manifest together at the same time. If both are present, this can be possible only on one condition — that they are convertible: their waves can oscillate from one to the other. So the meditator only comes to know why the mind is filled with conflicting emotions in the third body. A man comes and touches my feet in the morning and hails me as the blessed one — beloved master. The same man comes in the evening, abuses me and says, "This man is the devil himself." The next morning he again comes and addresses me as beloved master and touches my feet. Then others come and advise me not to pay any attention to his words as sometimes he calls me God and sometimes the devil.

I say that he is the only one fit to be relied upon. The man who speaks is not to be blamed. He is not making conflicting statements; rather, his statements belong to the same spectrum. They are rungs of the same ladder, the difference being only quantitative. In fact, as soon as he says "Beloved Master" he catches hold of one part.

The mind is made up of pairs of opposites, so where will the second part go? It will lie under the first waiting for it to exhaust itself. The first gets tired after all, because how long can this man keep on saying "Beloved Master"? When he is tired the second part comes up which prompts him to say, "This man is the devil himself." Now these are not two things; they are one.

Until the time comes when we are able to understand that all our conflicting emotions are forms of the same energy, we will not be able to solve man's problems. The greatest problem that confronts us is that when we love we hate also. We are ready to kill the person without whom we cannot live. He who is our friend is our enemy also deep within. This is our greatest problem, and wherever there are relationships this poses a big question. One thing to be well understood is that the underlying energy in the different emotions is the same; there is no difference whatsoever.

Ordinarily we look upon light and darkness as two opposite things, which is wrong. In scientific terms, darkness is the minimum state of light. If we try we will find light in darkness too. There is no darkness where light is not. It is a different matter if our instruments of investigation fail to recognise it. Our eyes may be incapable of discerning the light in the darkness, but light and darkness are on the same plane, they are different forms and vibrations of the one energy.

It will be easier to understand it in another way: we believe light and darkness to be absolutely opposed to one another, but we do not believe cold and heat to be opposed to each other to that extent. It would be interesting to carry out an experiment. Let one of your hands be heated over a stove and keep the other on ice. Now put both hands in a bucket of water at room temperature. You will find it difficult to decide whether the water is hot or cold. One hand will say it is hot and the other will say it is cold. You will be at a loss to decide because both hands are yours. In fact, cold and heat are not two different things; they are relative experiences.

If we call something cold it only means that we are warmer. That we call it warm only means we are colder: we are only expressing the quantitative difference of temperature between that object and ourselves — nothing else. There is nothing hot and nothing cold — or, you can say that that which is hot is cold also. In fact, hot and cold are misleading terms. We should speak in terms of the temperature; that is the right expression. The scientist also does not use the words hot and cold. He says that the temperature of a thing is so many degrees. Hot and cold are poetic words. They are dangerous for science because they convey nothing.

If a man enters a room and says it is cold we cannot know what he means. It is possible that this man has fever and the room feels cold to him though it is not at all cold. Therefore, until this man knows the condition of his body temperature his assessment of the temperature of the room is meaningless. So we can say, "Do not comment upon whether the room is hot or cold. Just say what is the temperature of the room." The degree gives no indication of hot or cold; it only informs you what the temperature is. If the temperature is less than your body temperature you will feel cold; if it is more you will feel hot. The same is true for light and darkness: it depends upon our ability to see.

The night seems dark to us but not to the owl. The owl finds the day very dark. It must be wondering, "How strange a creature man is! He keeps awake in the night." Generally man considers the owl foolish, but he does not know what the owl's opinion of him is. For the owl the day is the night and it is night when it is day. He must be wondering at the foolishness of man! He thinks, 'There are many wise men among human beings, yet they remain awake at night and when it is day they go to sleep. When it is the real time to be up and active these poor creatures go to sleep.' The owl's eyes are capable of seeing at night. Because it can see at night the night is not dark for it.

The vibrations of love and hate are like those of darkness and light: they have their own ratio. So when you begin to be aware of the third plane you will be in a strange condition: it will no longer be a matter of your own choice whether to love or to hate. Now you will know that these are two names of the same thing.

If you choose one you automatically choose the other; you cannot escape the second choice. So if you ask for love from a man of the third plane he will ask if you are prepared for hatred also. You will of course say, "No, I want love only. Please give me love!" He will reply that it is not possible because love is one form of the vibration of hate. In fact, love is the form that is pleasing to you, whereas hate is that form of the same vibrations which is displeasing to you.

So the man who awakes to the third plane begins to be liberated from the pairs of opposites. He will come to know for the first time that what he had looked upon as two opposites are one and the same. Two opposite branches became part of the same trunk of the tree. Then he will laugh at his stupidity for trying to destroy one in order to keep the other. But then he did not know that this was impossible and that deep down the tree was the same. But only after awakening to the second plane can the third plane be known, because the third body has very subtle vibrations. There are no emotions there only vibrations.

If you come to understand the vibrations of the third body you will begin to have a unique experience. Then you will be able to tell directly on seeing a person what vibrations surround him. Because you are not aware of your own vibrations it is not possible for you to recognise those of another person; otherwise, the vibrations emanating from the third body are gathered around every person's head. The halo depicted in pictures of Buddha, Mahavira, Rama and Krishna is the aura seen around their heads. These have special colours which have been detected. If you have the right experience of the third body you will begin to see these colours. When you begin to see these colours you will see not only your own but those of others as well.

In fact, the deeper we begin to see ourselves, the deeper we begin to see inside others also - to the same extent. Because we know only our own physical body we know only the physical bodies of others. The day we come to know our own etheric body we will begin to be aware of the etheric bodies in others.

Before you become angry you can know well in advance that you are going to be angry. Before you express love it can be easily predicted that you are making preparations for love. So what we call getting to know the feelings of others is not such a great thing after all. By becoming aware of one's own emotional body it becomes easy to grasp the feelings of others, because we begin to see all its variations. By awakening into the third plane things become very clear, because then we can see the colours of the personality also.

The colours of the clothes of *sadhus* and *sannyasins* were chosen by the colour seen from the third body. The choice was different in each case according to which body was emphasized. For instance, Buddha chose yellow because he stressed the seventh body. The aura around the person who has attained to the seventh plane is yellow; therefore, Buddha chose the colour yellow for his *bhikkhus*. It was because of this colour that Buddhist *bhikkhus* found it difficult to remain in India. The yellow colour is identified with death. And, in fact, it is the colour of death, because the seventh plane is the plane of ultimate death. So the yellow colour is connected with death deep within us.

The orange colour gives the feeling of life. Therefore, orange-robed *sannyasins* looked more attractive than the yellow-robed ones; they appeared alive. This colour is the colour of blood and the colour of the aura of the sixth body: it is the colour of the rising sun.

The Jainas chose white, which is the colour of the fifth body — the spiritual body. The Jainas insist on leaving God alone — on leaving God out of discussion and on leaving *nirvana* out of discussion — because scientific discussions are possible only up to the fifth body. Mahavira was a scientifically-minded man. Therefore, he talked about matters as far as they could be solved mathematically; beyond that he refused to talk. He did not wish to talk where his words were liable to err, so he refused to elaborate on mysticism. He said that we will not talk about it; let us move in and experience it. So he did not talk of the planes after the fifth. This is why he chose white; it is the colour of the fifth plane.

From the third plane you will start seeing colours which are due to the effect of the subtle vibrations within. In the very near future it will be possible to photograph them. If they can be seen by the naked eye it follows that they cannot escape the eye of the camera for long. Then we will develop a wonderful ability to assess people and their character.

There is a German thinker by the name of Luschev who has studied the effect of colour on millions of people. Many hospitals in Europe and America are using his experiments. The colour you choose deeply tells about your personality. A man with a particular disease prefers a particular colour; a healthy person chooses quite another colour; a tranquil man prefers yet another colour; an ambitious man quite another than a nonambitious person. With your choice you give a hint of what is happening within your third body. Now it is an interesting fact that if the colour that emanates from your third body is grasped, and if your preference of colour is then tested, it will turn out to be the same colour: you will choose a colour similar to the colour emanating from your third body.

Colours have wonderful meanings and uses. It was not known previously that colours could be so meaningful that they can even outwardly convey about your personality. Also, it was not known that the effect of colours can touch your inner personality. You cannot escape from them. For instance, the colour red: it is always connected with revolution. It is the colour of anger and it is difficult to escape from it. Therefore, the revolutionaries carried red flags. There is an aura of red around a wrathful mind. It is the colour of blood, the colour of murder, the colour of anger and of destruction.

It is very interesting that if everything in the room were coloured red the blood pressure of all of you sitting here would rise. If a man lives continuously with the colour red his blood pressure can never be normal. The colour blue causes the blood pressure to fall: it is the colour of the skies and of supreme tranquillity. If there is blue all around you your blood pressure will fall.

Leave aside man: if we fill water in a blue bottle and keep it in the sun the chemical composition of the water will change. The water absorbs the blue colour which then changes its composition. This water has an effect on man's blood pressure. Similarly, if we fill a yellow bottle with water and put it in the sun its characteristics will be different. The water in the blue bottle will remain fresh for days whereas the water in the yellow bottle will turn foul at once. The yellow colour is the colour of death and it disintegrates things.

You will begin to see the circles of all these colours around you. This will be on the third plane. When you are aware of these three bodies that very awareness will bring about a harmony between them. Then *shaktipat* of any kind will not be able to bring harmful results. The energy of *shaktipat* will enter your fourth body through the harmonious layers of the first three bodies; this will be the highway along which it will travel. If this path is not ready there can be many dangers. For this reason I said that the first three bodies should be strong and fit; then only growth happens smoothly.

If people who are established in the fourth, fifth, sixth or seventh chakra die, what will be the state of their chakras in the next birth? People of which plane stay in the realm of bodiless higher beings after their death? Do bodiless higher beings have to be reborn as human beings for the final attainment?

We will have to understand some things from afar. I talked to you about the seven bodies. Keeping these in mind, we can also divide existence into seven dimensions. In the entire existence, all the seven bodies are forever present. Awake or asleep, active or dormant, ugly or beautiful, they are always there. Take a piece of metal — say a piece of iron: all the seven bodies are present in it but all the seven are asleep; all the seven are dormant, non-active. Therefore, a piece of iron looks dead. Take a plant: its first body has become active, its physical body; therefore, we get the first glimpse of life in plants.

Then there is the animal: his second body has become activated. Movement which does not exist in plants starts in animals. The plant puts down its roots and stays in one place always. It is not mobile because for that the second body must be activated — the etheric body from which all movements come. If only the physical body is awakened it will be immobile, fixed. The plant is a fixed animal. There are some plants that move a little: that is a state between plant and animal. In many muddy areas of Africa there are certain plants that slide a distance of twenty to twenty-five feet in a year. By means of their roots they can clutch the ground and let it go and thus perform movement. This is the revolutionary link between the plant and the animal.

The second body has also begun to work in the animal. This does not mean that the second body has reached awareness; it only means it has become activated. The animal has no knowledge of it. Because of the second body being activated it experiences anger, it can express love, it can run, defend itself, it experiences fear, it can attack or hide and it can move.

In man the third, astral body is activated. Therefore, not only does he move bodily but also with the mind: he can travel with his mind. He travels in the past as well as in the future. There is no future for the animal, and for this reason it is never worried, never tense, because all anxiety is of the future. What will happen tomorrow is our greatest worry. But for animals there is no tomorrow; today is everything for them. Even today does not exist for them in a way, because what does today mean to one for whom tomorrow has no meaning? What is, is.

In man a more subtle movement has taken birth — the movement of the mind. It comes from the third, astral body. Now he can think of the future with the help of the mind. He can also worry about what will be after death — where he will go, where he will not go. He also reflects upon where he was before birth.

The fourth body is active in a few persons, not in all. If a person dies after his fourth body is activated he is born on the plane of the *devas,* the gods, where there are many possibilities for the activation of the fourth body. If the third body remains active, only then does a man remain as a man. From the fourth body birth on higher planes begins.

With the fourth there will be a difference that must be understood. If the fourth body is activated there is less possibility of acquiring a physical body again and more possibility of a bodiless being. But as I said, remember the difference between activation and consciousness. If the fourth body is merely activated and one is not conscious we call it the plane of the *pretas,* evil spirits; if it is activated as well as fully conscious we call it the plane of the *devas,* godly spirits. This is the only difference between *pretas* and *devas*. An evil spirit is not aware that its fourth body is activated whereas a godly one is. Therefore, the *preta* can cause a great deal of harm both to itself and to others with the activity of its fourth body, because unconsciousness can only bring harm. The *deva* will be the cause of many good deeds both to itself and to others, because awareness can only be beneficial.

He whose fifth body becomes active goes beyond the existence of *devas*. The fifth is the spiritual body. On the fifth plane activation and awareness are one and the same. No one can reach the fifth plane without awareness; therefore, activation and awareness take place simultaneously here. You can reach up to the fourth without awareness also. If you awaken the journey will take a different turn: it will go toward the *deva* plane, the plane of the gods. If you go on being unaware your journey will be in the realm of the evil spirits.

On the fifth plane activation and awareness are there simultaneously, because this is the spiritual body and unawareness is meaningless so far as self is concerned. *Atman* means consciousness; therefore, the other name of *atman* is consciousness. Here unconsciousness has no meaning.

So from the fifth body activation and awareness are one and the same thing, but before that the two ways are separate. The difference between male and female is there until the fourth; the difference between sleeping and waking is there until the fourth. As a matter of fact, duality and conflict are there only up to the fourth body. From the fifth the non-dual begins - the undivided. Unity starts from the fifth. Before this there is diversity, difference. The potential of the fifth comes neither from the plane of *pretas* nor from the plane of the *devas*. This should be understood.

The fifth body is not possible for *pretas* because theirs is an unconscious existence. They do not have that body which is necessary for awareness, and they do not have the first body which is the first step toward awareness. For this reason the *preta* has to return to a human form. Therefore, the human existence is in a sense at a crossroads. The plane of the *devas* is above it but not beyond it, because to go beyond it is necessary to come back to the human existence. The *preta* has to return in order to break its unawareness, because for this a human form is absolutely necessary. The *devas* have to return, because in their existence there is no suffering whatsoever. Actually it is an awakened existence. However, in such an existence there cannot be the pain and suffering that give birth to that longing for meditation. Where there is no suffering there is no thought of transformation or of attainment.

So the realm of *devas* is a static existence where there is no progress. This is a peculiarity of happiness: it blocks all further progress. In pain and suffering there is a longing for growth. Suffering stimulates us to find ways and means of freedom from pain and sorrow. In happiness all seeking stops. So this is indeed a very strange state of affairs, and people usually cannot understand this.

In the lives of Mahavira and Buddha there are descriptions of *devas* coming to them in order to be taught, but these are very exceptional happenings. It is strange that *devas* should come to human beings because it is an existence above the human existence. It seems strange but it is not, because the existence in heaven is a static existence from where there is no growth. If you wish to go ahead then just as you take a step back before you jump you have to step back to the human existence and then take a jump.

Happiness is peculiar in the sense that there is no further movement. Another thing: happiness becomes boring. There is no other factor that can cause as much boredom as happiness. Unhappiness is not boring; an unhappy mind is never bored. Therefore, an unhappy man is never discontented, nor is a society where pain and misery prevails. It is only the happy person or the happy community that is discontented. India is not as discontented as America. The reason is only this, that they are affluent and happy whereas we are poor and miserable. There is nothing to look forward to in America and there is no suffering to goad them to further growth. Besides, happiness is repetitive: the same forms of pleasure and enjoyment over and over again become meaningless.

So the realm of *devas* is the peak of boredom. There is no place more boring in the universe, and there is so much boredom there. But it takes time for the boredom to develop. Besides, it depends upon the sensitivity of the individual. The more sensitive a person the sooner he will get bored; the less sensitive a person the longer it will take. It is also possible that he may not get bored at all. The buffalo eats the same grass every day and is not tired of it.

Sensitivity is very rare. The boredom will be proportionate to the sensitivity of the person. Sensitivity always looks for the new: it seeks more and more that is new day by day. Sensitiveness is a kind of restlessness, and this in turn is a kind of aliveness. So the realm of the *devas* is a kind of dead existence, as is also is the realm of the *pretas*. But the realm of *devas* is more dead, because in the world of the *pretas* there is a lot of suffering and ways to inflict suffering as well as the pleasure of making oneself and others suffer. There are enough provisions for restlessness there, so there is no boredom at all.

The realm of *devas* is very peaceful: there is no disturbance of any sort. So ultimately the return from the realm of *devas* can only be out of boredom. Remember, it is above human life; sensitivity increases there. The pleasure that does not become boring to us over the years in the bodily life becomes stale and boring once it is enjoyed in the realm of *devas*.

This is why it is said in the *Puranas* that the gods yearn to be born as human beings. Now this seems very surprising because here on earth we long to go to the realm of the *devas*. There are even stories where some *deva* descends on earth to fall in love with a woman. These stories are indications of the state of mind. They show that in that realm there is happiness, but it is boring because there is just pleasure and enjoyment without a trace of pain or sorrow. Then it becomes boring. If one is given a choice between infinite happiness without a moment of sorrow and infinite sorrow and suffering, the wise man will choose the latter. We have to return from the realm of the *devas;* we also have to return from the realm of the *pretas*.

Human existence is at the crossroads: all journeys are possible from it. The man who attains the fifth body, however, has not to go anywhere. He enters a state in which there is no longer any birth through the womb; he is not reborn through the womb of any mother.

He who attains the self has ended his journey in a sense. The state in the fifth body is a state of liberation. But if he feels satisfied within himself, he can stop at this plane for an infinite number of ages, because here there is neither pain nor pleasure, neither bondage nor suffering. There is only one's own being — not the universal being, the all. So a person can go on living in this state for an infinite number of ages until a time comes when he grows curious to know the all.

The seed of inquiry is within us; therefore, it arises. If the meditator nurtures the curiosity of knowing the all from the very beginning, he can escape the danger of getting stuck in the fifth body.

So if you know the full science of the seven bodies you will know that the inquiry should be complete and ultimate from the very beginning. If you start with a goal of stopping midway, then when you reach the fifth you will feel you have come to the end, to your destination, and you will miss the point.

So the man of the fifth body has not to take birth but he is bound within himself: he breaks away from everyone but remains bound to himself. He is rid of the ego but not of the feeling of "I am." Ego is a claim against others.

Understand this well: When I say 'I' it is to dominate some 'you'. Therefore, when the I succeeds in dominating a you the ego feels victorious. When it is dominated by the I of another it is miserable. The I is always an effort to overpower the you. The ego exists always in contrast to the other.

Here at the fifth the other is no more and there is no longer any competition with it. This state of I-ness, *asmita,* is self-contained. This is the only difference between ego and *asmita*. Now I have nothing to do with you; there is no claim of I, but still there is my being. I no longer need to stand against the other, but "I am" although there is no you to be compared with.

For this reason I said ego will say 'I' and the being will say 'am'. This will be the difference. In "I am" there are two concepts: the I is the ego and the am, the being.

The feeling of I-ness is not against anyone; it is in favour of itself. The feeling is one of "I am," so let there be no one else in the world. Let there be a Third World War and let all perish but I should remain. So although there will be no ego in me the feeling of I-ness will still be: I know that I am, even though I will not say I to others, because for me there is no longer any you left to whom I can say it. So when you are absolutely alone and there is no other, then too you are — in a sense of being existent.

The ego disappears in the fifth body and thus the strongest link in the chain of bondage falls. But the feeling of I-ness remains — free, independent, boundless and without any attachments. But the I-ness has its own limits. All other boundaries fade away except the boundary of I-ness. At the sixth this too drops or is transcended. The sixth is the cosmic body.

The question of being born in a womb ends with the fifth body, but birth still must be taken. This difference should be properly understood. One birth is from within the mother's womb and one birth is from within oneself. This is why in this country we call the brahmin, *dwij* — twiceborn. This term was actually used for the *Brahma gyani,* one who knows the *Brahman* — the cosmic reality. To call an unenlightened person a brahmin is unnecessary. When a second birth of an entirely different kind was gone through a person was called *dwij* - twiceborn; an enlightened person was called a brahmin.

So one birth is from the womb of another and one is from one's own self. Once the fifth body is attained you cannot be born to another. Now you will have to be born through the fifth body into the sixth body. This is your journey, your own inner pregnancy, your own inner birth. Now there is no connection with an external womb or with any external means of creation. Now you have no father or mother; you are the father, you are the mother, and you are the child. This is entirely an individual journey. So when a person enters the sixth body through the fifth he can be called twiceborn and not before that. He is born without the external means of creation, without the help of an external womb.

One *rishi* of the *Upanishads* prays, "Oh Lord, open the golden covers of this inner womb within which the reality is hidden." The covers are definitely of gold. They are such that we do not want to throw them aside; they are such that we are eager to keep them. The I-ness is the most priceless cover that is over us. We ourselves will not want to part from it and there is no external obstruction to stop us. The cover itself is so lovable that we cannot leave it. Therefore, the *rishi* says, "Remove the golden covers and open the womb that makes a person twiceborn."

So *Brahma gyanis* were called twiceborn, and by *Brahma gyani* is meant one who has attained the sixth body. From the fifth to the sixth the journey is one of being twiceborn. The womb is different, the mode of being born is different. Now everything is wombless: the womb is one's own, and we are selfborn now.

From the fifth to the sixth there is a birth and from the sixth to the seventh there is a death. Therefore, one who has undergone the latter is not referred to as twiceborn; there is no meaning in it. Do you understand? It is easy to follow now.

From the fifth to the sixth there is birth through oneself; from the sixth to the seventh there is death through oneself. We were born through others — through the bodies of others — and the death that follows is also of others. This I shall explain.

If your birth is from another, how can your death be your own? How can this be? The two ends will be unrelated. If another gives me my birth, then death cannot be mine. When birth comes from another death too is from another. The difference is this, that first I appear through one womb and the second time I enter into another womb — but I am not aware. When I came into this birth it was apparent, but now my going is not apparent. Death precedes birth: you had died somewhere before you were born somewhere. Birth is apparent, but of death you are not aware.

Now you were born through a mother and father: you obtained a body, an apparatus that will run for seventy to a hundred years. After a hundred years this instrument will not work. The day it will stop working is predestined from the moment of birth. It is not so important when it will fall; what is important is that it will fall. With birth it is decided that you will die. The womb which brought you your birth brought along your death also. You have brought them both along together. In fact, death lies hidden in the birth-giving womb; there is only an interval of a hundred years.

In these hundred years you will complete your journey from one end to the other and go back exactly to the place from where you came. The death of your body is received from another at the time of your birth; therefore, death is also from another. So neither are you born, nor is it you who dies. In birth there was a medium and in death too the same will be the case. When you enter the sixth, cosmic body from the fifth, the spiritual body, you will be born for the first time. Then you will be self-born: your birth will be without a womb. But then self-death will at the same time await you — a wombless death also awaits you. Wherever this birth takes you, from there death will lead you even further ahead. The birth takes you to the *Brahman* and death to *nirvana*.

This birth can be very prolonged; it can be endless. Such a person, if he remains, will become God. Such a consciousness if it travels for long will be worshipped by millions; prayers will be offered to him. Those whom we call an *avatar, Ishwara,* son of God, tirthankara, are those who have entered the sixth plane from the fifth. They can remain in that plane for as long as they wish and they can be of great help. There is no question of any harm coming from them and they can be great indicators. Such persons are forever striving and working for others to travel through the preceding journey. The consciousness of people from the sixth plane can also relay messages in various ways, and those who have the slightest feel of such persons cannot place them anywhere lower than Bhagwan, the blessed one. Bhagwan they are: there is nothing lacking in their being Bhagwan because they have attained the sixth, cosmic body.

In this very life it is possible to enter the sixth plane through the fifth. Whenever anyone enters the sixth in this life we call him a Buddha or a Mahavira or a Rama or a Krishna or a Christ. And those who perceive them as such look upon them as God. For those who cannot see the question does not arise.

One man in a village recognises Buddha as *Ishwara;* to another he is nothing — absolutely ordinary. He catches a cold like us; he falls ill just like us; he eats, sleeps, walks and talks like us; he even dies the same as us. "Then what is the difference between him and us?" is how they argue. The number of those who do not see is infinitely greater than of those who do, so those who do appear to be mad, deluded, because they have no evidence whatsoever to offer as proof.

Actually there is no evidence. For instance, this microphone is before me. If you who are present cannot see it, how will I prove to you that it is there? If I say it is and you cannot see it, I will be judged mad. To see when others cannot see is a proof that you are not sound of mind.

We measure enlightenment also by majority of votes; here too we have the voting system! So by some people Buddha is felt as God and by some not. Those who cannot see him as God will say, "What madness is this? He is the son of King Shuddhodana and so-and-so is his mother and so-and-so his wife. He is the same Gautama, not somebody else." Even his own father could not see that Gautama has become a totally different man. He looked upon him as his son, and said, "Into what kind of foolishness have you fallen? Return to the palace. What are you doing? The kingdom is getting ruined and I am getting old. You return and take care of everything." The poor father failed to recognise that Buddha had become the master of an infinite kingdom. Those who had the eyes to see looked upon such people as a tirthankara, Bhagwan, or the son of God. They will make use of some such word to address people of the sixth body.

The seventh body is never attained in this body. In this body we can at the most stand on the boundary line of the sixth body from where we can see the seventh. That jump, that void, that abyss, that eternity, is visible from there, and there we can stand. Therefore, in the life of Buddha two *nirvanas* have been mentioned. One *nirvana* he attained under the bodhi tree on the banks of the river Niranjana: that was forty years before his death. This is called *nirvana*. That day he stood on the periphery of the sixth body - and he remained there for forty long years. The day he died is called the *mahaparinirvana;* that day he entered the seventh plane. Therefore, when anyone asked him, "What will happen to the *Tathagata* after death?" Buddha would reply, "There will be no *Tathagata*."

But this does not satisfy the mind. Again and again they would ask, "What will happen to Buddha in *mahaparinirvana*?" To this Buddha replied, "Where all activities cease, where all happening ceases, that is called *mahaparinirvana*." As long as something keeps happening in the sixth body it is the existence; beyond this is the non-existence. So when Buddha is not, nothing will remain. In a sense you may say he never was. He will fade away like a dream, like a line drawn on the sand, like a line drawn on water that disappears as it forms. He will be lost and nothing will remain. But this does not satisfy our minds. We say that somewhere, on some level, in some corner no matter how far away, he should exist. But in the seventh he becomes only the void, the formless.

There is no way of bringing new form beyond the seventh. There are people who stand on the borderline and see the seventh, who see that abyss; therefore, all that is known of the seventh plane is what is reported by those who stand at the boundary line. It is not an account of people who have gone there, because there is no means to give any account. It is just as if a man standing at the borderline of Pakistan would look and report that there is a house, a shop, a road, some people, and he can see the trees and the sun coming out. But this man is standing on the Indian border.

To go into the seventh from the sixth is the ultimate death. You will be surprised to know that the meaning of *acharya* in the olden days was one who teaches the final death. There are aphorisms which say, "*Acharya* is death." So when Nachiketa reaches the god of death he reaches the *acharya*. The god of death can only teach death and nothing else. *Acharya* is a designation from which only dissolution, disintegration and extinction can be taught.

...But before this death it is necessary for you to be born. Right now you don't exist. That which you consider as yourself is borrowed; it is not your real being. Even if you lose it, you were never the possessor. It is just as if I were to steal something and then give it in charity: since the thing did not belong to me, how can it be my donation? What is not mine I cannot give. So one whom we call a renunciate in this world is not a renunciate at all because he renounces that which is not his. And how can you be the renouncer of that which is not yours? To claim to have left that which is not yours is madness.

Renunciation takes place when you enter the seventh from the sixth. There you cast aside that which is you — because you have nothing else. You leave your very being.

The only renunciation that is meaningful is the entrance from the sixth plane to the seventh. Before that all talk of renunciation is childish. The man who says "This is mine" is foolish. The man who says "I left all that was mine" is also foolish, because he still claims to be the possessor. Only we ourselves are ours — but we have no understanding of this.

Therefore, from the fifth to the sixth you will know who you are and from the sixth to the seventh you will be able to renounce that which you are. And the moment someone renounces that which he is there is nothing more left to be attained, there is nothing more left to be renounced. Then there is no question left. Then there is infinite stillness, eternal silence. After that one cannot say that there is bliss or peace; one cannot say that there is truth or falseness, light or darkness. Nothing can be said. This is the state of the seventh.

If the fifth plane is attained in the physical body, in which form is the person reborn after his death?

To attain the fifth body and to be awakened is one and the same thing. Then you no longer need the initial bodies. Now you can work from the fifth plane; now you are an awakened person. Hence, there is no difficulty. The initial bodies are required only up to the fourth body. If the fourth is activated and awakened the person becomes a *deva* — a heavenly soul. If the fourth lies idle and asleep the person enters the realm of the *pretas* — the evil spirits. You will have to return to the human form from both of these states, because you have no idea of your identity as yet. And in order to know your identity you must still have a need for the other. Only with the help of the other will you be able to know yourself.

Right now to know yourself you need the other; without the other you will not be able to recognise yourself. The other will form the boundary from where you will know yourself. Therefore, up to the fourth plane you will have to take birth under any circumstances. After the fifth the other is not necessary; it has no meaning. In the fifth it will be possible for you to be without the previous four bodies. But with the fifth the process of an entirely new kind of birth begins, and that is the entrance into the sixth plane. This is a different matter altogether and does not involve the first four bodies.

When a person enters the fifth from the fourth plane, does he not acquire a physical body again after death?

No.

If a tirthankara desires to be born, can he take a physical body?

Now this is a different matter altogether. If a tirthankara wishes to be reborn a very interesting happening takes place: that is, before death he does not discard his fourth body. There is a way and a method of doing this, and that is by having the desire to be a tirthankara. So when the fourth body is falling away one desire has to be kept alive so that the fourth body does not drop. If the fourth drops, birth in the physical form is impossible.

Then the bridge, the connection through which you came, is no more. So the desire to be a tirthankara has to be kept alive through the fourth body. Not all who are worthy become tirthankaras; they go straight along their way without this. There are only a few who become such masters, and their number is fixed beforehand. There is a reason why their number is predetermined. It is predetermined that for a particular age so many tirthankaras would be enough for so many people.

So the desire of becoming a tirthankara has to be very strong. It is the last desire, and if it slips the matter is over. So the seed of desire that "I want to teach others" must be very strong. One must feel, "I will show others the way; I will explain to others, I must come back for others." Then the tirthankara can descend into a physical body. But this means that the fourth body has not been left yet. He steps onto the fifth but he fastens a peg in the fourth body. This peg can be quickly uprooted; hence, it is a very difficult task to maintain it there.

There is a process of making tirthankaras: they are made in mystery schools, it is not an individual happening. In the same manner that a school functions, a group of seekers meditate. Then from among them they find one who shows full promise of becoming a tirthankara; he can express what he knows, he can impart what he knows, and he can communicate it to others. So the whole school begins to work on his fourth body. He is told to concentrate on his fourth body so that it should not disintegrate because it will be useful in the future. Thus, he will be taught ways and means of saving his fourth body. And more labour and hard work goes into saving this body than in discarding it.

It is so easy to let go and allow the fourth body to dissolve. When all the anchors are pulled up, when the sails are all drawn and filled with the wind, when the vast ocean calls and there is bliss and bliss everywhere, you can imagine how difficult it must be to guard one small peg. It is for this reason that when we address a tirthankara we say: "You are most compassionate."

This was the only reason why a tirthankara was so called. The greatest part of his compassion was that when everything was ready for his departure he stayed back for those who were still at the shore and whose boats were not yet ready to sail. His boat is absolutely ready; yet he bears the sufferings of this shore, he endures the stones and the abuses. He could have left anytime; his boat was ready to set sail. Yet for no reason of his own he preferred to be amidst those who are capable of harassing and even killing him. So his compassion knows no limits. But the desire for this compassion is taught in mystery schools. Therefore, meditators working individually cannot become tirthankaras, because when the peg is lost they will not know about it. Only when the boat has sailed do they realise that the shore is left far behind.

Even persons who have attained the sixth plane — those whom we call *Ishwara* — sometimes help in the advent of a tirthankara. When they find one worthy enough not to be let off from the shore they try in a thousand ways to keep him back. Even *devas* who, as I said, are helpful in doing good, take part in this. They go on influencing such a one to save one peg. They tell him, "We can see the peg; you cannot. But you have to save it."

So the world is not anarchic, disorderly. There are profound arrangements; there is order within order. Efforts of all kinds are often made — but at times the plans go amiss, as in the case of Krishnamurti. Great efforts were made with him to fix a peg, but they failed. The whole school of seekers made a tremendous effort to preserve a peg in his fourth body, but all efforts failed. Other persons had a hand in this effort. There were also the hands of higher souls behind this — of persons of the sixth and the fifth planes, and awakened ones of the fourth plane. Thousands took part in it.

Krishnamurti was chosen as well as a few other children who showed promise of becoming tirthankaras, but the opportunity passed away without bearing fruit. The peg could not be fixed, and so the world lost the benefit of a tirthankara which could have been possible through Krishnamurti. But that is a different story....

8
THE ESOTERIC DIMENSIONS OF TANTRA

***You have said** that the difference of male and female ends with the fifth body. How do the positive and negative poles of electricity of the first four bodies become adjusted to bring about this happening? Please explain this in detail.*

In the context of the male and female bodies you have been told that the first body of the female is a female body while the second is male, and the exact opposite is the case with the male. Then the woman's third body is again female and the fourth male. I have told you before that the female body is incomplete; so is the male body. These two together make a complete body. This union is possible in two ways. If the external man combines with the external woman, together they create a unit. With this unit the work of procreation, of nature, goes on. If a man or woman turns inward and unites with the female or male within, a different journey begins which is the way towards the divine. The external union, however, is a journey toward nature.

When the first body of the male meets his second, etheric body which is female, these two make a unit. When the first body of a female meets her second, etheric body which is of the male element, they also form a unit. This is a wonderful unity. The external union can only be momentary. Very briefly it gives a period of happiness, then the sorrow of separation is infinitely greater. And this sorrow brings about a fresh yearning for the same pleasure which again proves to be momentary; then again there is the parting which is long and painful. So the outer pleasure can only be momentary whereas the union within abides forever. Once it takes place it never breaks.

Therefore, as long as the union within does not take place there is sorrow and pain. A current of happiness begins to flow within as soon as the inner union takes place. This pleasure is similar to that which is experienced momentarily in the outer union that takes place during lovemaking—a union which is so infinitesimal in its duration that it is over almost before it has begun. Many times it is not even experienced; it happens with such swiftness that it is not experienced at all.

From the viewpoint of yoga, when inner intercourse becomes possible the instinct for outer intercourse immediately disappears. The reason is that this inner union is completely satisfying and fulfilling. The images of coitus depicted on temple walls are indications in this direction.

Inner intercourse is a process of meditation. Therefore, opposition arose between the concept of internal and external intercourse. This was due to the fact that he who enters into inner intercourse once will lose all interest in outer intercourse.

This also should be remembered: when a woman unites with her male etheric body the resulting unit will be female; when the male unites with his female etheric body the unit will be male. This is because the first body absorbs the second body: the second merges in the first. But now these are male and female in a very different sense. It is not the outer man and the outer woman that we see: the outer man is incomplete, and therefore uneasy, unsatisfied. The external woman is also incomplete, and therefore restless, unfulfilled.

If we examine the development of life on earth we will find that in primal organisms the male and female are both present. For example, the amoeba: the amoeba is half male, half female. Therefore, there is no other creature more satisfied in this world. No such thing as discontent ever arises in an amoeba. This is also the reason why it has failed to develop: it has always remained an amoeba. So very elementary organisms in biological development do not have separate bodies for each sex. Both male and female are contained within the same body.

When the first body of the woman unites with her male, etheric body, a new woman comes into being who is a complete woman. We have no idea of the personality of a complete woman because all the women we know are incomplete. We have no estimate of a complete man because all the men we know are incomplete; they are all only half. As soon as this unit is completed a supreme satisfaction pervades—a satisfaction in which all discontent diminishes and finally disappears. Now it will be difficult for this complete man and complete woman to establish any external relationships, because outwardly there are only half men and half women with whom their personalities do not feel harmony. However, it is possible for a perfect man—one whose first two bodies have united within—to form a relationship with a perfect woman, one whose first two bodies have also united.

Tantra has tried many experiments for this relationship. Therefore, *tantra* had to go through a great deal of harassment and misunderstandings. We could not understand what *tantrikas* were doing—naturally it was beyond our understanding. When a woman and a man who are united to the inner complementary body make love under the circumstances of *tantra,* it is nothing more than ordinary intercourse for us. We could never evaluate what was happening.

But this is a very different kind of happening, and this was a very great help to the seeker. It had a great significance for him. The external union of a complete man and a complete woman was the beginning of a new meeting; it was a journey toward a new union. One kind of journey was already over: the incomplete woman and incomplete man have been completed. A particular plateau of fulfilment was then reached, because now there was no thought of desire.

When a complete man and a complete woman meet in this way, they experience for the first time the bliss, the pleasure, of the union of two whole beings. Then they begin to understand that if such a perfect union could take place within themselves there would be a torrent of unbounded bliss. The half man enjoyed the union with the half woman; then he united with the half woman within himself and he experienced unlimited bliss. Then the complete man united with the complete woman. Then it is but logical that he should set out to attain a perfect woman within himself, so he set out in search of the perfect woman within where the meeting of the third and fourth bodies takes place.

The third body of the man is again male and the fourth female; the woman's third body is female and the fourth male. *Tantra* has taken care to see that man does not stagnate after the first perfection is achieved. There are many sorts of perfection within us. Perfection never obstructs, but there are many kinds of perfections which are imperfect compared to the further perfections that lie ahead. However, they are perfections in relation to the preceding imperfections. The previous imperfections may have disappeared, but we still have no idea of the greater perfections that lie ahead. This may create a hindrance.

Therefore, many surprising methods have been developed in *tantra* which cannot be immediately understood. For instance, when there is intercourse between a complete man and a complete woman there will be no loss of energy: there cannot be, because each forms a complete circuit within his or her own self. There will be no discharge of energy from the partners; for the first time they will experience pleasure without loss of energy.

The pleasure experienced in the physical intercourse at the time of orgasm is invariably followed by the experience of pain. The gloom, the anguish, the fatigue, the remorse that follows with the loss of energy is inevitable. The pleasure passes in a moment but the loss of energy takes twenty-four to forty-eight hours or more to be regained. Until the energy is regained the mind is filled with agony.

Tantra has evolved strange and marvellous methods for intercourse without ejaculation, and it has worked very courageously in that direction. We shall have to talk separately on this subject some other time as *tantric* practice forms a complete network in itself. And since this network has been broken the entire science gradually became esoteric. Also, it is difficult to talk about *tantric* practices openly and directly, because our moral beliefs have made this very difficult. Moreover, our foolish "wise" men who know nothing but who are capable of saying anything have made it impossible to keep any precious wisdom alive. The practices of *tantra* thus had to be given up or else it was hidden and *tantric* experiments had to go underground. For this reason the current of *tantric* knowledge no longer flows clearly in our lives.

The intercourse between a complete man and a complete woman is a very different kind altogether. It is an intercourse in which there is no loss of energy. An entirely new happening takes place which can only be hinted at. When an incomplete man and an incomplete woman meet, both undergo a loss of energy. The quantity of energy after their intercourse is much less than it was prior to it.

Quite the opposite is the case in the union of a complete man and a complete woman. The quantity of energy after their intercourse will be more than was there before it. The energy of both increases. This energy lies within them, and it becomes awakened and active by the nearness of the other partner. In the first ordinary sexual act also, ejaculation happens by coming together of a man and a woman. In the second meeting of a complete man and a complete woman, their own individual energy becomes awakened and active in the presence of the other; whatever lies hidden within each one's own self manifests fully. From this happening there is a hint whether a union of the complete man and complete woman can take place within. The first union is a union of two incomplete beings. Now the second phase of the work begins to bring together their third and fourth bodies.

The third body of the man is again male and the fourth female; the third body of the woman is again female and the fourth male. Now in the union of the third and the fourth only the male will remain within the male; his third body will become prominent. Within the female the female will remain prominent. Then the two complete females will merge into one, because now there will be no boundary between the two to separate them. The male body is required to keep them apart. Similarly, between the two male bodies a female body is required to keep a distance between them.

When the female of the first and second bodies meets the female of the third and fourth bodies, at the very instant of meeting they will merge into one. Then the woman achieves perfect femininity in double measure. No greater womanhood than this is possible, because after this there is no further growth of femininity. This will be the perfect feminine state. This is the perfect woman who has no desire even to meet the perfect man.

In the first completeness there was the enchantment of meeting a second complete person, and the meeting created more energy. Now that too is over. Now even meeting God will be meaningless in a sense. Within the man also both the males will merge into one. When the four bodies unite, what remains in the male is the male and what remains in the female is the female. From the fifth body onwards there is no male and no female.

Therefore, the happening that takes place in a man and a woman after the fourth plane will be different; it is bound to be. The happening is the same but their attitude towards it is different. The man will still be aggressive and the woman will still be surrendered. After the attainment of the fourth body a woman lets go completely; not even an iota will be withheld in her surrender. This surrender, this letting go, will take her to the journey of the fifth plane where a woman is no longer a woman because in order to remain a woman it is necessary to keep something back.

In fact, we are what we are because we hold back a little of ourselves. If we were to let ourselves go completely we would become something we never were before. But there is a holding back in one's being all the time. If a woman gives in completely even to an ordinary man, there will be a crystallisation within her and she will go beyond the fourth body. This is why women have many a time crossed the fourth body with their love for very ordinary men.

The word *sati* has no other esoteric meaning. *Sati* does not mean a woman whose eyes do not fall on another man; *sati* means that woman who no longer has the female factor left within her to look at another man.

If a woman becomes so completely surrendered in love to even an ordinary man, she does not have to go through this long journey. All her four bodies will combine and stand at the doorstep of the fifth. Therefore, it was the women who went through this experience who said, "The husband is God." This does not mean that they actually thought that the husband was God; it means that the doors of the fifth opened for them through the medium of the husband. There was no mistake in what they said; what they said was absolutely correct. What another meditator obtains through great effort she obtains with ease through her love. The love for one person alone takes her to that state.

Take the case of Sita: she belongs to the category of women whom we call *sati*. Now Sita's surrender is unique. From the point of view of surrender she is perfect; her surrender is total. Ravana is an incomplete man whereas Sita is a complete woman. The radiance of a complete woman is such that an incomplete man cannot dare to touch her. He cannot even set eyes on her, and only an incomplete woman can be seen in a sexual way by him.

When a man approaches a woman sexually the man is not entirely responsible. This incompleteness of the woman is also inevitably responsible. When a man sexually touches a woman in a crowd he is only half responsible. The woman who invites it is equally responsible. She provokes it, invites it, and because she is passive her aggression goes unnoticed. Since the man is active it is very evident that he touched her. But we cannot see the other side's invitation to it.

Ravana could not even raise his eyes toward Sita and Ravana held no meaning for Sita. Yet after the war Rama insisted on the fire test from Sita to confirm her purity. Sita did not resist. Had she refused to go through the test she would have lost her position as *sati*. She could have insisted that they both pass through the fire test, because if she was alone with another man Rama too was roaming the woods alone—and who knows what women he may have met!

But this question never arose in Sita's mind. She readily went through the fire test. Had she questioned Rama's authority even once she would have fallen from her position - because then the surrender would not have been total; there would have been something slightly lacking in it. And had she raised the question even once and then passed through the fire, she would have been burnt; she would not have gone unscathed. But her surrender was total. For her there was no other man. We, however, think it a miracle that she passed through the fire unharmed.

If an ordinary person also passes through fire while in a particular inner state, he will not burn. If in the state of hypnosis a man is told that fire will not burn him, he can walk on it and not be burnt.

An ordinary *fakir* walks on fire in a particular state of mind when the energy circuit is complete within himself. The energy circuit breaks with doubt. If a doubting thought crosses his mind even once, if he doubts that maybe he will be burnt, the circuit breaks and he is bound to get burnt. If two *fakirs* jump into the fire and seeing them you feel, "If these two can jump and not be affected, how can I burn?" then if you too jump into the fire, you also will not be affected by it. A whole line of people can thus pass through fire and not be burnt. The one who doubts will not dare enter the fire; he will stand aside. But the one who sees so many passing through unaffected thinks, "If so many are unharmed, why should the fire harm me?" So for this reason he can go through and the fire does not touch him.

If the circuit within us is complete, even fire has no means of touching us. So if fire did not affect Sita it is quite conceivable. After the fire test, when Rama turned her out of his kingdom, even then she did not question him. She had passed the fire test to prove her chastity. But Sita's surrender is so total, so complete, that for her there was no reason to question.

If a complete woman reaches a perfection of love for one person she will jump over the first four steps of spiritual practice. For a man it is very difficult because he does not have a surrendering mind. But it is interesting to know that even aggression can be perfect. However, for aggression to be perfect many things are involved and not you alone. In surrender, however, you alone are responsible for its perfection and other things do not matter at all. If I wish to surrender to someone I can do so entirely without telling him. But if I have to be aggressive toward someone, that someone will also be involved in the final result.

Therefore, in our talk about *shaktipat* you may have felt that there is something slightly lacking in women, that there is a slight difficulty as far as they are concerned. I had told you that there are rules of compensation in life. In the case of the woman, her shortcoming is made up for by her ability to surrender. A man is never able to love completely no matter how much he loves someone. The reason is that he is aggressive and has less ability to surrender. So if a woman's first four bodies become complete and merge into one unit she can surrender very easily at the fifth. And when a woman in this fourth state crosses these two steps of inner intercourse and becomes perfect, no power on earth can come in her way. Then no one except God exists for her. Actually, the one she loved in her first four bodies had also become God for her, but now, whatever is, is God.

There is a beautiful incident in Meera's life. Once she went to Vrindavan. There the priest of the great temple did not look at women, so women were not allowed inside that temple. Bells in hand, immersed in her Lord Krishna, Meera went right inside, however. The other people in the temple hastened to tell her that the temple was closed to women as the priest did not look at women. To this Meera said, "That is very strange. I was under the impression there was only one man in the world—Krishna. Who is this other man? Is there another man? I would like to see him."

They rushed to the priest and told him about Meera. When he heard all they had to say he came running to Meera, fell at her feet, and said, "It is meaningless to call her a woman for whom there is only one man. The matter of man and woman is finished for her. I touch your feet and ask forgiveness. Seeing ordinary women I looked upon myself as a man. But for a woman of your calibre my being a man has no meaning."

When a man reaches the fourth body he becomes a perfect man. He will have crossed the two steps toward attaining this perfection. From then onwards there is no woman for him; the word woman holds no meaning for him. Now he is only a force of aggressiveness, just as a woman who attains perfect womanhood in the fourth body becomes only the energy of surrender. Now they are only an energy of aggressiveness and an energy of surrender respectively. Now they no longer hold the name of man or woman; they are only energies.

Man's aggressiveness developed into various yoga practices and woman's surrender blossomed into various paths of *bhakti,* devotion. Surrender becomes *bhakti,* aggressiveness becomes yoga. Both male and female are the same; there is no difference between them now. The difference of man and woman is now merely external and applies only to the physical body. Now, whether the drop falls into the ocean or the ocean falls into the drop, the final result is the same. The drop of the man will jump into the ocean and merge with it. The drop of the woman will become an abyss and call upon the whole ocean to fill her. She will surrender and the whole ocean will drop into her.

Even now she is negative; she is completely a negativity. She is the womb that holds the entire ocean within itself. The entire energy of the universe will enter into her. Man, even at this stage, cannot be receptive. He still maintains the quality of strength, so he will take a jump and drown in the ocean. In the intimate depths of their beings their personalities will carry this male-female differentiation — right until the very end of the fourth body.

The realm of the fifth plane is absolutely different, however. There only the soul remains. There is no longer any discrimination based on sex, and henceforth, the journey is the same for all. Until the fourth there is a difference, and that too is only one of whether the drop falls in the ocean or the ocean into the drop. But the final outcome is the same. It makes no difference whether the drop falls in the ocean or the ocean into the drop. Until the last limit of the fourth body the difference is very apparent, however. There, if a woman wishes to jump into the ocean she will create difficulties for herself, and if a man wishes to surrender he will land himself in trouble. So you should beware of the possibility of such an error.

In one of Your discourses You had said that a prolonged intercourse leads to the formation of an electrical circuit between the man and the woman. What is this circuit, how is it formed and what are its uses in relation to the first four bodies? Also, in so far as meditation alone is concerned, what is the form of the above-mentioned happening?

As I said before, woman is half and so is man. Both are energies, both are electricity. The woman is the negative pole, the man the positive pole. Whenever the negative and positive poles of electricity meet and form a circuit light is created. This light is of various kinds: it may not be visible at all, it may be visible only sometimes, or it may be visible to some and invisible to others. But a circuit is formed all the same. But the union of man and woman is so momentary that no sooner is the circuit formed than it breaks. Therefore, there are methods and systems of prolonging intercourse. If intercourse exceeds half an hour the electrical circuit can be seen encircling the couple. Many pictures of this have been taken. There are many primitive tribes whose sexual union lasts for long; hence the circuit is formed.

Ordinarily it is difficult to find this energy circuit in the civilised world. The more tension-ridden the mind, the more momentary the intercourse. Ejaculation takes place quicker when the mind is tense. The greater the tension, the quicker the ejaculation, because a tension-ridden mind is not looking for intercourse but for release. In the West sex serves no greater purpose than a sneeze. A tension is thrown out, a load is unburdened. When the energy is thrown out a load is unburdened. When the energy is thrown out you feel dissipated. To relax is one thing, to feel dissipated is quite another. Relaxation means the energy is within and you are resting, and to feel dissipated means energy is thrown out and you lie exhausted. You are weakened with the loss of energy and you think you are relaxing.

So as tension increased in the West sex became a release from tension, a freedom from the pressure of an internal energy. There are thinkers in the West who are not ready to consider sex as being any more valuable than a sneeze. The nose tickles, you sneeze, and so the mind is relieved. In the West they are not ready to give sex any more recognition than this. They are correct also, because what they are doing with sex is no more than this.

In the East people are slowly coming to this point...because the East is also becoming tense. Somewhere, in some distant mountain cave, we might find a man who is not tense. He lives in a world of mountains and streams, trees and woods, and is as yet untouched by civilisation. There, even now, the energy circuit is formed during intercourse.

There are also *tantric* methods with which anyone can produce such an energy circuit. The experience of this circuit is wonderful because it is only when the energy circuit is formed that you get the feeling of oneness. This oneness is never experienced before the formation of this circuit. As soon as the circuit is formed the couple engaged in intercourse is no longer two separate entities. They become a flow of one energy, one power. Something is experienced as coming and going and revolving; the two separate entities disappear.

Depending upon the intensity of this circuit, the desire for intercourse will lessen and its interval will increase. It can happen that once the circuit is formed, for one full year there may not be any desire for repetition, because a fulfilment has happened.

Or take it this way: a man eats a meal and then vomits it. Then he will not get any satisfaction from the meal. Satiation happens not by eating food but by digesting it. Generally we feel that the act of eating brings satiation. It is not so; satiation only comes when the food is digested.

Intercourse is of two types: one that is of merely eating and another is that of digesting. What we generally know as intercourse is merely eating and vomiting, nothing is digested. If something is digested its satisfaction is long and deep. Absorption takes place only when the energy circuit is formed, however. The energy circuit indicates that the minds of the two partners have merged and become absorbed into one another. Now there are not two; they become one. There are two bodies but the energy within each has become one; the energy has jumped and intermingled.

This condition of sexual absorption leaves a deep state of satisfaction: this is what I mean. It is very useful for yoga and for the meditator. If such inner intercourse is possible for the meditator the need for intercourse becomes very much reduced. Then the intervening period leaves him free for his inner journey. Once the inner journey starts and the inner intercourse takes place with the woman or man within, the external woman becomes useless, the external man becomes useless.

For a householder the term *brahmacharya,* celibacy, means that his act of intercourse should be so fulfilling that it leaves years of *brahmacharya* in between. Once this period of *brahmacharya* is attained and the seeker sets out on the inward journey, the outer necessity for intercourse fades away.

I am saying that this is the case for a householder. For those initiated into *sannyas,* the traditional kind of *sannyas,* for those who have not accepted a householder's life, the meaning of *brahmacharya* is *antarmaithun,* sexual union between the inner male and female. For them there is a need for inner intercourse. Such a person will directly have to start finding a means for inner intercourse, or else he will shun the outer woman only in name while his mind will keep running, and he will lose more energy in his efforts to keep away from the outer woman than he would by intercourse.

So the path is a little different for the traditional *sannyasin*. The difference is only this: sexual union with the outer woman is the initial step for the householder; he then meets the inner woman in the second step, whereas the traditional *sannyasin* unites directly with the inner woman within himself. The first step is not for him.

Therefore, it is foolish in the traditional concept of *sannyas* to make anyone and everyone a *sannyasin*. Actually, initiation into traditional *sannyas* is only possible when we can look within the person to see whether his first body is in a state of readiness to meet the woman of his second body. If it is so, only then should the initiation into *brahmacharya* be granted; otherwise this will only bring about madness and nothing else.

But there are persons who go on initiating indiscriminately. There is one guru of a thousand *sannyasins,* another of two thousand, and they do not know what they are doing. Are those whom they initiate ready and fit for inner intercourse in meditative states? Not at all — they do not even know that there is anything like inner intercourse. This is why, whenever a traditional *sannyasin* comes to me, his most profound and intimate trouble is sex. Householders I meet have other troubles too, but I have yet to come across a traditional *sannyasin* whose trouble is anything but sex.

Sex is one of the many worries of a householder, but it is the one and only affliction of the traditional *sannyasin*. Therefore, his whole mind is centred around this one point. His guru shows him many remedies to save himself from the outer woman, but he has no idea of how a meditator can meet the woman within. Therefore, it becomes impossible to discard the outer woman. He can only make a show of shunning her — and it is very very difficult.

The bioenergy has to move somewhere. If it can go within, only then can it be prevented from flowing outwards. If it does not go in, it is bound to flow out. It makes no difference whether the woman is present in substance or in imagination; it can flow out with the help of an imaginary woman also. The same goes for women, but here again there is a little difference between the two which should be kept in mind.

Sex is not such a problem for a female seeker as for a male seeker. I am acquainted with many Jaina nuns, and for them sex does not pose a big question. The reason is that a woman's sex is passive. Once it is awakened it becomes a problem; if it is not awakened she can go through a lifetime and never feel that there is any problem.

A woman requires initiation — even in sex. Once a man takes a woman into sex the energy rises sharply within her. But if this does not happen she can remain a lifelong virgin. This is very easy for her because of her passive nature. Her own mind is non-aggressive; she can wait and wait indefinitely. For this reason I feel that it is dangerous to initiate a married woman unless she is taught to unite with the man within her.

A virgin girl can be initiated. She is in a better position than a boy. She can wait indefinitely until she is taken into sex, because she is not aggressive. And if there is no aggression from without, gradually the inner man will begin to unite with the outer woman. Her second body is a male body which is aggressive.

So inner intercourse is much easier for a woman than a man. Do you understand what I mean? The second body of a woman is male and this body is aggressive. Therefore, even if a woman does not find an outer man it does not matter to her. And if she does not experience sex from an outside source the man within will begin to be aggressive. Her etheric body will begin to invade her; then she will turn inward and become immersed in inner intercourse.

For a man inner intercourse is difficult, because his aggressive body is the first whereas his second body is female. This body cannot assert itself over the first. Only when the first body goes to it will it receive him.

These are the differences, and once they are understood we will have to change all our arrangements. If the householder succeeds in creating the electric circuit in intercourse it will be very helpful to him. The same energy circuit will be formed in the case of inner intercourse also. The energy circuit surrounds an ordinary man only at the time of ordinary intercourse. The same energy will surround the man who has united with his second body twenty-four hours a day. The circle of energy will become wider and wider at every plane.

No image was made of Buddha until five hundred years after his death, and this kind of phenomenon has happened many times throughout history. Instead an image of the bodhi tree was carved and was worshipped in the temples, but the place beneath the tree where Buddha was supposed to have sat was left vacant. Now those who study history and mythology are very much intrigued over why Buddha's image was not carved: why was Buddha symbolised by a tree? And why was his image then installed after five hundred years? Why was the place beneath the tree depicted as empty all that time? This is a mystery which neither the historian nor the mythologist can solve.

In fact, those who had observed Buddha very keenly stated that on observing him with one-pointed attention Buddha could not be seen: only the tree remained and the aura of the energy. His physical body disappeared. Now, for instance, if you observe me keenly I too will disappear and only the chair will remain. So those who saw him deeply claimed that Buddha could not be seen, but those who did not, claimed that he could be seen. However, the statement of the former was more authentic. For five hundred years the word of those who said that Buddha was never visible, and that there was only the tree and the empty place beneath it, was honoured. But this concept worked only as long as there were people who could see deeply. When this calibre of people began to diminish it became difficult to worship the tree alone without Buddha. Five hundred years after Buddha his idol was installed. This is a very interesting fact.

Those who saw Jesus deeply also could not see him; they could see only light. Those who saw Mahavira deeply could also see only light, and so it was with Krishna also. If people of this calibre are observed with full alertness only the light of the energy will be visible; no person as such will be seen there.

After every two bodies the vital energy increases. After the fourth body it attains a fullness. At the fifth body there is only energy. At the sixth body this energy will appear not separate but as one with the stars and the skies. At the seventh plane even this will disappear. First matter will disappear, then energy.

On which plane does the meditator reach the no-thought state? Are thoughts possible without identifying the consciousness with objects or is identity essential for thought?

The perfect no-thought state is attained in the fifth body but small glimpses begin from the fourth body. Thoughts continue in the fourth body but one begins to observe the gaps between two thoughts. Before the fourth there are thoughts and thoughts and only thoughts; we do not see the gap between the thoughts. In the fourth the intervals begin to appear and the emphasis changes. If you have observed gestalt images you will be able to understand this. Suppose there is a picture of a flight of steps: it can be so drawn that if you look attentively you will observe the steps going up; then if you look again you will see the steps coming down. But the most interesting part is that you cannot observe the steps going up and down simultaneously. You can see only one of the two. When you observe the second picture the first picture will have vanished.

We can make a picture in which two faces can be seen facing each other, complete with nose, eyes and beard. First it will appear as if two men are facing each other. Now paint the faces black leaving the intervening space white. Now you will say that there is a flower pot in this intervening space, and the nose and eyes become the outlines of the pot. You will not be able to see the pot and the two faces at one time. When you see the two faces the pot will not be seen; when the pot is observed the faces will vanish. No matter how hard you try to see them all together the gestalt will change its emphasis. When your emphasis shifts to the faces the pot will vanish; when the emphasis is on the pot the faces will vanish.

Up to the third body the gestalt of our mind has its emphasis on thought. Rama comes, so Rama is visible and his coming is visible. The empty space between Rama and his coming, or the empty space before Rama's coming and after Rama's going, is not visible to us. The emphasis is on Rama's coming; the intervening space is not observed. The change starts from the fourth body. All of a sudden it will strike you that Rama's coming is no longer very important. When Rama was not coming there was the empty space; when Rama has gone there is the empty space. The empty space begins to come within the focus of your mind: faces disappear; the pot becomes visible. And when your attention is on the empty space you cannot think.

You can do only one of the following two things: as long as you see thoughts you will think, but when you see the empty space you will be empty within. However, this will keep alternating in the fourth body. Sometimes you will see the two faces and sometimes the pot: that is, sometimes you will see thoughts and sometimes the gap. Silence will come and so will thoughts.

The difference between silence and emptiness is only this: silence means thoughts have not yet ended, but the emphasis is changed. The consciousness has shifted from thought and takes pleasure in silence, but thought still remains. It is only that the consciousness has shifted: the attention has shifted from thoughts. Then the attention is on silence. But thought returns sometimes — and when it manages to draw your attention, again silence is lost and thought begins.

In the last moments of the fourth body the mind will keep alternating between the two. On the fifth plane all thoughts will be lost and only silence will remain. This is not the ultimate silence, because this silence exists in comparison to thought and speech. Silence means not speaking; emptiness means a state where there is neither silence nor speech. Neither the faces remain nor the flower pot; only the blank paper. Now if you are asked whether the faces are there or the flower pot, you will say neither.

The state of no-thought occurs in its totality in the fifth body. At the fourth we get glimpses of this state; it will be observed off and on between two thoughts. At the fifth the no-thought state will become evident and thoughts will disappear.

Now the second part of your question is, "Is identification necessary for the formation of thoughts, or can thoughts occur without any identification?" Up to the third body identification and thought come simultaneously. There is your identification and there is the coming of thought: there is no interval between the two. Your thoughts and you are one — not two. Now when you are angry it is wrong to say that you are angry. It would be more correct to say that you have become anger, because in order to be angry it should also be possible for you not to be angry. For instance, I say, "I am moving my hand." Then suppose you say, "Now stop your hand," and I say, "That is not possible; the hands keep moving" — then you may well question what I mean when I say, "I am moving my hand." I should say, "The hand is moving," because if I am moving the hand I should be able to stop it. If I cannot stop my hand I cannot claim to be its owner. It has no meaning. Because you cannot stop your thoughts, your identification with them is complete up to the third body. Up to there you are thought.

So up to the third body, by hitting someone's thoughts we are hitting the person himself. If you tell such a person, "What you say is wrong," he will never feel that what he says is wrong; he will feel he is wrong. Quarrels and fights take place not because of a statement but because of the I — because there is complete identification. To attack your thoughts is to attack you. Even if you say, "It is all right if you do not agree with my way of thinking," within you will feel that you have been opposed. Many times it happens that the idea in question is left aside and we begin to fight for it merely because we put forth the view and not for any other reason. You support it merely because you have put it forth as your viewpoint — because you have declared it as your scripture, your principle, your argument.

Until the third body there is no distance between you and your thoughts. You are the thought. In the fourth, wavering begins. You will begin to get glimpses of the fact that you are something apart and your thoughts are something apart. But so far you are unable to stop your thoughts, because deep within the roots the association still exists. Above on the branches you feel the difference. You sit on one branch and the thoughts on the other and you see they are not you. But deep within you and thoughts are one. Therefore, it seems that thoughts are separate, and it also seems that if my association with them is broken thoughts will stop. But they do not stop. At some deeper level the association with thoughts will continue.

Changes begin to take place on the fourth plane. You begin to get a vague notion of thoughts being different and you being different. You still cannot proclaim this, however, and the thought process is still mechanical. You cannot stop your thoughts, nor can you bring them about. If I can say to you, "Stop anger and show that you are the master," it can also be said, "Bring about anger and prove that you are the master." You will ask, "How can this be done? We cannot bring about anger." The moment you can you are its master. Then you can stop it at any moment. When you are the master the process of bringing on anger and stopping it are both in your hands. If you can bring on anger you can stop it also.

It is also interesting to note that stopping it is a little difficult, but bringing it on is easier. So if you want to be the master first begin by bringing on anger, because this is easier. In the situation of bringing it on you are tranquil, but in the situation of having to stop it you are already angry and so you are not even aware of yourself. Then how will you stop it? Therefore, it is always easier to start the experiment by bringing on anger rather than by stopping it. For instance, you begin to laugh but then you find that you cannot stop laughing; it is difficult. But if you are not laughing and you want to bring on laughter you can do it in a minute or two. Then you will know the secret of laughter — from where it comes and how — and then you will know the secret of stopping it also, and it can be stopped.

At the fourth plane you will begin to see that you are separate and thoughts are separate; that you are not your thoughts. Therefore, whenever the no-thought state occurs — as I said before — the witness also comes, and wherever there are thoughts the witness will be lost. In the intervals between thoughts, that is, in the gaps between thoughts, you will realise your separate identity from the thoughts. Then there is no association between you and the thoughts. But even then you will be a helpless observer. You will not be able to do much, though all efforts are to be made in the fourth body only.

So I have defined two possibilities of the fourth body — one that is natural and the other that is obtained through meditations. You will be alternating between these two. The first possibility is thought and the second is understanding. The moment you attain the second potential of the fourth body—*vivek,* or understanding — the fourth body will drop as well as the identification of consciousness with mind. When you attain the fifth body two things will drop: the fourth body and this identification.

In the fifth body you can bring on thoughts or not bring them on, as you wish. For the first time thoughts will be a means and will not depend on identification. If you wish to bring on anger you can bring on anger; if you wish to bring on love you can do so. If you do not wish to bring on anything you are at liberty not to do so. If you wish to stop anger that is half-formed you can order it to stop. Whatever thought you want to bring will come to you, and that which you do not wish to bring will not have any power to invade your mind.

There are many such instances in the life of Gurdjieff. People considered him a peculiar man. If two people were sitting before him, he would look toward one with the utmost anger and toward the other with the utmost love. So quickly would he change his expression that the two would carry away different reports about him. Though both had met him together, one would say, "He looks like a dangerous man," while the other would say, "How full of love he is." This is very easy on the fifth plane. Gurdjieff was beyond the understanding of people around him. He could instantly bring any kind of expression to his face. There was no difficulty for him in this, but there was difficulty for others.

The reason behind this is that in the fifth body you are the master of yourself; you can bring about any feeling you please. Then anger, love, hatred, forgiveness, all your thoughts, become mere playthings; therefore, you can relax when you please. To relax after play is very easy but to relax from life is difficult. If I am only playing at anger I will not sit in anger after you leave the room. If I am playing the game of talking I will no longer be talking after you go. But if talking is my life-breath, then I shall keep on talking even after you leave. Even if nobody listens, I will listen. I will keep on talking because that is my very life; it is not a play after which I can relax. It is my very life, it has taken hold of me. So such a man will talk even at night. In dreams also he will gather a crowd and speak. In dreams also he will quarrel, he will fight and do all that he has been doing in the daytime. He will keep doing this all the twenty-four hours, because that is his life, that is his very existence.

Your identification breaks in the fifth body. Then for the first time you are at peace, you are empty, by your own free will. But when the need arises you think also. So in the fifth body, for the first time you will be putting your power of thinking to use. It would be better to say that before the fifth body thoughts make use of you; after the fifth you make use of thoughts. Before that it is not correct to say, "I think." In the fifth body you also come to know that your thoughts are not your own: thoughts of people around you also enter your mind. However, you are not even aware that the thoughts you think to be your own could be someone else's.

A Hitler is born and the whole of Germany is permeated with his thoughts, but each German feels it to be his own thought. A very dynamic person diffuses his thoughts into the minds of others and they become echoes of the same. This dynamism is as serious as it is deep. For example, it is two thousand years since Jesus died. The thought waves that he left in the world still grasp the minds of Christians who think that these are their own thoughts. The same is the case with Mahavira, Buddha, Krishna and others. Any kind of dynamic person's thoughts, whether they are of a good person or an evil one, can catch hold of the human mind. The hold of Tamerlane and Genghis Khan upon our minds has not yet been released, nor has the hold of Krishna and Rama. Their thought waves move forever around us, and you are able to catch those thought waves that are conducive to your particular state of mind.

It always happens that a man who is very good in the morning becomes evil by noon. In the morning he moves in the waves of Rama; in the afternoon he may be caught by the waves of Genghis Khan. Receptivity and time cause the difference. The beggar always comes to beg in the morning, because the effect of evil vibrations is at the minimum at the time of the rising sun. As the day progresses and as the sun gets tired of its long journey in the skies the influence gains strength, so the beggar has no hope of charity from others in the evening. If a beggar asks a man early in the morning to give two rupees he will not be able to refuse right away; as the day progresses it is more difficult to say yes to the beggar. By evening the man is tired with the day's work so now he is fully prepared to refuse. The condition of his mind is quite different now; so also is the entire atmosphere of his surroundings. So the thoughts we feel to be our own also do not belong to us.

This you will experience only in the fifth body, and you will be surprised to see the way thoughts come and go. The thought comes, then it goes; it catches hold of you, then it leaves you alone. There are a thousand kinds of thoughts — and very contradictory ones too; therefore, there is confusion in our minds. Every single person is confused. If thoughts were entirely yours there would be no question of confusion. Your one hand catches hold of Genghis Khan and the other catches hold of Krishna, so there is bound to be confusion. Both of these sets of thought waves lie in wait for you, and as soon as you show your readiness they enter within. They are present all around you.

All this you will come to know when your identification with thoughts breaks completely. The biggest change will be that until this time you will have thoughts, but now you will have thinking. There is a difference between the two. Thoughts are atomic: they come and go and they are always alien. To say that thoughts are always alien is quite correct. Thinking is ours, but thoughts are alien. This thinking will start within you after the fifth body. Then you will be able to think; you will no longer be merely collecting the thoughts of others. Therefore, the thinking of the fifth body is never a burden upon you, because it is your own. This thinking that is born in the fifth body may be called wisdom or understanding or whatever you like to call it.

At the fifth plane you have your own intuition, your own understanding, your own intelligence. At the fifth the influence of all outside thoughts will end, and in this sense you will be the master of yourself; you will attain your being; you will become your self. Now you will have your own thoughts, your own power of thinking, your own eyes and your own vision. After this only what you wish will come to you; what you do not wish will never come near you. You can think just what you want to think; other thoughts cannot invade you. Now you will be the master. Here the question of identification does not arise.

In the sixth body thinking is also not required. Thoughts are necessary up to the fourth body; thinking and wisdom are necessary in the fifth. On the sixth plane even these end, because there they are not required at all. You become cosmic; you become one with the *Brahman*. Now there is no other.

In fact, all thoughts are always related to the other. The thoughts before the fourth body are unconscious links with others. The thoughts of the fifth body are conscious links but they are still related to others. After all, why are thoughts necessary? They are required only to establish a relationship with others. Until the fourth they are unconscious links; at the fifth they are conscious links. But at the sixth no "other" remains for establishing links. All relatedness is finished; only the cosmic remains. I and thou are now one. Now there is no place, no reason for thought to exist.

The sixth is the *Brahman,* the cosmic reality, where there are no thoughts. In the *Brahman* there are no thoughts; therefore, it can be said that in the *Brahman* there is knowing. Actually, the thoughts which exist up to the fourth body are unconscious thoughts; they contain a deep ignorance. It shows that we need thoughts to fight with this self-ignorance. At the fifth there is knowing of the self within, but we are still ignorant about that which is other to us; the other is still there for us. Therefore, there is the need to think in the fifth body. At the sixth there is no inside or outside, there is no I or thou, there is no this or that. Now there is no distance to justify thoughts. Now what is, is. Therefore, at the sixth there is only knowing, not thoughts.

At the seventh knowing also does not exist, because he who knew is no more and that which could be known is no more. So even knowing is not on the seventh plane. The seventh plane is not knowing-less, but beyond knowing. If you like you can call it a state of ignorance also. That is why it is always the case that a man of ultimate consciousness and an absolutely ignorant person seem identical, because their behaviour is often similar. This is why there is always a great similarity between a small child and an old man who has attained enlightenment: they are not actually the same but superficially they seem alike. Sometimes an enlightened sage acts in a childlike way; sometimes in the behaviour of a child we get a glimpse of saintliness. Sometimes an enlightened one looks like an absolutely ignorant person, an absolute fool, and it would seem that no one could be as foolish as he. But the sage has gone beyond knowledge and the child is still below knowledge. The similarity lies in the fact that they both are outside of knowledge.

In which body is that obtained which You refer to as samadhi?

Actually there are many types of *samadhi*. One *samadhi* will take place between the fourth and the fifth body. Remember, *samadhi* is not a happening of one plane; it always happens between two planes, it is the twilight period. One may just as well ask whether twilight belongs to the day or the night. Twilight belongs neither to the day nor the night, it is a happening between day and night. So is *samadhi*.

The first *samadhi* occurs between the fourth and the fifth planes. This *samadhi* leads to self-realisation, *atma gyan*. One *samadhi* occurs between the fifth and the sixth planes; this in turn leads to *Brahma gyan* — cosmic knowing. The *samadhi* that occurs between the sixth and the seventh planes is the *samadhi* that leads to *nirvana*. So generally speaking there are these three *samadhis* that occur between the last three *shariras,* the last three bodies.

There is one false *samadhi* that has to be recognized also. It occurs in the fourth body, but is not *samadhi* though it seems like it. In Japan the Zen Buddhist term for it is *satori*. It is false *samadhi*. It is that state which a painter or a sculptor or a musician reaches when he is completely immersed in his art; he experiences a great bliss. This is a happening on the fourth, the psychic plane. If when looking at the morning sun or listening to a melody or looking at a dance or looking at the opening of a flower the mind is completely drowned in the happening, a false *samadhi* takes place. Such a false *samadhi* can be brought about by hypnosis or false *shaktipat*. Such a false *samadhi* can be brought about by alcohol and drugs like marijuana, lsd, mescaline, hashish.

So there are four types of *samadhi*. Actually there are three authentic *samadhis* and they happen in a sequence. The fourth is an absolutely false experience that appears like *samadhi*. In this there is no actual experience — only a feeling of *samadhi* that is misleading. Many people are misled by *satori*. This false *samadhi* occurs in the fourth — the psychic plane. It is not the transitional process between the fourth and the fifth plane; it happens well within the fourth body. The three authentic *samadhis* occur outside the bodies in a transitional period when we pass on from one plane to another. One *samadhi* is a door, a passage.

Between the fourth and the fifth bodies happens the first authentic *samadhi*. One attains self-relaxation. We can get stuck here. Usually people stop at the false *samadhi* in the fourth body because it is so easy. We have to spend very little energy, making no effort at all, and it is obtained just like that. The majority of meditators, therefore, stagnate here. The first real *samadhi,* which takes place on the journey from the fourth to the fifth body, is very difficult; and the third, from the sixth to the seventh, is the most difficult of all. The name chosen for the third *samadhi* is *vajrabhed* — piercing of the thunderbolt. It is the most difficult one because it is a transition from being into non-being; it is a jump from life into death; it is a plunge from existence into non-existence.

So there are actually three *samadhis*. The first you may call *atma samadhi,* the second *brahma samadhi,* and the last *nirvana samadhi*. The very first and false *samadhi* you may call *satori*. This is the one you should guard against, because it is very easily attainable.

Another method to test the validity of the *samadhi* is that if it takes place within the plane it is false; it must take place between the planes. It is the door; it has no business to be inside the room. It must be outside the room, adjoining the next room.

Why has the serpent been chosen as a symbol of kundalini? Please explain all the reasons. In the symbol used by Theosophy, a coiled serpent with his tail in the mouth is shown. In the symbol of the Ramakrishna Mission, the tail of the serpent touches the hood. Please explain the meaning of these.

The serpent symbol for the *kundalini* is very apt and meaningful. Perhaps, there is no better symbol than this. Therefore, not only the *kundalini* but also the serpent has undergone a great many travels in the symbol form. Nowhere in the world is there a religion in which the serpent has not been depicted somewhere. This is because the serpent has many qualities that tally with the *kundalini*.

The very first thing that occurs to the mind at the mention of the serpent is the motion of sliding — crawling. The very first experience of *kundalini* is that of something within. You feel as if something has moved within, just as a serpent moves. Another thing that comes to mind with the very notion of a serpent is that it has no legs, yet it moves. It has no means of movement — it is sheer energy — yet it travels. The third thing that comes to the mind is that when a serpent sits it forms coils. When the *kundalini* lies asleep within us it too rests in the same manner.

When a long thing has to accommodate itself in a small place it has to coil up; there is no other way for it. A very big power is seated on a very small centre so it can only coil itself up. Now when the snake gets up it unwinds the coils one by one; as it rises the coil unwinds. In the same way we feel *kundalini* unwinding within when the *kundalini* energy rises within us.

The serpent sometimes in playfulness catches its tail in its mouth. This holding of the tail in the mouth is also a significant symbol. This is a valuable symbol and many recognised it as such. It is valuable because it suggests that when the *kundalini* is fully awakened it will become circular and begin to form its own circuit within. Its hood will catch hold of its own tail; the serpent will become a circle. Now when a symbol is made to depict male *sadhana,* male spiritual practice, it will catch the tail by its mouth; it will be aggressive. If the symbol is arrived at by female *sadhana,* female spiritual practices, the tail will just be touching the hood. This is a surrendering tail — one that is not held in the mouth. This is the only difference and no more.

The hood of the serpent also became purposeful. The tail is very narrow whereas the hood is very broad. When the *kundalini* awakens fully it reaches up to the *sahasrar*. It opens and spreads like the hood of the serpent; it expands enormously. It is as if many flowers bloom in it. Then its tail becomes very small.

When the serpent stands up it is a wonderful sight; it stands erect on the tip of its tail. It is almost a miracle. The serpent is an invertebrate, a creature with no bones, and yet it can perform this act. It can only be with the help of the vital energy within it, because there is no other substantial means for it to stand erect. It stands by the strength of its own will-power; it has no material strength to rely on. So it is also when the *kundalini* awakens: it has no physical support; it is an immaterial energy.

These were the reasons why the serpent was chosen as a symbol. There are many other reasons too. For instance, it is an innocent creature; hence, the Hindu god Shiva — who is also called "the innocent Shiva" — carries it on his head. On its own the serpent never troubles anybody, but if it is disturbed it can be very dangerous. The same applies to the *kundalini*. It is a very innocent power; it does not trouble you on its own. But if you disturb it the wrong way you will find yourself in trouble. It can prove very dangerous. So the symbol of a serpent reminds us that it is dangerous to disturb the *kundalini* in the wrong way. Keeping all this in mind, there was no other symbol more apt than that of the serpent.

All over the world the snake stands as the symbol of wisdom. Jesus has said, "Be clever and intelligent like a snake and as innocent as a dove." The snake is a very intelligent creature — very alert, very watchful and very sharp and quick. These are all its qualities. The *kundalini* is also like this. You reach the ultimate peak of wisdom through it; it is very swift, and also very powerful.

In the old days, when this symbol was chosen for the *kundalini,* perhaps, there was nothing better than the serpent. Even now there is nothing better. Perhaps, in the future there may be a new symbol - like the rocket. Some future concept may grasp the *kundalini* as being like the rocket. Its journey is the same; it travels from one sky to another, from one planet to another, and there is a void in between. It can become a symbol. The age decides the symbol.

This symbol was chosen when man was very close to the animal kingdom. All our symbols of those times have been taken from animals, because that was all that our knowledge consisted of so we tried to find symbols in them. The serpent was thus the most apt symbol to define the *kundalini*.

In those days we could not say that *kundalini* is like electricity; when we talk today we can say so. Five thousand years ago *kundalini* could not be talked about in terms of electricity because there was no notion of electricity. But the snake has the quality of electricity. This is hard for us to believe because many of us have no experience of the snake. We may have no experience of the *kundalini* whatsoever, but we hardly have any experience of snakes either. The serpent is a myth for us.

Recently a survey was taken in London and it was found that seven hundred thousand children had never seen a cow. Now these children who have not seen a cow cannot possibly have any idea of a snake. So their whole way of thinking and reflecting — and their symbols — will be quite different.

Now the serpent is obsolete: it is no longer an important part of our life. Once upon a time it was very near to us; it was our neighbour and was with us all the twenty-four hours of the day. It was then that man noticed its agility, its intelligence, its movements, and the ease with which it carried itself about. It was then that man realised also how dangerous a creature it could be. There are stories of a serpent guarding an infant, and it is so innocent .... There are instances when it has bitten the most fierce person and killed him, so dangerous it can be. So both of these possibilities are in it.

When man was very close to the serpent he must have watched it closely. The subject of *kundalini* also began at about the same time, and both the serpent and the *kundalini* were found similar in their qualities. But all symbols are meaningful, and if they have come to us through the ages there is a suitability, a rhythm in them. But now it is bound to break. The symbol of the serpent will not last long. We shall not be able to call the *kundalini* serpent power, because now where is the poor serpent? It is no longer our neighbour; we have no connection with it. We do not even see him on the roads. So as we have no connection with it whatsoever, this question arises. It could never arise before when it was the only symbol.

It is said that when the kundalini awakens it eats the flesh and drinks the blood. What does that mean?

There is a meaning to this. This description is almost literally true. Actually, when the *kundalini* arises many transformations take place within the body. Whenever a new energy arises in the body its old composition undergoes a complete change. It is bound to change; the body functions in so many unknown ways of which we are not conscious. For example, take the case of a miser. Miserliness is a quality of the mind, but his body will also become a miser. His body will begin to collect those substances that may be required by it in the future. It will keep on accumulating without any reason until it reaches a point where it becomes a harassment and a discomfort.

Now let us consider another man who is a coward. His body will gather all the elements that are conducive to fear. Suppose the body wants to tremble in fear and it does not have the necessary requirements—what will it do? You demand fear from the body and it does not have the necessary glands and hormones: what will it do? So the body keeps a ready store as it knows your requirements. The body of a fearful man gathers glands of fear to facilitate his indulgence in fear. The man who perspires with fear will have very strong perspiration glands; he has a capacity to perspire profusely. This arrangement is absolutely necessary because his demands can be many in the course of a single day. So the body stores things according to the requirements of our mind—and more.

When the mind changes the body changes also. When the *kundalini* rises there will be a complete change in your body. In that transformation your flesh may decrease and so also your blood, but it will decrease strictly to your requirements. So the body will be completely transformed. Only as much flesh and blood as is necessary for the body will remain; the rest will be burnt away. Then only will you feel light; then only will you be able to fly in the inner sky. This will be the difference.

What has been said is correct. The meditator has to have a special diet and a special arrangement for living, or else he will find himself in difficulties. When the *kundalini* rises a lot of heat is produced within because it is an electric force; it is an energy that is of a very high voltage. Just as I told you that the serpent is a symbol of *kundalini,* fire too is a symbol of *kundalini* in some places. This too is a very good symbol.

So the *kundalini* will burn like fire within you and the flames will rise high. A lot of things will burn in this. A certain dryness can result from the awakening of the *kundalini*. Therefore, the personality should be very harmonious and some channels of juicy qualities should be developed. For instance, take an angry person: if his *kundalini* awakens he will find himself in difficulty. He is a dry and coarse person, so if a fire should burn within him he will be in trouble. A loving person has a deep chemical harmony. There is a smoothness of chemical harmony within him. He will not be adversely affected by the awakening of the *kundalini*.

Whatever has been said has been said with regard to all these details. Things have been put rather roughly because the art of expression in the old days was not very developed and the approach was raw. So what has been said is very true: the flesh will burn and so will the blood and marrow, because you will change completely; you are going to be an entirely new person. All of your patterns, your composition, have to undergo a change. The meditator has to keep this in mind and prepare himself accordingly.

9

OCCULT DEPTHS OF KUNDALINI AND SPIRITUALITY

In the Nargol meditation camp You said that the practices of yoga—asanas, pranayamas, mudras and bandhas—were discovered in the state of meditation. In different states of meditation, different postures are formed by the body from which the depth of meditation of the meditator could be told. Conversely, can the same inner state be brought about by forming the necessary postures? In that case, can meditation be attained by the use of various asanas, pranayamas, mudras and bandhas? What is their use and significance?

First came the experience of meditation. With the experience of meditation it was found that the body assumed many postures. Actually, whenever the mind is in a particular state the body takes an appropriate corresponding posture. For instance, when you are filled with love your face, your expression, is one way, and when you are angry your expression becomes altogether different. In anger you grind your teeth and clench your fists and the body is ready for fight or flight. When you are in a forgiving mood the eyes are soft and the palms of the hand open. When a man is filled with forgiveness his fists will never clench. Just as clenching the fist is a preparation to fight, opening the fist and spreading out the palm is an indication of freedom from the urge to fight; it is an assurance of protection. To clench the fist is to frighten the other person.

The nature of the body is that it works in accordance with the state of mind. The body follows the mind: it always follows behind. So ordinarily we know what a man will do in anger and what he will do in love—also what he will do in a state of trust. But we do not know how he will react to the deeper states of mind.

When deep states are created within the mind a great deal takes place in the body also. Various *mudras* (gestures) and also many *asanas* (postures) happen that tell of the changes within. In fact, the *asanas* are formed at the time of preparation for particular inner states. *Mudras* are formed later and they give information about a person's inner state.

When changes occur within, the body has to find an equivalent adjustment to the inner changes. When the *kundalini* awakens within, the body will have to assume all kinds of unusual positions to make way for the energy. The spine will bend itself in many ways in order to allow the energy to ascend. The head also takes different positions when the *kundalini* awakens. The body assumes such postures as we have never taken before. It is just like when we are awake the body takes an erect position and when we sleep the body has to lie down—it cannot stand or sit.

Now suppose there is a man who has not known what it is to sleep since he was born: he will never lie down. If after thirty years he wants to fall asleep he will lie down for the first time. For the first time the condition of his mind will have changed in this respect and he will go to sleep. However, he will be very much intrigued by the new posture, as his body has never before assumed it. Up to now he used to sit, stand, walk, but never did he lie down. Now he has to lie down so that the necessary conditions of sleep can take place within him. When the body is lying down the mind finds it easier to slip into a particular condition. But different people have different ways of lying down because the state of mind of each person is different.

For instance, a man from a tribal area will not put a pillow under his head, but for a civilised person it is impossible to sleep without one. A tribal person does so little thinking that the flow of blood to his head is much less. For sleep it is essential that the flow of blood toward the head be as little as possible. If it is too much you will not be able to sleep. If the nerves of the brain do not relax it will be difficult for you to relax; the blood will keep on flowing to the brain. Then you add one more pillow and then another. The more educated and civilised a person is, the more he is cultured, the greater the number of pillows that he requires under his head. The neck should be almost vertical to prevent the flow of blood toward the brain.

The posture of the body corresponds to one's state of mind. So with the awakening of the energy within and its movements in several ways *asanas* begin to form. The different *chakras* also take the body into different asanas. Thus, various postures are formed. As a particular state begins to form within, the expressions of your hands, face and eyes change. This happens in meditation. As a result, the reverse has also come into man's attention: that is, when performing these *asanas* is it possible to go into meditation? It is necessary to understand this.

In meditation these processes take place; yet they are not inevitable. In other words, all meditators do not pass through the same body processes. One condition has to be born in mind: every meditator's state of body and mind is different from the states of body and mind of others—therefore, all will not pass through the same *asanas*. For instance, if the flow of blood is less toward the head of one meditator and if a greater flow is required for the awakening of the *kundalini,* he will at once without knowing, go into *shirshasana,* the headstand posture. All meditators will not go into this *asana* because the rate of the flow of blood is different in each; each one has different requirements. So *asanas* will form according to the need of each meditator.

When we ourselves select *asanas* and practise them, then we do not know which particular *asana* is useful or necessary for us. *Asanas* can be harmful as well as helpful. If they are not required in the case of a particular meditator they can prove harmful—if they are needed they will be of help. One difficulty is that this is an uncertain thing. Another difficulty is that when something is happening within and simultaneously something begins to happen outwardly as well, then the energy will move outwardly. When we perform an act from the outside it may remain nothing more than a physical performance.

Now as I said, in anger the fists clench automatically. But it is not necessarily the case that you can bring on anger by clenching your fists. We can put on an act of anger while there is no anger whatsoever within. Yet if we want to provoke anger within, clenching of fists could be helpful, but we cannot say for sure that anger will result. If we have to choose between clenching and not clenching the fists the possibility of bringing on anger is definitely more with a clenched fist. This little help is possible.

When a person is in a state of tranquillity his hands will take on the necessary *mudra*. But if a person practises the formation of this *mudra* of the hands it cannot be said for certain that his mind will attain peace. Yet particular states of the body help the mind to be peaceful. The body will show its readiness to cooperate; then it is left to the mind to do the needful. But changing the body does not mean that the mind will change, and the reason is that the state of mind precedes the state of the body. That is why when the mind changes the body follows suit, but an initial change in the body can at best create a possibility of a change in the mind. It is not a certainty.

So there is always the danger of delusion. A man may keep on performing *asanas* and *mudras* and think he has done everything; such cases have happened. For thousands of years people have been doing *asanas* and *mudras* thinking that they were practising yoga. Then gradually the concept of meditation was lost in yoga. By the words yoga *sadhana,* what comes to mind is *asanas, pranayamas,* etcetera. If you ask someone what yoga is he will think of *asanas, pranayamas,* and so on. Therefore, I always insist that if the requirements of a meditator are properly understood certain body positions can prove helpful to him. But the result is not certain. This is why I am always in favour of working from within and not from without.

If something begins from within we can understand its meaning. Suppose a meditator sits in meditation and I feel that inwardly he wants to burst out crying but he is holding it back. I can see that if he cries for ten minutes he will also begin to move and catharsis will take place. However, he is afraid that he may burst out crying so he stops himself. Now if he is told not to stop himself but to cry, he will at first pretend to cry. But within two or three minutes it will become authentic as the impulse to cry was pushing to break out from within. The process of crying will break the barrier and what was to flow out will do so.

Another meditator feels like dancing but he holds himself back. If we tell him to dance, at first he will only be acting: as yet the dance will not have come from within. Once he begins to dance it will give the dance an opportunity to break out. Soon this will start and the dance within will merge into the dance without. But if there is no cause for dance within him and we tell the meditator to dance, he will keep on dancing but nothing will happen.

So many things have to be considered. There are many many conditions to all that I have told you. If you keep these in mind you will understand. If you do not want to be burdened with all this, the best way is to start from within and let things happen spontaneously. Do not stop the outer happening, do not fight with it. Then things will happen of themselves.

In the meditation experiments You are presently conducting, what are the physical and psychic differences brought about by sitting or standing for the experiment?

It makes a great difference. As I told you before, deep within every condition of the body is connected with a particular state of mind that corresponds with it. If we tell a man to remain awake when he is lying down it will be difficult for him to do so; if we tell him to be alert when he is standing this will be easy. If we tell him to sleep when he is standing it will be difficult; if we tell him to sleep when he is lying down it will be easy.

So there is a double process in which there is the fear that the meditator may fall asleep or become drowsy. If he stands this will help to dispel this fear. If he stands the possibility of drowsiness is less.

The second part of the experiment is the witnessing attitude—awareness. Initially it is difficult to maintain awareness lying down. Later on it is easy. It is always easy to maintain witnessing when you stand. The initial process of hypnosis, which will take you into a trance instead, is very much reduced by standing up.

There are two or three things more. When you stand the movements of the body are free; when you lie down your movements will not be so free. When you sit half the body will not be able to participate at all. Suppose your legs want to dance and you are sitting, then the legs cannot dance. You will not even know what they need because the feet have no way of expressing themselves. There are subtle hints which we fail to catch. If you are standing the feet will begin lifting themselves and you will know they want to dance. But if you are sitting this hint is not possible to be conveyed.

Actually, the tradition of sitting for meditation was specifically meant to suppress all the resulting movements of the body. *Siddhasana, padmasana* and *sukhasana* had to be practised extensively before meditation was taught in order that the body movements could be stopped. So the possibility of the energy rising within is there from the beginning. A great deal happens as a result. You feel to dance, sing, jump, run. These emotional actions are always associated with madness. Mad persons cry, laugh, dance or jump. As the meditator does the same he will, therefore, appear mad.

Not to appear mad in the society, *siddhasana, padmasana* and other sitting postures were intensely practised in order that the body would be in full control. Then the meditator would not look mad to the world. Now the sitting postures of *padmasana, sukhasana* and *siddhasana* are such that they cause your legs to become stiff. Your weight is greater near the ground while away from the ground it becomes lesser. Your bottom becomes heavy like a temple or a pyramid: broad at the bottom, narrow at the top. Then the possibility of movement is very minimal—almost nil.

Maximum movement is possible when you stand—when there is nothing that keeps you fixed. When you cross your legs and sit you form an immovable base. A large part of your body is fixed by gravity which then catches hold of it. Then you place your hand in such a way that the possibility of movement is minimised. The spine too is kept straight and fixed. Before you would be allowed to go into meditation this type of *asana* first had to be perfected over a long practice period.

According to my approach the matter is just the opposite. In my viewpoint there is not much fundamental difference between us and those who are mad. We are all suppressed madmen; ours is a suppressed insanity. You can say that we are insane in a normal way or that we are "normally insane." There is so much in common between us and the insane. Those who go a little further in their insanity find themselves in trouble, but insanity lies within all of us and it tries to find its own outlets.

When you are angry you are temporarily in madness. At such a time you do things you would never dream of doing when you are conscious. You shout abuses, throw stones, break furniture. You can even jump from the roof; you can do anything. If an insane person does these things we can understand, but when a "normal" person does this we merely say that he was angry. Now this was the same "normal" man, and if these things were not within him they would not have come out. All this is inside of us and we are all guarding it. My understanding is that before going into meditation it is necessary that all this should be thrown out from within. The more you are relieved of this insanity, the lighter your mind will be.

Therefore, whereas the old method of *siddhasana* took years to yield results, this new method performs the same task in a few months. The old method took many births for its fulfilment; this one may take only months. The inner madness has to be released, but in the old method the catharsis was carried out in the etheric body instead of the physical. Now this is something altogether different, because laughing, crying, dancing, etcetera are all within you, and it is absolutely necessary that this should come out.

If you have trained your physical body extensively to be absolutely still for hours on end, then you will carry out the catharsis through your etheric body. Then it will not be visible to others but only to you. You have now protected yourself from society; now no one will know when you dance or sing as you will only do so within. This dancing and singing will be as if in a dream. You will dance within, cry within, laugh within, but your physical body will give no evidence of what is happening inside you. It will sit still with not a trace of the inner happening.

My opinion is that it is not worth undergoing so much trouble for such a small thing. There is no point in making a seeker spend years in physical discipline before taking him into meditation. There are other possibilities also. If a man becomes very proficient in controlling his body and succeeds in suppressing his physical body completely, there is a possibility that no vibrations will arise in the etheric body and it may become absolutely inert. Under such conditions it is possible that no deeper process will take place within you but you will succeed in merely sitting like a statue. Now under such conditions, when all processes are suppressed within, there is a fear of the individual becoming insane.

In the past the meditators have been found going insane. The method I advocate, however, if practised even by a madman for a month or two, will bring him out of his madness. There is no likelihood of a normal person becoming mad when practising this method, because in my method we are not suppressing the insanity within us, we are bringing it out. The old methods of meditation have turned many into madmen, and this fact was covered up in beautiful words. We would say of such a person, "He is ecstatically mad; he is God-intoxicated; he has become a saint." But the fact remained that he had gone absolutely mad. He had suppressed some things within himself so badly that they became completely out of his control.

This method does two things. The first task it carries out is to throw out all the rubbish that is within you by means of catharsis. You have first to become weightless — so weightless that not the slightest trace of madness remains within; then you travel within. So what apparently seems like madness in this method is intrinsically a process of making you free of all madness. I prefer that what is within you should come out, and with it the burden, the tension, the anxiety.

The most interesting fact is that when madness comes upon you, you have no control over it. But you are the master of the madness that you bring on by yourself. Once you are aware of this fact madness can never take hold of you.

Take a man who is dancing and singing or laughing and shouting of his own free will: he is doing all that a madman would do. There is only this difference: to the madman things are happening by themselves whereas the meditator is bringing them about. Without the full cooperation of the meditator this madness cannot last a moment. He can stop the moment he wishes to. Now this man can never go mad, because he has lived madness, seen madness, become familiar with madness. Now this has become a voluntary happening for him; madness is now within the scope of his control.

Our culture has trained us in such a way that madness is beyond our control; it has become non-voluntary. Thus, when it happens to us we cannot do anything about it.

I consider this method very valuable for the future humanity, because the whole civilisation is heading every day toward complete insanity. Everyone will need this technique to get rid of his madness; there is no other way.

If one throws out his madness in this way during an hour of meditation, people will gradually get used to this mode of meditation. People will know that this man is doing meditation. However, if a person performs a similar act on the roadside he will be locked up in a jail. If he releases his anger among people all his relationships will become ugly and broken.

This madness must come out one way or the other, or else he will be in difficulty. If he does not allow it to be released voluntarily this madness finds a hundred ways of erupting. Sometimes a man becomes completely drunk in order for the madness to come out of him; sometimes he expresses his madness in a frenzy of mad dancing. But why go through all these disturbances? Now the new modes of dancing, like the twist, etcetera, are not accidental happenings. Inwardly the body wishes to move and we have not left any room for movement. Thus it makes arrangements for itself and then weaves further webs within these arrangements.

Meditation is throwing the madness without these alternative arrangements. In meditation we are merely throwing out that which we know is within us and which we know should be thrown out. If we teach this method of catharsis to children along with the education there will be a sharp drop in the number of mad people. Madness can be removed forever. But instead we see it increasing day by day. As our society progresses further it will get more and more rampant.

Our culture teaches us to suppress. Etiquette does not allow us to weep loudly or to laugh loudly; it does not allow us to dance or to scream as we please. It puts pressures on us from all sides with the result that all that needs to happen within us is suppressed. Then one day the accumulated pressure of these emotions explodes and the situation goes beyond our control.

Thus, catharsis is the first step in our method of meditation, and through it we release all our pent up emotions within.

It is for this reason that I advise standing during the experiment, because then you will be aware of the slightest movement within and you will be able to move freely. The meditator should be in a closed room. He should not only stand, but he should be absolutely naked so that not a strip of cloth can become a cause of obstruction to him. He should be absolutely free to let all movements happen. There should not be the slightest obstacle in any part of his personality to hinder his movements. Then he will make quick progress and that which takes years and even lives to bring about through hatha yoga and other yogas will happen within the course of a few days by this method.

The long drawn out yoga practices will not do for the world; now people do not have days or even hours to spare. We need methods that yield quick results. If a man makes a seven-day commitment, by the end of that period he should begin to feel that something has happened to him. He should become a different man in seven days' time. If an experiment gives results only in seven births, no one will ever go near such an experiment. The old methods claimed results after so many births. They used to say, "Carry out the practices in this life and the result is bound to come in another life." Those were very patient and persevering people. They carried out meditation even though the result was promised in later lives. Now you will not find a single man like this. If the result is not attained this very day, no one is willing to wait even until tomorrow.

And who can rely on tomorrow? Ever since the atom bomb fell on Hiroshima and Nagasaki our tomorrow has vanished. Thousands of American girls and boys refuse to go to college. They say, "Will the world remain intact by the time we finish our education? One never knows what might happen tomorrow." They feel it is a waste of time. They run away from schools and colleges. They argue with parents: "In the six years we spend at the university will the world still exist? Do you guarantee it? Why should we not make full use of these six precious years of our lives?"

Where tomorrow has become so uncertain it is meaningless to talk in terms of many births. No one is ready to listen, no one does listen. So I say practise today and feel the result immediately. If a man is willing to give me an hour for this experiment, he should get the feeling of the results after this very hour. Then only will he be able to give me an hour of his time tomorrow; otherwise it is uncertain that he will do it tomorrow. So requirements have changed for this age. In the world of the bullock cart everything moved slowly, so also meditation moved at a very slow pace. Now it is the jet age; now meditation cannot afford to be slow. It has to pick up speed.

Please explain the significance and meaning of the following with respect to the energy of kundalini: prostrating on the ground in obeisance to a holy person, touching his feet with the head or hands, offering worship at holy places, the blessings of a divine person given by touching the head or back of a seeker, the covering of the head by Sikhs and Mohammedans on entering the gurudwara or mosque.

There are many reasons for these things. As I said before, when we are filled with anger we feel like beating up someone; we feel like putting his head under our feet. Since this is rather impractical we do the next best thing: we throw a shoe at him. It is very difficult to get a man of five feet six inches under our feet so we throw a shoe at his head as the symbol of the urge of anger within ourselves. But no one ever questions what is the reason behind this shoe throwing. And this is not an act indulged in by any one sect or one country; it is universal. It is a fact that whenever one man is angry with another, his overpowering desire is to bring the head of the latter under his foot.

When man was still primitive, perhaps he rested only after placing his foot on his opponent's head since man had no shoes. So when you are in a state of anger you feel like putting your foot on someone's head. However, the opposite is true also: when you are filled with trust and reverence you feel to place your head at someone's feet. There are many reasons for this as there are for the former situation.

There are moments when you feel to prostrate yourself, and these are the very moments when you feel the vital energy flowing from someone toward you. In fact, whenever you want to receive any kind of flow you have to bow down. If you want to fill your pot from the river you must bend down. One must bend in order to receive the flow of any current because all currents flow downwards. So if you feel that something is flowing from someone, the more your head is bowed at that moment the more receptive it becomes.

Secondly, the energy flows from the pointed extremities of the person: for example, from the fingers and toes. The energy does not flow out from all places. The bioenergy, or the energy of *shaktipat,* or for that matter any energy that flows out from the body, flows from the tips of the fingers and toes. It does not flow from the entire body but only from the pointed extremities. So he who has to receive the energy will put his head at the feet of the master and he who means to give the energy will put his hands upon the head of the one who is to receive.

These are very occult and deeply scientific matters. It is only natural that many will imitate the action. Thousands of people place their heads at the feet of others without any purpose, and there are thousands who place their hands on people's heads also without any meaning. Thus, a very deep principle gradually became a mere formality. When a formality continues for a long time people are bound to rebel against it. They will say, "What is this nonsense? What comes out of placing your head at someone's feet? And what happens by merely touching the head?" Ninety-nine per cent of the time it is just nonsense; one per cent is still meaningful, however.

There was a time when it was a hundred per cent meaningful because then it was spontaneous. You did not have to touch someone's feet because you thought you should. Sometime, when you feel you must fall at someone's feet, do not hold yourself back: fall! And it was not that the other person had to place his hand on the recipient's head. It happens that in some moments the hand becomes very heavy and something is ready to flow out of it. If the other was ready to receive, then only was the hand placed on the head. But over a long period everything turns into a mere ritual which becomes meaningless. And when it becomes meaningless it is criticised. These criticisms then hold a great deal of appeal because the science behind the tradition is lost. So this is a very meaningful gesture, but it is meaningful only when there is an alive master and a receptive disciple.

A man falls at the feet of a Buddha, a Mahavira, and experiences unique delight; he feels a downpour of grace upon him. No one will be able to see it from outside because this is entirely an inner happening. It is a reality for the one who has already experienced it. If others ask proof of it he has none to give. In fact, this is the difficulty with all occult phenomena: the individual has the experience but he has no proof of it to put before others. Then this person appears to be a blind believer. He says, "I cannot explain it, but something has happened." Those who have not experienced refuse to believe this because they have not felt anything. Then they feel that this poor man is under an illusion.

If a person like that falls at the feet of Jesus, nothing will happen to him and he will begin to proclaim loudly that this is all nonsense: he put his head at the feet of Jesus and nothing happened. It is just like a pitcher with an open brim which bows down into the water. Upon returning it then says, "I bowed down and was filled." Now another pitcher whose brim is closed may set out to try it for itself. It may go deep into the river but it will return empty. Then it will maintain that it is all false and that no one gets filled by being dipped into the river. It will proclaim, "I bent myself over, I dipped myself in, but I came back empty."

It is a twofold happening. It is not enough that the energy flows from a person; it is equally important that you are empty and open. Many a time the flowing of the energy from somebody is not as important as your preparedness, your openness to receive it. If you are open enough, then even if the energy is absent in the person before you, the higher sources of energies above the person will begin to flow toward you and reach you. So the most surprising thing is that if you let yourself go wholeheartedly even before a person who has nothing to give you will receive energy from him. But the energy does not come from him; he is only a medium and he is completely unaware of the happening that has taken place.

Now the second part of your question is about entering the gurudwara or mosque with the head covered. Many *fakirs* prefer to cover their heads and then practise meditation. It has its uses. When the energy awakens there is a possibility of the head becoming very heavy. If you have covered your head with a cloth this energy is not likely to flow out. Then this energy will create a circuit within you and thus intensify your meditation. So this tying of the head proved very useful. If you meditate with your head covered you will feel the difference at once. Then what could be accomplished in fifteen days can be accomplished in five.

When the energy reaches the head there are chances of its becoming diffused and scattered. If it can be tied and if a circuit is then formed your experience will be much more deep. But at present this covering of the head in mosques and gurudwaras is a mere formality; it has no meaning now. The fact remains, however, that there is a lot of meaning behind this custom.

Now it is understandable that some energy can be received by touching someone's feet or through his hand being raised in blessing. But a man bowing before a grave or before an image in a temple, what can he gain? There are many things in this also to be understood. Behind the creation of images and idols lies a very scientific arrangement.

Suppose I am about to die and there are a few people around me who love me, who have seen something in me, who have searched and found something in me. Now these people may ask me in what way they should remember me. So before I die a symbol can be established between us. It could be anything—an idol, a stone, a tree, even a platform, or my grave, my *samadhi,* or a piece of clothing of mine, or my slippers—anything. But this should be decided beforehand between us; it is an understanding between us. It cannot be decided upon by any one part alone; I should be a witness. My acceptance, my endorsement, is necessary regarding the symbol. Then I can say that if they go in front of the symbol and think of me I will be present in the bodiless state. This promise I have to give, and all the work proceeds in accordance with this promise. And this is absolutely true.

Therefore, there are temples that are living temples and temples that are dead. The dead temples are those that are created by only one side; there is no assurance from the other side. It is our desire to make a temple of Buddha—but this will be a dead temple because Buddha has not given any promise regarding it. There are living temples that have an assurance from the other side also, and at their foundation lies the declaration of some holy person.

There is a place in Tibet where Buddha's assurance has been fulfilled since the last two thousand five hundred years. This place is now in difficulty, however. There is a group, a committee of five hundred lamas, and when one of these five hundred dies it is very difficult to replace him. This number of five hundred is constant; it can neither be more or less. When one of them dies one more is chosen, but only with the approval of the four hundred and ninety-nine. And if even one of the four hundred and ninety-nine refuses to accept him he cannot be taken. This committee of five hundred lamas gathers together on a particular mountain on the night of Buddha Poornima—the full-moon night in May when Buddha's birthday is celebrated—and at the exact given time Buddha's voice is heard. This event will not happen at any other spot and with any other people. It happens exactly according to a promised arrangement.

It is just as if you would make a resolve before sleeping at night that you will get up in the morning at five o'clock: then you do not need any alarm to awaken you. At five o'clock sharp you will suddenly get up. This is something amazing—and you can check it by your watch. The watch may be wrong but not you. If your resolve is firm you will surely get up at five.

If you make a firm resolve to die on a certain day of a certain year, no power on earth can stop you: you will die in the moment decided upon. If your resolution is very profound and intense you can fulfil your promises even after death. For instance, the appearance of Jesus after death: it was a promise fulfilled. This has caused a lot of difficulty for Christians, because they do not know what happened afterwards and thus they are not sure whether Christ was resurrected or not. However, this was a promise by him to certain disciples which was fulfilled after death.

In fact, places where certain living promises are still being fulfilled over thousands of years have slowly turned into *tirths,* holy places of pilgrimage. Then by and by the promises were forgotten. Only one thing remained in people's memories—that they have to go and visit these places; that was all.

There are promises that Mohammed made; there are promises that Shankara made. So also are the promises made by Buddha, Mahavira and Krishna, and these are tied to special places, to special moments and to a special time. But we can still establish a relationship with them. So you will have to bow down again at these places and surrender yourself completely; then only can you establish this connection.

Holy places, temples, *samadhis,* all have their uses, but as with other things these useful places ultimately become a tradition, and then they become dead and useless. Then they have to be torn down so that new promises can be made that would give rise to new places of pilgrimage, new idols, and new temples. The old has to be broken down because it has become dead. We have no idea of the processes that have been working through them.

There was a yogi in South India. An English traveller came to him. At the time of his departure he told the yogi, "I am leaving now and, perhaps, I shall never return to India. But if I want to see you what shall I do?"

The yogi picked up a picture of himself and handing it to him said, "Whenever you close yourself in a room and concentrate for five minutes on this picture without blinking the eyelids, I will be there."

Now the poor man could not contain himself throughout the journey. He was possessed with one thought: to try out the experiment as early as possible. He did not believe such a thing could happen—but it happened. The given promise was fulfilled astrally. There is no difficulty in this. An awakened man can fulfill his promise even when he is dead. Therefore, pictures become significant and also statues. The reason for their significance is that through them some promises could be fulfilled. So there was a complete science behind the creation of images and idols.

An idol cannot be made just in any way; there is a complete method behind it. Now if you were to observe the images of the twenty-four tirthankaras of the Jainas you would be in difficulty because they are all alike; only their symbols are different. Mahavira has one sign, Parshwanath another,

Neminath yet another, and so on. If these symbols are removed it is impossible to tell one tirthankara from another. However, it cannot be that they all looked alike. It is, therefore, possible that the tirthankaras that followed used the image of the first tirthankara as their prototype. So there was no need to make different images; there was one image of the tirthankaras that was used by all.

But this did not satisfy the devotees who were devoted to different tirthankaras, so they appealed to their special tirthankaras for at least a sign, a token to differentiate him from the others. Thus, different symbols were created for the different tirthankaras but the image remained the same. One has a lion, the other something else, and so on. So there is this difference in their symbols—and this too is a part of a promise given. Only the particular tirthankara connected with the symbol could be contacted.

So these are agreed upon symbols and they work. For instance, the sign of Jesus is the cross; this will work. Now Mohammed refused to have his idol made. In fact, so many images were created during the time of Mohammed that he wanted to give his followers an entirely different kind of symbol. He told them, "Do not make a statue of me. I will establish a relationship with you without a statue. Do not make a statue of me; do not make a picture of me. I will be related to you without a picture or a statue." This was a very deep and courageous method, but ordinary people found it very difficult to establish contact with Mohammed.

Therefore, after Mohammed the Mohammedans built mausoleums and tombs for thousands of their saints. They did not know how to establish connections with Mohammed directly so they did it by making a tomb of some Mohammedan saint. Nowhere in the world are tombs and graves so extensively worshipped as by the Mohammedans. The only reason was that they had nothing of Mohammed to hold onto in order to establish contact with him directly. They could not make an image of him so they had to create other images and they began to establish relationships through these.

All this is a totally scientific process. If this is understood scientifically the results can be miraculous, but if followed blindly, suicidal.

What is the occult significance of the process performed during prana pratishtha, the installation of an idol?

It holds a great significance. The very term *prana pratishtha*—occult installation of an idol—means that we have created a new image based on an old promise. Now we must discover through indications whether the old promise has been duly fulfilled. We on our part should follow the old arrangement faithfully; we should not look upon an idol as a mere idol but as a living entity. We should make all arrangements for it as we would for a living person, and then we will begin to get hints and signs by which we can know that the occult installation of the idol has been accepted. But this second aspect has completely vanished from our knowledge. If these signs are not present, then although we have done the idol installation it has not been successful. There must be proof that the idol installation has been successful. So for this reason, some special occult indications were fixed. If these signs were found it was understood that the idol installation has been accepted by the occult forces and that it is now alive and active.

Now suppose you have installed a new radio in your house. The first thing is that the radio itself should be in good condition; all its components should be in the proper place. Then you connect it with electricity, and yet you find it does not pick up any station. That means it is not working. It is a dead instrument and it will either have to be repaired or replaced. The idol too is a receiving point of a sort through which a physically dead enlightened man fulfils the promise he has made to others. But if you keep an image and you do not know about the indications that confirm the installation, then you will never know whether the image is living or dead.

The process of installation of an idol has two parts. The first part is fulfilled by the priest. He knows how many *mantras* are to be repeated, how many threads are to be tied, what conditions are required for its worship, what type of worship is to be performed, etcetera. This is half of the work. The second part of this ceremony can only be carried out by a person of the fifth plane. When this person pronounces that the image is alive, then only does it become living. This has become nearly impossible in modern times; therefore, our temples are not living temples but dead places. The new temples of today are certainly dead places.

It is impossible to destroy a living temple because it is not an ordinary event. If it is destroyed it only means that that which you thought to be alive was not alive, as for instance, the Somnath temple. The story of its destruction is a very strange one and it is indicative of the science of all temples. There were five hundred *pujaris*—priests—in its service, and they were certain that the image within was a living one, so they were certain it could not be destroyed. The priests carried out their part of the task, but this was one-sided because there was no one who could actually find out whether the image was dead or living.

One day the surrounding kings and princes sent word to the temple warning them about the coming of the Mohammedan invader Gajanawi and offered them protection, but the priests declined their help saying that the idol that protected all was beyond their protection. The princes asked their forgiveness and kept away—but it was a mistake: the idol was a dead idol. The priests were under the illusion that a great power stood behind the image, and as they considered it to be living it was wrong even to think of its protection. Gajanawi came and with a stroke of his sword broke the idol into four pieces. Even then it did not occur to the priests that the idol was a dead one. This cannot happen to a living idol; not a brick could have fallen if the image within were living. If the temple were a living one it could not have been touched.

But usually temples are not living ones because there are great difficulties in keeping them alive. A temple becoming alive is a great miracle. It is a part of a very profound science. Today, however, there is no one alive who knows this science and who can carry out its various requirements. Nowadays the class of people who run temples as shops has become so large that if there is someone who knows this science he will not be allowed even on the premises of the temple. Temples are now run along business lines, and it is in the interest of the priests that the temple remains dead. Living temples are not beneficial for a *purohit,* a priest. He wants a dead god in the temple whom he can lock up, and then he wants to keep the key himself. If the temple is connected with higher powers it will be impossible for the priest to remain there. So priests are instrumental in the creation of these dead temples as this provides them with a flourishing business. In reality, living temples are very few.

A great effort was made to keep the temples alive, but the numbers of priests and pundits in all religions, in all temples, was so great that it made it difficult to do so. This is what always happens ultimately. This is the reason why there are so many temples; otherwise there would be no need for so many. If the temples and places of pilgrimage created in the times of the *Upanishads* had still been alive in Mahavira's time there would have been no need for Mahavira to build new temples. But the temples and sacred places were completely dead by then and there was a network of priests around them which could not be broken. These temples could not be entered so there was no other way except to make new temples. Today even Mahavira's temples are dead and the same kind of network of priests surrounds them.

If the living principles of religion had been saved so many religions would not have come into being in this world. But these cannot be saved, because all kinds of disturbances gather around and ultimately cause them to lose all their potential. Then, when the conditions on one side are broken, the promise on the other side also breaks. It is a mutual understanding arrived at by two parties. We have to keep our side of the agreement; then only does the other side respond; otherwise the promise will not be fulfilled and the matter ends there.

For instance, if while leaving my physical body I say to you, "Remember me and I shall be there"—but if you never think of me or if you throw my picture into the dustbin and forget all about it, how long will our agreement last? And if this agreement is broken on your part there is no need for me to keep it. So such agreements are always broken.

So the occult process of installation of an idol holds a meaning, but its significance is based on various tests and indications that determine whether the idol installation has been a success or not.

In some temples, water trickles down naturally over the images. Is this a sign that such a temple is a living temple?

No. The validity of a living temple has nothing to do with this. The water will trickle whether there is an image underneath it or not. These are false proofs, and because of them we assume that a temple is a living one. Where not a drop of water falls, still there are temples that could be and are living temples.

In spiritual quest, deeksha, initiation, holds a very important place. Its special ceremonies are carried out under special conditions. Buddha and Mahavira used to give initiation. How many types of initiation are there? What is their significance and use and why are they needed?

A little talk on initiation will be useful. For one thing, *deeksha,* initiation, is never given; initiation takes place, it is a happening. For example, a person stays with Mahavira and it takes years for his initiation to take place. Mahavira tells him to stay, to be with him, to walk with him, to stand in such a way, to sit in such a way, to meditate such a way. Then a moment comes when the person is fully prepared. Then Mahavira is only the medium. Perhaps, it is not proper even to say that he is the medium—rather, in a very deep sense he remains only a witness and initiation takes place in front of him.

Initiation is always from the divine, but it can happen in the presence of Mahavira. Now the person to whom it is happening sees Mahavira in front of him, but the divine he cannot see. It happens to him in front of Mahavira so naturally he becomes grateful to Mahavira—and this is fitting also. But Mahavira does not accept his gratitude. He can only accept his gratitude if he acknowledges that he initiated him.

So there are two types of initiation. One is that which happens and which I call "right" initiation, because in this you establish your relationship with the divine. Then your journey through life takes a new turn: you become someone else now; you are no longer the same that you were; everything within you is transformed. You have seen something new. Something new has happened to you, a ray has entered you, and now everything within you is different.

In the real initiation the guru stands aside like a witness and he can confirm that initiation has taken place. He can see the full process but you see only half. You can only see what is happening to you; he sees that from where the initiation takes place. So you are not a complete witness of the happening; all you can say is that a great transformation has taken place. But whether initiation has taken place or not, whether you have been accepted or not, that you cannot say for certain. Even after you are initiated you will still wonder, "Have I been accepted? Have I been chosen? Have I been accepted by the divine? Can I now take it that I am his? On my part I have surrendered, but has he taken me to him?" This you cannot know at once. You will come to know after some time, but this interval can be long also. So the second person, whom we call the guru, can know this because he has watched the happening from both the sides.

Right initiation cannot be given, nor can it be taken. It comes from the divine; you are merely the recipient.

Now the other type of initiation, which we may call false initiation, can be given as well as taken. The divine is completely absent there; there is only the guru and the disciple. The guru gives, the disciple takes, but the third, real factor is absent.

Where there are only two present—the guru and the disciple—the initiation is false. Where three are present—the guru, the disciple and he from whom it takes place—everything changes. This giving of initiation is not only improper but also dangerous, fatal, because in this illusion of initiation right initiation cannot take place. You will merely live under the illusion that initiation has taken place.

A seeker came to me who had been initiated by someone. He said, "I have been initiated by such and such a guru and I have come to you to learn meditation."

I asked him, "Why then did you take initiation? And if you did not even attain meditation, what have you obtained from your initiation? All you received is clothes and a name. If you are still seeking meditation, then what is the meaning of your initiation?"

The truth is that initiation can only happen after meditation. Meditation after initiation has no meaning. It is like a man who proclaims that he is healthy and still he knocks at the physician's door and asks for medicine. Initiation is the acceptance obtained after meditation. It is a sanction given of your acceptance—a consent. The divine has been advised of you and your entrance into his realm has happened. Initiation is only a confirmation of this fact.

Such initiation is now lost, and I feel it should be revived again: initiation where the guru is not the giver and the disciple is not the recipient—and the giver, God. This can be; this should be. If I am a witness to someone's initiation I do not become his guru. Then his guru is the divine. If he is grateful it is his business. But to demand gratefulness is senseless and to accept it is meaningless.

Gurudom, the web of the so-called gurus, was created by giving a new form to initiation. Words are whispered in the ears, *mantras* are given, and anybody initiates anyone. Whether he himself is initiated is also not certain; whether the divine has accepted him is not known. Perhaps, he too has been initiated in the same manner. Someone had whispered into his ears, he whispers into someone else's, and this one in his turn will whisper into someone else's ears again.

Man creates lies and deceptions in everything—and the more mysterious a happening the more deceptions there are, because there is nothing substantial to show as proof.

I intend carrying out this method also. About ten or twenty people are preparing for it. They will take initiation from the divine. The others who are present will be the witnesses, and their work will be to confirm whether the initiation has been accepted by the divine; that is all. You will experience but you will not be able to recognise at once what has taken place. It is so unfamiliar to you, how will you recognise that the thing has happened? Confirmation can be made by the presence of the enlightened one. This alone is the basis of its evaluation.

So the supreme guru is the *paramatman*—God only. If the gurus in between would step back initiation would be easier, but the intermediary guru stands fixed. His ego exults at making a god of himself and displaying himself. Many kinds of initiations are given around this ego. They have no value, however, and in terms of spirituality they are all criminal acts. If some day we should start punishing spiritual criminals, these should not go unpunished.

The unsuspecting seeker takes it for granted that he has been initiated. Then he goes about with pride that he has received his initiation, that he has received his *mantra,* and that all that was to happen has happened to him. So all his search for the right happening stops.

When anyone approached Buddha he was never initiated immediately; sometimes it took years. Buddha would keep on postponing by telling him to perform this practice and that. Then, when the moment came, he would tell him to stand up for initiation.

There were three parts to Buddha's initiation. One who came for it went through three types of surrender. First he said, "I surrender unto Buddha—*Buddham sharanam gachchhami.*" By this he did not mean Gautama Buddha; this meant surrendering himself to the awakened one.

Once a seeker came up to Buddha and said, "I surrender unto buddha." Buddha listened and remained silent.

Then someone asked him, "This man says, 'I surrender unto buddha,' and you were only listening to him?"

Buddha replied, "He is not surrendering to me, he is surrendering to the awakened one. I am a mere excuse. There have been many buddhas before me, there will be many after me. I am just an excuse. I am just a peg. He is surrendering himself to the awakened one, so who am I to stop him? If he surrenders to me I shall certainly stop him, but he has said three times that he is surrendering himself unto the awakened one."

Then there is the second surrender which is still more wonderful. In this the person says, "I surrender myself to the assembly of the awakened ones—*Sangham sharanam gachchhami.*" Now what does this assembly mean? Generally, the followers of Buddha take it to mean Buddha's assembly, but this is not the meaning. This assembly is the collective gathering of all awakened ones. There is not only one Buddha who has become awakened; there have been many buddhas before and there will be many buddhas after who will awaken. They all belong to one community, to one collectivity. Now the Buddhists think this term means an association of Buddhists, but this is wrong.

The very first invocation, in which Buddha explains that the seeker surrenders himself to the awakened one and not to him as a person, makes everything clear. The second invocation makes it all the more clear. In this the person offers himself to the community of awakened ones.

First he bows down to the awakened one who is right there in front of him. As he is right there it is easy to approach him, to talk to him. Then he surrenders himself to the brotherhood of the awakened ones that have awakened since long and whom he does not know, and to those who will awaken in the future and whom he does not know. He surrenders to all of them and he proceeds a step further towards the subtle.

The third surrender is to *dhamma*—religion. The third time the seeker says, "I surrender unto the *dhamma*—*Dhammam sharanam gachchhami.*" The first surrender is to the awakened one, the second is the brotherhood of the awakened ones, and now the third surrender is to that which is the ultimate state of awakening—to the *dhamma*. That is, to our nature, where there is no individual, no community; where there is only the *dhamma,* the law. He says, "I surrender unto that *dhamma*."

When these three surrenders were completed then only the initiation was recognised. Buddha was only a witness of this happening. This was not a matter of mere repetition. When these three were completed—and Buddha could see whether they had been completed—only then was the individual initiated. Buddha remained a witness to the happening.

So later on also Buddha would tell the seeker, "Do not believe what I say just because I am an awakened one; do not believe what I say just because I am famous or because I have many followers or because the scriptures confirm it. Now only believe what your inner understanding tells you."

Buddha never became a guru. At the time of his death, when he was asked for his final message, he said, "Be a light unto yourself. Do not go after others; do not follow others. Be a light unto yourself. This is my last message."

Such a person as Buddha cannot be a guru. Such a person is a witness. Jesus has said many a time, "On the final day of judgment I shall be your witness." In other words, on the last day Jesus will testify, "Yes, he is a man who had striven to become awakened. This man wanted to surrender to the divine." This is talking in symbols. What Christ meant to say is also this: "I am your witness, not your guru."

There is no guru; therefore, beware of the initiation where someone becomes your guru. The initiation where you become immediately and directly connected with the divine is a unique initiation. Remember, in this initiation you have not to leave your house and go away, you have not to become either a Hindu or a Mohammedan or a Christian, nor are you required to be tied to someone. You remain where you are in your full freedom; the change will take place only from within. In the false type of initiation you will be tied to a religion: you will be a Hindu or a Mohammedan or a Christian. You will be a part of an organisation. Some belief, some religious order, some dogma, some person, some guru, will catch hold of you and they will kill your freedom.

That initiation which does not bring freedom is no initiation. That initiation which gives you absolute freedom is alone the right initiation.

You have said that Buddha attained mahaparinirvana, but also that Buddha is to come once again in human form and will be known as Maitreya. How is it possible to take on a human form after reaching nirvana? Please explain this.

This is somewhat difficult; therefore, I did not speak about it yesterday. It requires a detailed explanation; yet I will now give you a brief explanation.

It is not possible to return after reaching the seventh plane. There is no rebirth after the seventh body. It is a point of no return; you cannot come back from there. But it is also true that Buddha has said he will come again in the form of Maitreya. Now both these things seem contradictory: I say you cannot return after the seventh body and Buddha has promised to come again. Buddha attained the seventh body and merged into the *nirvana*—then how is this possible? There is another way. Now you will have to know and understand a few things.

When we die only the physical body drops; the rest of the six bodies remain with us. When a person reaches the fifth plane, the first four bodies drop away and only three remain—the fifth, the sixth and the seventh. In the fifth body a person can make a resolve to keep his second, third and fourth bodies, and this can happen if the resolve is very intense and deep. And for a person like Buddha this was an easy matter: he can leave behind forever his second, third and fourth bodies. Like a mass of energy these bodies of Buddha keep on moving in space.

All the feelings that Buddha had acquired in his infinite lives are the property of the second—the etheric body. And the impressions of all the *karmas* that Buddha had in his previous lives are accumulated in the third—the astral body. The fourth body carries all the achievements of Buddha's mind. All of his achievements beyond the mind have been expressed by him through the mind as all expressions are given through the mind. Whenever a man wishes to make known his attainments of the fifth or even the seventh body he has to make use of his fourth body—because the vehicle of expression is the fourth body. So the one who has heard Buddha more than anyone or anything else is in his own fourth body. Whatsoever he has thought, lived and known is collected in his fourth body.

These first three bodies disintegrate very easily. When a person enters the fifth body these three bodies are destroyed. When a man enters the seventh body all the previous six bodies are destroyed. But if a person of the fifth plane so desires he can leave all the vibrations of these three bodies in space. It is just as we are now making stations in space: this collection of Buddha's second, third and fourth bodies will go on moving in space until they manifest themselves in an individual by the name of Maitreya.

So when a person of the required state for Maitreya is born these three bodies of Buddha will enter into him. Until then they will await his coming. When these three bodies enter into that person he will attain the calibre of Buddha, because they are an accumulation of all the experiences, all the emotions, desires and activities of Buddha.

Now, for instance, suppose I leave my body behind here and it is well preserved.

In America a man died about three or four years ago. He left a trust of millions of dollars and he willed that this be used to preserve his body until the time when science discovers the secret of bringing a dead body back to life. Millions of dollars are spent to preserve his body so that it should not deteriorate. His body is preserved by a scientific process. If by the end of the century we succeed in reviving the dead this body will be brought back to life. But the soul will be different; it cannot be the same.

The body will be the same: his eyes, his colour, his features, his way of walking, all of his physical habits, will be the same. In a sense, the man who is dead will be represented in the body. If the man was centred around his physical body—which he must have been or else this keen desire to preserve the body would not have been there—without any idea of the other bodies, another soul can act for him. It will act exactly in the same way as the dead man, and scientists will then say that it is the same man come back to life. All his remembrances and recollections that are stored in the physical brain will awaken once again: he will be able to recognise the pictures of his mother and his son who have long been dead; he will recognise the town where he was born; he will point out the place where he died; he will also name the people that were present when he died. The soul will be different although the brain content will be the same.

Now scientists claim that very soon they will be able to transplant memory. This will be possible. If I die the whole of my recollections and memories are lost with me. But now it is possible to save the whole mechanism of my memories at the time of my death just as we preserve eyes for transplanting. Tomorrow someone will be able to see with my eyes. And it is not that I alone can love with my heart—someone else may also love with my heart tomorrow. Now it is not possible to promise that "My heart is forever yours," because this very heart can make the same vow to another in the distant future.

In the same way memory will also be transplanted. It will take time to bring this about because it is very delicate and very subtle. But in future, as we donate eyes to an eye bank there will be memory banks also. Then my memory will be transplanted into a small child who will then know all that I had to learn. He will grow up already knowing so many things because my memory will be a part of his cerebral make-up.

Then my thoughts will be his, my remembrances will be his, and in certain matters he will think the same way I do, because he will have my brain.

Now Buddha has experimented in a different direction—a direction which is not scientific but occult. Through some methods efforts have been made to preserve his second, third and fourth bodies. Buddha does not exist any more; the soul that lived within was lost at the seventh plane. But before the soul was merged into the seventh, arrangements were made to see that these three bodies—the second, third and fourth—did not die. The momentum of Buddha's determination and promise was instilled into them. It is just as if I were to throw a stone with enough force for it to travel fifty miles; then I die soon after throwing the stone. But my death cannot interfere with the movement of the stone. It has the force I gave it to travel fifty miles, and it will do that whether I am there or not. The strength I exerted will keep the stone going.

Buddha has given a momentum to these three bodies and they will live. He has also told how long they can remain. Now the time is ripe for Maitreya to take birth. This very experiment was carried out upon J. Krishnamurti so that he would attain these three bodies of Buddha. First this experiment was carried out on Nityananda, the elder brother of Krishnamurti, but he died in the process. This is a very unique process—one which is difficult to go through.

An effort was made to separate Nityananda's second, third and fourth bodies and replace them with Maitreya's. Then Nityananda died. Then this same experiment was tried on Krishnamurti, but this also could not succeed. Then it was tried on one or two more people: George Arundale was one upon whom the experiment was tried by some who knew of this mystery. Among those who knew of this secret, Madame Blavatsky was the most profound woman of our century as far as the knowledge of occult science is concerned. Annie Besant was another; Leadbeater also had a lot of understanding in occult matters. There are very few people who had this understanding.

These few people knew that now the power behind the three bodies of Buddha was about to diminish. If Maitreya would not take birth these bodies would not be able to hold on any longer; they would disperse. Now their momentum is about to end. Someone should now be ready to absorb these three bodies. Whoever absorbs these will in a way cause the rebirth of Buddha. The soul of Buddha will not come back, but the soul of the individual will take on the bodies of Buddha and work accordingly. That person will at once involve himself in the mission of Buddha.

Not every person can be in this state. Whoever he is he should at least be of a level of consciousness that is almost as high as was Buddha's. Only such a one will be able to absorb his three bodies; otherwise he will die. So the experiment was unsuccessful, because there were many difficulties in the process. Endeavours still go on. Even today there are small esoteric groups who are trying to bring down these three bodies of Buddha. But now there is no extensive propaganda about it, because that proved harmful.

There was a possibility of the three bodies descending into Krishnamurti. He was worthy of it and this was widely advertised. This propaganda was done in good faith. It was done for the reason that when Buddha's advent took place he should be quickly recognised. It was also done in order to revive the past-life memories of those now living who existed at the time of Buddha so that they could recognise that this was the same man. But this propaganda turned out to be detrimental to the process. It created a reaction in the mind of Krishnamurti, who has a modest, reserved and sensitive personality. It was difficult for him to be in a crowd. If this experiment had been carried out silently in a secluded place, if nobody would have known about it until the happening took place, it is very likely that the happening would have taken place.

But it did not take place. Krishnamurti refused to let go of his second, third and fourth bodies to be replaced by the three bodies of Buddha. This was a great blow to the occult science of our times. Such a vast and intricate experiment had never been performed in this world anywhere except in Tibet. This process has been carried out in Tibet for a long time, and many souls work through the medium of other bodies.

I hope you have understood what I said. There is no contradiction in it even though sometimes you might feel that there is. It is possible that you may feel something to be contradictory because I have talked from a different angle, but it is not so.

An Invitation To Experience

OSHO
Never Born
Never Died
Only Visited This
Planet Earth Between
Dec 11, 1931 - Jan 19, 1990

Osho is an enlightened Mystic.

During the course of thirty years of talks to seekers and friends, Osho would answer their questions, or comment on the teachings of the world's great sages and scriptures. His talks continue to bring fresh insight to everything, from the obscure Upanishads to the familiar sayings of Gurdjieff, from Ashtavakra to Zarathustra. Osho speaks with equal authority on the Hassids and the Sufis, the Bauls, Yoga, Tantra, Tao and Gautama the Buddha. And ultimately, Osho concentrates on transmitting the unique wisdom of Zen, because, He says, Zen is the one spiritual tradition whose approach to the inner life of human beings has weathered the test of time and is still relevant to contemporary humanity. Zen is another word for the original Hindi word Dhyana. In English you may translate it as 'meditation', but Osho says this is a poor translation. So call it Dhyana or Zen or whatever you may wish - Osho's emphasis is on ***experiencing***.

Osho settled in Pune in 1974, and disciples and friends from all over the world gathered around Him to hear His talks and practice His meditation techniques for the modern man. Western therapeutic group processes, classes and trainings were gradually introduced so bridging the wisdom and understanding of the East with the scientific approach of the West. And now Osho Commune International has evolved into the world's largest centre for meditation and spiritual growth, and offers hundreds of different methods for exploring and experiencing the inner world.

Every year, thousands of seekers from all over the world come to celebrate and meditate together in Osho's buddhafield. The commune grounds are full of lush green gardens, pools and waterfalls, elegant snow-white swans and colourful peacocks, as well as beautiful buildings and pyramids. Such a peaceful and harmonious atmosphere makes it very easy to experience the inner silence in a joyful way.

For detailed information to participate in this Buddhafield contact:

OSHO COMMUNE INTERNATIONAL

17, Koregaon Park, Pune-411001, MS, India
Ph: 020 628562 Fax: 020 624181
E-mail: commune@osho.net / Website: www.osho.com

BOOKS BY OSHO

english language editions

EARLY DISCOURSES AND WRITINGS
A Cup of Tea
Dimensions Beyond The Known
From Sex to Superconsciousness
The Great Challenge
Hidden Mysteries
I Am The Gate
The Inner Journey
The Long and the Short and the All
Psychology of the Esoteric
Seeds of Wisdom

MEDITATION
The Voice of Silence
And Now and Here (Vol 1 & 2)
In Search of the Miraculous (Vol 1&.2)
Meditation: The Art of Ecstasy
Meditation: The First and Last Freedom
The Path of Meditation
The Perfect Way
Yaa-Hoo! The Mystic Rose

BUDDHA AND BUDDHIST MASTERS
The Book of Wisdom
(combined edition of Vol 1 & 2)
The Dhammapada (Vol 1-12)
The Way of the Buddha
The Diamond Sutra
The Discipline of Transcendence (Vol 1-4)
The Heart Sutra

BAUL MYSTICS
The Beloved (Vol 1 & 2)

KABIR
The Divine Melody
Ecstasy: The Forgotten Language
The Fish in the Sea is Not Thirsty
The Great Secret
The Guest
The Path of Love
The Revolution

JESUS AND CHRISTIAN MYSTICS
Come Follow to You (Vol 1-4)
I Say Unto You (Vol 1 & 2)
The Mustard Seed
Theologia Mystica

JEWISH MYSTICS
The Art of Dying
The True Sage

WESTERN MYSTICS
Guida Spirituale On the Desiderata
The Hidden Harmony
The Fragments of Heraclitus
The Messiah (Vol 1 & 2) Commentaries on
Khalil Gibran's The Prophet
The New Alchemy: To Turn You On
Commentaries on Mabel Collins' Light on the Path
Philosophia Perennis (Vol 1 & 2)
The Golden Verses of Pythagoras
Zarathustra: A God That Can Dance
Zarathustra: The Laughing Prophet
Commentaries on Nietzsche's Thus Spake Zarathustra

SUFISM
Just Like That
Journey to the Heart (same as Until You Die)
The Perfect Master (Vol 1 & 2)
The Secret
Sufis: The People of the Path (Vol 1 & 2)
Unio Mystica (Vol 1 & 2)
The Wisdom of the Sands (Vol 1 & 2)

TANTRA
Tantra: The Supreme Understanding
The Tantra Experience
The Royal Song of Saraha
(*same as* Tantra Vision, Vol 1)
The Tantric Transformation
The Royal Song of Saraha
(*same as* Tantra Vision, Vol 2)
The Book of Secrets: Vigyan Bhairav Tantra

THE UPANISHADS
Behind a Thousand Names Nirvana Upanishad
Heartbeat of the Absolute Ishavasya Upanishad
I Am That Isa Upanishad
The Message Beyond Words: A Dialogue with the Lord of Death
Philosophia Ultima Mandukya Upanishad
The Supreme Doctrine Kenopanishad
Finger Pointing to the Moon
Adhyatma Upanishad
That Art Thou Sarvasar Upanishad,
KaivalyaUpanishad, Adhyatma

Upanishad
The Ultimate Alchemy
Atma Pooja Upanishad (Vol 1& 2)
Vedanta: Seven Steps to Samadhi
Akshaya Upanishad

TAO
The Empty Boat
The Secret of Secrets
Tao: The Golden Gate (Vol 1& 2)
Tao: The Pathless Path (Vol 1& 2)
Tao: The Three Treasures (Vol 1- 4)
When the Shoe Fits

YOGA
The Path of Yoga (previously Yoga: The Alpha and the Omega Vol 1)
Yoga: The Alpha and the Omega (Vol 2-10)

ZEN AND ZEN MASTERS
Ah, This!
Ancient Music in the Pines
And the Flowers Showered
A Bird on the Wing (same as Roots and Wings)
Bodhidharma: The Greatest Zen Master
Communism and Zen Fire, Zen Wind
Dang Dang Doko Dang
The First Principle
God is Dead: Now Zen is the Only Living Truth
The Grass Grows By Itself
The Great Zen Master Ta Hui
Hsin Hsin Ming: The Book of Nothing
Discourses on the Faith-Mind of Sosan
I Celebrate Myself: God is No Where,
Life is Now Here
Kyozan: A True Man of Zen
Nirvana: The Last Nightmare
No Mind: The Flowers of Eternity
No Water, No Moon
One Seed Makes the Whole Earth Green
Returning to the Source
The Search: Talks on the 10 Bulls of Zen
A Sudden Clash of Thunder
The Sun Rises in the Evening
Take it Easy (Vol 1) Poems of Ikkyu
Take it Easy (Vol 2)Poems of Ikkyu
This Very Body the Buddha *Hakuin's Song of Meditation*
Walking in Zen, Sitting in Zen
The White Lotus
Yakusan: Straight to the Point of Enlightenment
Zen Manifesto : Freedom From Oneself
Zen: The Mystery and the Poetry of the Beyond
Zen: The Path of Paradox (Vol 1, 2 & 3)
Zen: The Special Transmission

ZEN BOXED SETS
The World of Zen (5 volumes)
Live Zen
This. This. A Thousand Times This
Zen: The Diamond Thunderbolt
Zen: The Quantum Leap from Mind to No-Mind
Zen: The Solitary Bird, Cuckoo of the Forest
Zen: All The Colors Of The Rainbow (5 vol.)
The Buddha: The Emptiness of the Heart
The Language of Existence
The Miracle
The Original Man
Turning In
Osho: On the Ancient Masters of Zen (7 vol.)
Dogen: The Zen Master
Hyakujo: The Everest of Zen - With Basho's haikus
Isan: No Footprints in the Blue Sky
Joshu: The Lion's Roar
Ma Tzu: The Empty Mirror
Nansen: The Point Of Departure
Rinzai: Master of the Irrational

**Each volume is also available individually.*

RESPONSES TO QUESTIONS
Be Still and Know
Come, Come, Yet Again Come
The Goose is Out
The Great Pilgrimage: From Here to Here
The Invitation
My Way: The Way of the White Clouds
Nowhere to Go But In
The Razor's Edge
Walk Without Feet, Fly Without Wings and Think Without Mind
The Wild Geese and the Water
Zen: Zest, Zip, Zap and Zing

TALKS IN AMERICA
From Bondage To Freedom
From Darkness to Light
From Death To Deathlessness
From the False to the Truth
From Unconsciousness to Consciousness
The Rajneesh Bible (Vol 2-4)

THE WORLD TOUR
Beyond Enlightenment *Talks in Bombay*
Beyond Psychology *Talks in Uruguay*
Light on the Path *Talks in the Himalayas*
The Path of the Mystic *Talks in Uruguay*
Sermons in Stones *Talks in Bombay*
Socrates Poisoned Again After 25 Centuries *Talks in Greece*
The Sword and the Lotus *Talks in the Himalayas*
The Transmission of the Lamp *Talks in Uruguay*

OSHO'S VISION FOR THE WORLD
The Golden Future
The Hidden Splendor
The New Dawn
The Rebel
The Rebellious Spirit

THE MANTRA SERIES
Hari Om Tat Sat
Om Mani Padme Hum
Om Shantih Shantih Shantih
Sat-Chit-Anand
Satyam-Shivam-Sundram

PERSONAL GLIMPSES
Books I Have Loved
Glimpses of a Golden Childhood
Notes of a Madman

INTERVIEWS WITH THE WORLD PRESS
The Last Testament (Vol 1)

INTIMATE TALKS BETWEEN MASTER AND DISCIPLE - DARSHAN DIARIES
A Rose is a Rose is a Rose
Be Realistic: Plan for a Miracle
Believing the Impossible Before Breakfast
Beloved of My Heart
Blessed are the Ignorant
Dance Your Way to God
Don't Just Do Something, Sit There
Far Beyond the Stars
For Madmen Only
The Further Shore
Get Out of Your Own Way
God's Got A Thing about You
God is Not for Sale
The Great Nothing
Hallelujah!
Let Go!
The 99 Names of Nothingness
No Book, No Buddha, No Teaching, No Disciple
Nothing to Lose but Your Head
Only Losers Can Win in This Game
Open Door
Open Secret
The Shadow of the Whip
The Sound of One Hand Clapping
The Sun Behind the Sun Behind the Sun
The Tongue-Tip Taste of Tao
This Is It
Turn On, Tune In and Drop the Lot
What Is, Is, What Ain't, Ain't
Won't You Join The Dance?

COMPILATIONS
After Middle Age: A Limitless Sky
At the Feet of the Master
Bhagwan Shree Rajneesh: On Basic Human Rights
Jesus Crucified Again, This Time in Ronald Reagan's America
Priests and Politicians: The Mafia of the Soul
Take it Really Seriously

GIFT BOOKS OF OSHO QUOTATIONS
A Must for Contemplation Before Sleep
A Must for Morning Contemplation
India My Love

PHOTOBOOKS
Shree Rajneesh: A Man of Many Climates, Seasons and Rainbows *through the eye of the camera*
Impressions... *Osho Commune International Photobook*

BOOKS ABOUT OSHO
Bhagwan: The Buddha for the Future *by Juliet Forman*
Bhagwan Shree Rajneesh: The Most Dangerous Man Since Jesus Christ *by Sue Appleton*
Bhagwan: The Most Godless Yet the Most Godly Man by Dr. George Meredith
Bhagwan: One Man Against the Whole Ugly Past of Humanity by Juliet Forman
Bhagwan: Twelve Days That Shook the World *by Juliet Forman*
Was Bhagwan Shree Rajneesh Poisoned by Ronald Reagan's America? *by Sue Appleton*
Diamond Days With Osho *by Ma Prem Shunyo*

GIFTS
Zorba the Buddha Cookbook

STERLING

LIBRARY

OF

OSHO

VISION